GROUNDWATER EXPLOITATION
IN THE HIGH PLAINS

DEVELOPMENT OF WESTERN RESOURCES

The Development of Western Resources is an interdisciplinary series focusing on the use and misuse of resources in the American West. Written for a broad readership of humanists, social scientists, and resource specialists, the books in this series emphasize both historical and contemporary perspectives as they explore the interplay between resource exploitation and economic, social, and political experiences.

John G. Clark, University of Kansas, General Editor

GROUNDWATER EXPLOITATION IN THE HIGH PLAINS

Edited by David E. Kromm
and Stephen E. White

Foreword by Gilbert F. White

 University Press of Kansas

Published by the University Press of Kansas (Lawrence, Kansas 66049), which was
organized by the Kansas Board of Regents and is operated and funded by Emporia State
University, Fort Hays State University, Kansas State University, Pittsburg State
University, the University of Kansas, and Wichita State University

Library of Congress Cataloging-in-Publication Data

Groundwater exploitation in the High Plains / edited by David E. Kromm
    and Stephen E. White
        p.   cm. — (Development of western resources)
    Includes bibliographical references and index.
    ISBN 0–7006–0537–1 (hardcover)
    1. Water, Underground—Great Plains.   2. Irrigation—Great Plains.
3. Water-supply—Great Plains—Management.   4. High Plains Aquifer.
5. Ogallala Aquifer.   I. Kromm, David E.   II. White, Stephen E.
III. Series.
TD223.G763   1992
333.91'04'0978—dc20   91–40798

British Library Cataloguing in Publication Data is available.

Printed in the United States of America

10   9   8   7   6   5   4   3   2   1

The paper used in this publication meets the minimum requirements of
the American National Standard for Permanence of Paper for Printed
Library Materials Z39.48-1984.

FOREWORD

Because the High Plains is widely regarded as a prime example of ground-water exploitation, a careful analysis of the situation now prevailing and of alternative prospects is especially valuable. From the beginning, deep pumping of water from the Ogallala Aquifer has provoked questions about how farmers and the responsible public agencies deal, or should deal, with that finite, exhaustible resource.

This volume advances the analysis in two important respects, making it significant for other parts of the world as well as for the Great Plains. Kromm, White, and their colleagues examine the evolving conditions of the use of water in a regional framework that recognizes the distinctive subregions of the High Plains. Important differences are identified, and the value of such an approach is demonstrated. The study also brings to bear an essential array of disciplinary skills and perspectives. Hydrogeo-logic, technologic, economic, institutional, legal, and historic methods are employed. The coherent combination of these approaches and related tools is an extremely difficult task.

The more fragile the resource and the more complex the exploitive practices, the more desirable it is to pursue a regional approach and to place it in a broader framework. Beginning with the early efforts of Walter Firey to understand the processes by which people use and exhaust a resource, the challenge is to deepen that knowledge and to show how it can help fashion a truly sustainable human occupancy of the High Plains. That will involve consideration of related dryland use and climate as well as the sustainability of resources in adjoining regions. This is an important step in that direction.

Gilbert F. White
Boulder, Colo.
October 11, 1991

CONTENTS

TABLES, FIGURES, AND ILLUSTRATIONS

Tables

Figures

Illustrations

PREFACE

The story of the American High Plains is very much the story of water. Changing perceptions of the region express prevailing views of water availability. Known as the Great American Desert and later the Dustbowl, the region attracted settlers whenever abundant rain fell for a few years. The variability of the region's climate is reflected in these changing perceptions and by the corresponding periods of in- and out-migration. Indeed, the High Plains is both wet and dry, both garden and desert.

Farmers sought stability in irrigation. Early irrigators diverted water from rivers and built dams to impound water. Limited surface water and precipitation restricted irrigated land to a few thousand acres. Groundwater was to become the central fact of life for the region. As early as 1854 a large aquifer had been identified, but adequate means to bring the water to the surface did not appear for another fifty years. The introduction of more sophisticated pumps, well-drilling equipment, and rural electrification led to an irrigation boom in Texas during the 1930s. As additional energy sources became available and methods of distributing water and applying it to the fields improved, irrigation spread rapidly through those portions of Oklahoma, New Mexico, Kansas, Colorado, and Nebraska underlain by aquifers. Large-scale irrigation was commonplace by the early 1970s.

New problems arose. The water was being pumped mostly from the High Plains aquifer, which receives minimal recharge except for areas of sandy soils. Fear struck the region as wells began to dry up. Many farmers could no longer irrigate their crops, and some towns had to haul water as heavily used parts of the aquifer became depleted. Would millions of acres of farm land lose its water supply? Would the integrated agribusiness economy of irrigated crops, feedyards, and beef-processing plants collapse? Would the High Plains become depopulated as the wells ran dry? Everything seemed to hinge on the availability of groundwater.

The contributors to this book address the salient groundwater issues in the High Plains. The evolution of irrigation technology and its socioeconomic impact are traced and the major groundwater problems explored. Legal and institutional conditions are discussed and the importance of differences among the laws and policies of the states considered. Technological change plays a major role in the drama of the High Plains, and in this book both irrigation technologies and techniques for monitoring groundwater are examined.

The writers show that environmental conditions, legislation, institutional arrangements, and economic constraints vary substantially throughout the High Plains, as do the availability of water, the depth to the aquifer, and pumping costs. Management strategies that work in one area may be inappropriate in other areas. The resultant range and complexity of management issues are illustrated through case studies of the Nebraska Sandhills, northwest Kansas, and the Texas High Plains.

Once we know where we are and what we have, some notion of what we can expect emerges. Basing their response on a review of the material presented in the book, the two editors provide a look at the future of the High Plains in the concluding essay. It is certain that water, especially groundwater, will continue to be the key.

The editors acknowledge the tremendous assistance given us in more than a dozen years of groundwater research in the High Plains. Our scholarly efforts have been financially supported by the Kansas Water Resources Research Institute, the General Service Foundation, and, most significantly, the Ford Foundation. The experiences in the Ogallala region made possible by these grants stimulated our desire to produce this edited volume.

We give our heartfelt thanks to Cherryle Glanzer, Donna Rose, and Bobbie Kromm, who professionally prepared the final manuscript and index for this book, and to the many student assistants and office personnel who contributed to each and every chapter.

CHAPTER ONE

The High Plains Ogallala Region

David E. Kromm and Stephen E. White

THE PHYSICAL SETTING

Many people understand the concept of the High Plains as a distinct part of the United States, but few could locate the region precisely. The essence of the region was permanently captured by Walter Prescott Webb (1931), who defined it sixty years ago in terms of an association of physical features: "A plains environment is characterized by a plane, or level, surface, is treeless, and is subhumid. The High Plains have all three characteristics." To the east he saw the humid prairie plain and to the west arid mountains. Webb perceived the unity of the region in terms of its flatness, absence of trees, and insufficient rainfall. Most people today feel comfortable with this notion.

Fred Shannon (1940) lamented Webb's imprecise boundaries. He saw much inconsistency in the areas Webb included and excluded at various times and observed that the High Plains is not always flat, treeless, and subhumid. Possibly both Webb and Shannon are right. Webb described the main natural conditions known at the time, and Shannon argued that they are not uniform or consistent in appearance. We might still ask just where the region begins and ends and what it is like. Fenneman (1931) defined the High Plains physiographically as a very flat remnant of a former great fluviatile plain bounded by escarpments on all sides except for a piedmont in the west. From east to west the High Plains is a zone of transition between a more humid area with a tallgrass prairie and trees and a mountainous area with lowland aridity. The High Plains–mountain boundary is sometimes clear, but to the east a gradation toward taller grasses and more and more trees occurs, along with perennial streams and rivers.

Precipitation plays a major role in defining the plains environment and also contributes to the uncertainty of the regional boundaries. The area is called subhumid or semiarid, denoting whether the observer sees it as somewhat wet or somewhat dry, and precipitation varies greatly from year to year. Kraenzel (1955) correctly noted that the plains are not

1

half dry and half wet but that "some years they are dry and even arid; other years they are very wet; and still other years they are wet or dry at the wrong times from the standpoint of agricultural production and yields. It is this undefinable aspect of semiaridity that gives the Plains their distinctiveness." It is no surprise that in the world climatic scheme, the north-south line dividing the dry steppe from the humid continental in the north and the humid subtropical in the south runs through the heart of the High Plains.

Variability describes the climate well. Rosenberg (1987) wrote that a "wide range of weather conditions can occur within the period of a day, from one day to the next, from season to season, and from year to year." He attributed this instability to continentality and air masses. The High Plains is distant from the oceans and the Great Lakes, bodies of water that moderate climatic conditions. This remoteness marks the climate as continental since air and land heat and cool more quickly than water, a process leading to temperature extremes greater than those in coastal areas. Rosenberg (1987) noted that Amarillo in the Texas High Plains has the same daily minimum temperature in January as Detroit, which lies 500 miles north, and that the same normal daily maximum temperature for July occurs in north-central South Dakota and in Jacksonville, Florida. Most of the air masses that cross the High Plains originate in the north, bringing dry polar air that is very cold in the winter, or in the Gulf of Mexico, bringing moist and usually warmer air in the summer. Shifts in wind direction bring in new air masses and often abrupt changes in the weather. Because air masses from the Gulf of Mexico prevail in the summer, the greatest rainfall is during the growing season from April to September (Rosenberg 1987).

As one would expect in a zone of variability, many of the changes and associated weather phenomena are threatening. The main climatic hazards of the High Plains are tornadoes, hail, wind, frost, flood, and drought. Tornado alley, the most frequent path for tornadoes, lies in Kansas and Oklahoma at the eastern fringe of the High Plains. The "hail center" of the United States is in the High Plains of Nebraska, Colorado, and Wyoming, where as many as nine days with hailstorms occur on the average each year (Rosenberg 1987). Rosenberg called the plains the "windiest region in the country"open as it is to the free sweep of air masses from north and south." Strong winds endanger crops and livestock and damage buildings. In the winter the wind-chill factor is a well-known index of danger to residents. A temperature of 20°F with a wind speed of 25 miles per hour has the same cooling power as −10°F with a 5-mile-per-hour wind. Great care must be taken because human flesh freezes quickly when exposed to low temperatures with even moderate winds (Dale 1967). As air masses shift quickly, spring frosts are common after an extended period of relatively warm weather, restricting the growing of fruit trees and threatening planted crops.

There may be too much or too little precipitation. Heavy rainfall, especially in the spring, fills drainage courses and often floods adjacent lands. As downpours are more frequent than gentle showers, building in floodplains or obstructing natural drainage can have severe consequences. Yet drought is a normal feature of the High Plains. Average precipitation, in the sense of the long-term mean for a specific location, seldom occurs, but human activity tends to reflect the supposed norm in terms of such widely diverse practices as the planting of moisture-demanding crops, lawn grasses, and ornamental trees and shrubs. When several years of below-normal precipitation come in a row, the resulting drought conditions have significant adverse effects. Sweeten and Jordan (1987) pointed out that "rainfall probabilities are more important than average rainfall as a basis for decision making in water management." The inevitability of drought in the High Plains does not lessen the hardship that it brings.

Dale (1967) labeled the positive aspects of the High Plains climate as climatic resources. He highlighted the "prevalence of favorable weather for outdoor work," noting that at Colby and Garden City, Kansas, the possibility of a dry day "ranges from about 92 percent in the Christmas week to 75 percent at Garden City and 65 percent at Colby in June." Other climatic resources include abundant sunshine, low relative humidity, and a tendency toward cool evenings during the hot summer months. The heat promotes rapid growth of agricultural crops. The winds power windmills that pump water primarily for livestock and sweep the air of human-induced and natural pollutants (Rosenberg 1987). For many people the changes in the weather are stimulating and make life more interesting. The weather most certainly is a major topic of daily conversation.

Webb believed that the climate, specifically the deficiency in precipitation, was the most important characteristic in determining a plains environment. Today, groundwater rather than precipitation helps define the region. Groundwater supports millions of acres of irrigated agriculture as well as municipalities and manufacturing. Green (1973) referred to the "land of the underground rain" in writing about the Texas High Plains. Much of the region is underlain by the High Plains aquifer, the largest underground water reserve in the country. Since very few natural lakes or rivers with large flow are found in the High Plains, groundwater provides most of the water in the region.

The topography of the High Plains is almost as uniform as the climate is variable. Reisner (1986) wrote, "the landscape is relentlessly the same: the same flatness, the same treelessness, the same curveless thirty-mile

Field in Gaines County, Texas, that conveys the sense of flatness and dryness characteristic of the High Plains.

stretches of road." The relative flatness of the land provides one of the strongest images of the region. Although elevations generally exceed 4,000 feet in the west and fall below 2,000 feet in the east, the gentle slope and rolling hills make the change imperceptible. The High Plains is a remnant of a vast plain formed by sediments deposited by streams flowing east from the Rocky Mountains (Weeks 1986). Webb attributed the absence of pronounced erosional features to the sod cover, which mats and protects the surface. The modest precipitation, paucity of perennial rivers, and limited glaciation also contribute to the nearly featureless plain. Perhaps the most distinctive topographic area of the High Plains is the Sandhills of Nebraska. Approximately 19,300 square miles of sand dunes create an uneven landscape, with dunes reaching as high as 400 feet and having slopes as steep as 25 percent (Bleed and Flowerday 1989).

Soils and vegetation in the High Plains reflect the limited precipitation. Soils are lightly leached, resulting in a relatively dark color and a horizontal zone of alkaline salt accumulation not far below the surface. The color ranges from almost black in the east to brown in the west, in part because of the closer proximity of the carbonate zone to the surface in the western reaches (Kraenzel 1955). The level of fertility is high. Soils formed under subhumid conditions with grassland vegetation tend to have abundant organic matter because of the decomposition of grasses and their root systems (Baltensperger 1985). Alluvial soils in the floodplains of rivers and streams are well suited to agriculture. In the Sandhills and sandy areas, thin, coarse-textured soils are the rule. According to the Comprehensive Soil Classification System, the chief soil order found in the High Plains is mollisols, with aridisols in the drier west, entisols in areas of sandhills and along some rivers, and discontinuous zones of alfisols to the south (Figure 1.1). Mollisols are defined by their dark-brown to black surface horizon and a dominance of calcium. They are formed under grass in climates with a seasonal water deficiency and are among the most naturally fertile soils in the world. Aridisols experience extended periods of inadequate water for plants and together with alfisols are not darkened by humus. Entisols lack soil horizons and are associated with a parent material of sand and with recent stream deposition (Strahler and Strahler 1987).

The High Plains is in the grassland biome. Grasses prevail, though trees and shrubs may be found along watercourses. Indeed, treelessness goes along with the semiarid climate and level topography in defining the High Plains. The natural vegetation is short grass, but most of that has given way to cropped fields or improved pasture. The degree of coverage ranges from continuous to discontinuous; in the eastern fringes and during wet years one finds tall grasses and to the west and in dry years sagebrush.

The precise extent of the High Plains has not yet been defined. Despite the problems of delineating a transitional zone, we felt that we must use some agreed-upon area in order to give structure to the region and to provide a base for reporting statistical data. The focus of this study is on groundwater, and the contributors deal specifically with that part of the region underlain by the High Plains aquifer—the greater part of the High Plains in Texas, Oklahoma, Kansas, and Nebraska. The specific boundaries used are those defined in the High Plains–Ogallala Aquifer Regional Resources Study (High Plains Associates 1982). The region consists of about 220,000 square miles in 184 counties in Texas, New Mexico, Oklahoma, Colorado, Kansas, and Nebraska (Figure 1.2)—because of the limited use of water for irrigation in Wyoming and South Dakota, that part of the area was not included in the High Plains Study. The region will be referred to as the High Plains throughout the book, though terms like "High Plains aquifer region," "plains," or "Ogallala region" may be used on occasion.

SETTLEMENT PATTERNS

The geographer John Holmes (1981) has argued that a reasonable definition of sparsely populated lands designates a density that ranges between

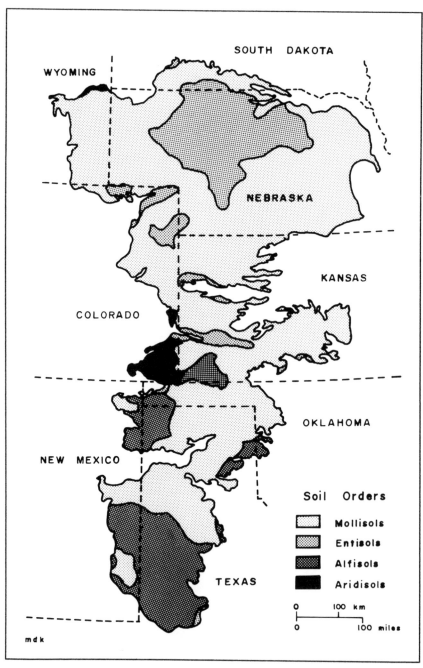

Figure 1.1. Soils Overlying the High Plains Aquifer. *Source:* U.S. Geological Survey; U.S. Department of Agriculture

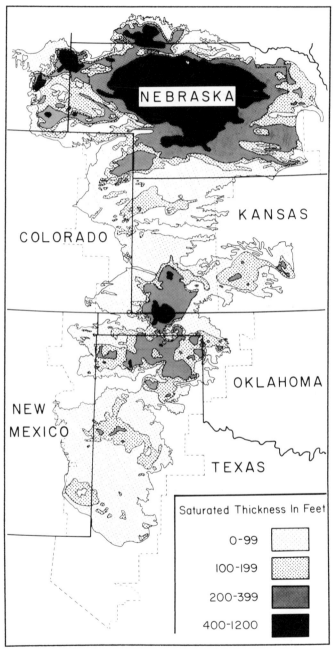

Figure 1.2. Saturated Thickness of High Plains Aquifer, 1980.
Source: U.S. Geological Survey. Reprinted with permission
from *Journal of Geography* (Kromm and White, 1987).

two and ten persons per square mile. Using this guideline, much of the High Plains aquifer region can be classified as sparsely populated; 131 of 184 or 71 percent of the counties had fewer than ten persons per square mile in 1990 (Figure 1.3). In 1990 the total population of the entire region was just under 2.2 million people or slightly less than the population of metropolitan St. Louis (Table 1.1).

Areas of greatest density include portions of the Texas Panhandle, centered on Amarillo and Lubbock, the Platte River valley, counties that fringe the eastern portion of the aquifer in Nebraska, and a few individual counties that have relatively large towns such as Finney (Garden City) and Ford (Dodge City) in Kansas, Curry (Clovis and Portales) in New Mexico, and Scotts Bluff (Scotts Bluff) in Nebraska.

Brunn and Zeigler (1981) have identified several generalizations that characterize the settlement patterns of sparsely populated areas in the United States; they described the High Plains situation well. Sparsely populated areas (1) tend to have a larger proportion of low-order central places than more densely settled areas, (2) tend to have county boundaries that are organized in a regular fashion (like rectangles), (3) have county seats that are centrally located, and (4) have a high degree of urban primacy (large gaps in population exist between the largest city and the second-largest city within a multicounty area).

Not only do residents of the High Plains live in a sparsely populated area, but many are isolated from other major population nodes and few are near any part of the interstate highway system. For example, residents in most of western Nebraska, western Kansas, and portions of eastern Colorado live more than 150 miles from a metropolitan area, and much of the High Plains is more than 50 miles from an interstate highway. However, Brunn and Zeigler (1981) argued that relative isolation with respect to the national urban system has diminished in recent years because of the diffusion of space-adjusting technologies such as jet aircraft, cable TV, satellite transmission, and computers. Although relative isolation as de-

Table 1.1. Population in the High Plains Aquifer Region

	1960	1970	1980	1990
Colorado	81,608	76,205	77,434	71,869
Kansas	184,427	183,141	188,462	194,873
Nebraska	636,226	621,296	647,477	612,105
New Mexico	122,539	122,726	130,099	130,608
Oklahoma	91,793	90,378	100,551	90,892
Texas	994,291	961,334	1,080,042	1,097,559
High Plains Aquifer Region	2,110,884	2,055,080	2,224,065	2,197,906

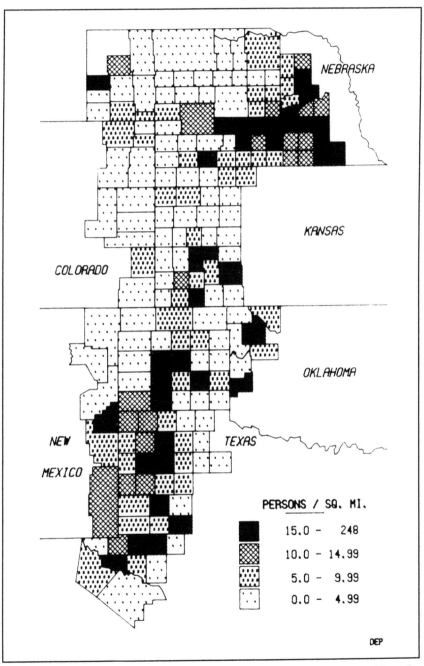

Figure 1.3. High Plains population density, 1990. *Source:* U.S. Census of Population, 1990

fined in terms of communication has declined, physical isolation remains a constant reality.

The cultural geographer Cotton Mather (1972) has described "transience" as one of the major identifiable characteristics of human activity in the Great Plains. Mather noted that though "vast volumes of people, livestock, and inanimate commodities move across the Great Plains . . . to a large degree the area is simply a transit region." He argued that for over 125 years the major settlement trails, railroad lines, and now the interstate highways are oriented east-west and serve to move people through the region, thus reducing the potential for internal integration. He painted a picture of a region that people tend to travel through rather than to settle. Mather's observations were recorded before the widespread expansion of irrigation in Kansas, Colorado, and Nebraska. Evidence now shows that irrigated agriculture has provided the High Plains with an economic base that reduces transience, sparseness, and isolation by encouraging the growth and redistribution of population.

Although the High Plains is a sparsely populated region, the Ogallala portion is not becoming depopulated rapidly. In the wake of severe economic downturns in both agriculture and energy in the 1980s, depopulation in the High Plains has gained much attention. Deborah and Frank Popper's widely publicized study criticized past policies that encouraged settlement in the High Plains (1988 and 1987). The Poppers have predicted that in the near future "the most likely possibility is a continuation of the gradual impoverishment and depopulation. . . . The small towns in the surrounding countryside will empty, wither, and die. The rural Plains will be virtually deserted. A vast, beautiful, characteristically American place will go the way of the buffalo" (1987). They have recommended that the federal government establish buy-back programs, but their recommendations have not been favorably received by many of the residents.

Analyses such as the Poppers' frequently overlook the intraregional complexity of the variables that influence population change. The 184-county Ogallala region actually experienced a 4.1 percent population increase between 1960 and 1990, gaining more than 87,000 inhabitants. However, the pattern of population change has fluctuated somewhat from decade to decade and from state to state. The 1950s witnessed a gain of 14.8 percent; the 1960s saw a period of stagnation (2.6 percent decline); and the 1970s experienced an increase of 8.2 percent. According to the 1990 Census Bureau's totals, the region declined by 1.2 percent between 1980 and 1990 (Table 1.2). Although the region lost some population during the 1980s the decline was small and does not support a rational basis for adopting a buffalo-commons mentality. The Ogallala region has not experienced massive depopulation despite the farm crises, declining energy production, declining water levels, and bank failures. Region-

Broken Bow, in central Nebraska, like many smaller communities in the High Plains, appears as an attractive island in an ocean of fields and pasture.

wide, the demographic changes have been subtle since 1960. Nearly 60 percent of the region's 2.22 million inhabitants lived in urban areas in 1980 (Figure 1.4). Only 16.4 percent resided in incorporated places having less than 2,500 people, and 23.8 percent lived in the country.

Population change, however, varied significantly throughout the region (Figure 1.5). At the state level, the greatest percentage of increase between 1960 and 1990 occurred in Texas (10.4 percent), followed by New Mexico (6.6 percent) and Kansas (5.7 percent); population losses occurred

Table 1.2. Population Change in the High Plains Aquifer Region (in percentages)

	1960–70	1970–80	1980–90	1960–90
Colorado	− 6.6	+ 1.6	− 7.2	− 11.9
Kansas	− 0.7	+ 2.9	+ 3.4	+ 5.7
Nebraska	− 2.4	+ 4.2	− 5.6	− 3.8
New Mexico	+ 0.2	+ 6.0	+ 0.4	+ 6.6
Oklahoma	− 1.5	+11.3	− 9.6	− 1.0
Texas	− 3.3	+12.4	+ 1.6	+10.4
High Plains Aquifer Region	− 2.6	+ 8.2	− 1.2	+ 4.1

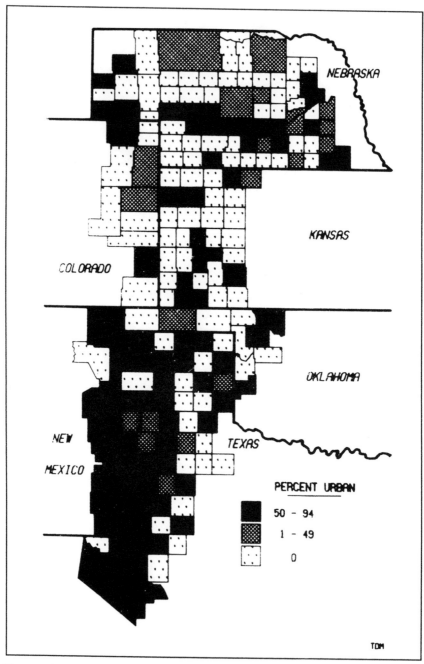

Figure 1.4. High Plains Urban Population, 1980. *Source:* U.S. Census of Population, 1980

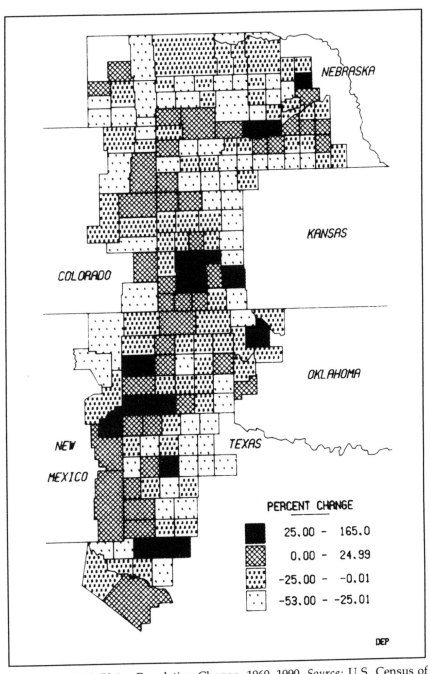

Figure 1.5. High Plains Population Change, 1960–1990. *Source:* U.S. Census of Population, 1990

Most towns that are stable or expanding rely heavily on irrigation-related business. Imperial, in southwestern Nebraska.

in Nebraska (−3.8 percent), Oklahoma (−1.0 percent), and Colorado (−11.9 percent). Within individual states, the primary-growth areas include the Platte valley of Nebraska, southwestern Kansas, and the most northern and western counties in the Texas Panhandle. Areas with a high percentage of losses are the Sandhills in Nebraska, south-central Nebraska, northwestern Kansas, eastern Colorado, and the eastern-most counties in the Texas Panhandle.

A study by Jan and Cornelia Flora (1988) suggested that the occurrence of medium-sized farms in predominantly wheat-growing High Plains counties was related to a community's economic vitality and population stability. Farmers who operated medium-sized farms used more labor per unit of agricultural output than those with larger operations, tended to buy supplies locally, and were less likely to be absentee farm operators. Research by Albrecht and Murdock (1985) has also shown that irrigated agriculture is more frequently associated with smaller farms and large population than is dryland agriculture. Thus irrigated agriculture may have a direct impact on local economic viability because it is capital intensive and an indirect impact on population stability and growth by supporting smaller farms.

THE HIGH PLAINS AQUIFER

The lifeblood of the High Plains economy is the High Plains regional aquifer (see Figure 1.2), which underlies about 174,000 square miles in eight states and 161,300 square miles in our 184-county, six-state region (Weeks 1986). The aquifer sustains 20 percent of the irrigated acreage and provides 30 percent of all irrigation water pumped within the United States. In 1980 the regional aquifer supported over 170,000 irrigation wells that pumped 18 million acre-feet of water to 14 million acres of crops (Weeks 1986). Over 95 percent of the water pumped from the aquifer is used for irrigation (Gutentag et al. 1984; Weeks and Sun 1987).

The High Plains regional aquifer is actually composed of several water-bearing formations. The most important geologic unit is the Ogallala formation, which underlies about 134,000 square miles. The Ogallala is composed primarily of unconsolidated, poorly sorted clay, silt, sand, and gravel laid down about ten million years ago from the Rocky Mountains by fluvial deposition (Bittinger and Green 1980). After deposition, several important rivers (the Platte, Republican, Niobrara, Smoky Hill, Arkansas, and Canadian) cut channels deep enough to reach the Ogallala formation. Where this occurs, a significant portion of the stream-flow is provided directly by the Ogallala formation, thus permitting the movement of water in the streambed even during dry years in areas where the water table has not been lowered by groundwater depletion. Other geologic units in the High Plains aquifer include the Brule formation and the Arikaree group (Tertiary), consisting of alluvial, dune sand, and valley-fill deposits of Quaternary age, and the deeper Dakota formation of the Cretaceous (Gutentag et al. 1984).

The U.S. Geological Survey has estimated that the total amount of drainable water in the High Plains aquifer is approximately 3.25 billion acre-feet (Weeks 1986). An acre-foot is the volume of water that would cover an area of one acre to a uniform depth of one foot. The volume of drainable water is a function of the saturated thickness and areal extent of the aquifer as well as of its specific yield. Specific yield refers to the percentage of water that can be removed from a water-bearing formation with current technology. The average for the entire aquifer is about 15 percent; thus if irrigators withdrew 1.5 acre-feet of water for each acre of land over the aquifer, the water table would drop 10 feet.

The volume of drainable water from state to state varies highly because saturated thickness, specific yield, and areal extent of the aquifer are not uniform. Nebraska has almost two-thirds (65 percent) of the High Plains groundwater; Texas has 12 percent, Kansas 10 percent, Colorado 4 percent, Oklahoma 3.5 percent, and New Mexico, South Dakota, and

Wyoming less than 2 percent each. Eighty-seven percent of all the groundwater is concentrated in three states.

Although Nebraska has about 65 percent of the water, it contains only 37 percent of the area underlain by the aquifer. On the other hand, Texas has over one-fifth of the aquifer's surface area but only 12 percent of the drainable water (Weeks 1986). Importantly, the physical characteristics of the aquifer affect the volume of water not only among states, but they also vary significantly on the local scale. For example, some farmers in north Finney County, Kansas, have no drainable water, but those in the southern portion of the county 25 miles away have more than 200 feet of saturated thickness, enough water to permit irrigation for over one hundred years at 1980s' depletion rates (Kromm and White 1981).

Donald Green has noted that in the Texas High Plains the theory that the Ogallala was an inexhaustible source of water from distant mountains prevailed well into the 1950s (Green 1973). The theory quickly vanished, however, as irrigation expanded and water tables systematically fell. The issue of groundwater depletion is at the heart of the future economic survival of the High Plains (see chap. 3). However, four important terms—saturated thickness, groundwater recharge, groundwater flow, and depth to the water table—provide a context for better understanding the depletion problem.

Saturated thickness represents the vertical distance between the water table and the base of the aquifer; that is the depth of the saturated zone. The total volume of saturated material in the High Plains aquifer has been estimated to be 21.8 billion acre-feet. The saturated thickness varies from zero in several areas where the aquifer is unsaturated to more than 1,000 feet in west-central Nebraska. Although the mean saturated thickness for the entire aquifer is about 200 feet, only a few places outside Nebraska have thicknesses that exceed the mean, notably, areas in southwestern Kansas, the northern portion of the Texas Panhandle, and extreme southeastern Wyoming. The mean saturated thickness for Texas is only 112 feet, and many areas in Texas have less than 100 feet of saturated thickness (Sweeten and Jordan 1987). In many places saturated thickness has declined. About 29 percent of the area over the High Plains aquifer has experienced water-table declines of more than 10 feet since preirrigation development.

Precipitation is the primary source of water for recharging the Ogallala. With low rainfall and high evapotranspiration, however, recharge is negligible throughout most of the High Plains. Estimated recharge rates range from a high of 6 inches per year in sandy areas of Nebraska and southcentral Kansas to just .024 inch per year in parts of Texas. The long-term average recharge rate is probably about a few tenths of an inch per year for the High Plains region (Gutentag et al. 1984).

Frequently, people think that an aquifer is an underground river and may have the misperception that water freely flows underground over long distances in short periods of time. In fact, an aquifer is a porous rock structure that contains water. Groundwater does flow through the High Plains aquifer but at an average rate of only one foot per day, slightly more than the length of one football field per year (Gutentag et al. 1984), and at a rate of only seven inches a day in Texas (Sweeten and Jordan 1987). The direction of flow is generally from west to east, following the slope of the water table. Irrigators in Colorado need not worry about their water flowing downhill to benefit Kansas irrigators as it would take about 145 years for it to flow east a mere 10 miles.

A very important characteristic of the aquifer is the depth of the water table below the earth's surface. This depth affects the feasibility of exploiting water because of its direct association with energy costs. The relationship between depth to the aquifer and energy costs is almost linear (Gutentag et al. 1984). An irrigator who must pump water from 100 feet below the ground uses only about one-third of the energy that an irrigator uses who pumps from a depth of 300 feet. Energy costs are the primary consideration in the decision to irrigate. Survey research (Kromm and White 1985; Taylor, Downton, and Stewart 1988) suggests that irrigators throughout the High Plains are more concerned about high energy costs than about groundwater depletion.

Depth to the water varies significantly throughout the High Plains and can also vary greatly within individual counties. A highly generalized map reveals no obvious patterns (Figure 1.6). Each state has shallow and deep water, although Texas does have a greater share of its aquifer more than 200 feet below the surface and even some sizable areas where the depth exceeds 300 feet.

IRRIGATED AGRICULTURE

Irrigated agriculture sustains the High Plains and is central to an integrated agribusiness economy that demands seeds, fertilizers, pesticides, agricultural machinery, and credit. It supplies cotton to support gins and denim mills and feedgrains to support cattle feedlots and meat-packing plants. Without irrigation, vast tracts of land now cultivated would be in pasture or extensively farmed with dryland techniques; the regional economy would be much smaller and far less active. Herodotus observed more than two thousand years ago that Egypt is a gift of the Nile River; likewise, the contemporary High Plains is largely the gift of the huge aquifer system. The common thread is water, which, by virtue of irrigated agriculture, nurtures life in a dry region.

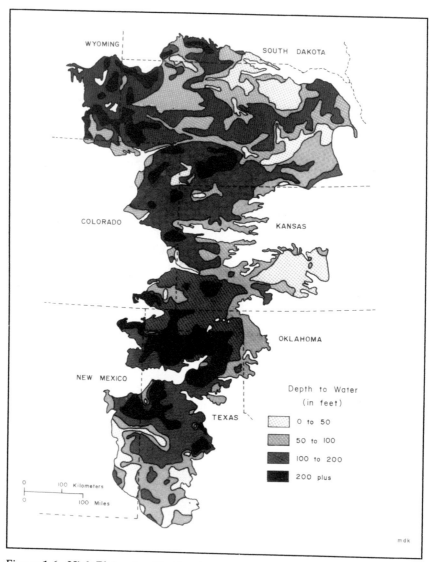

Figure 1.6. High Plains Aquifer Depth to Water in 1980. *Source:* U.S. Geological Survey

Two common scenes in the High Plains: furrow irrigation (top), and center pivot irrigation (bottom).

Irrigated agriculture is not a homogeneous activity in the High Plains. From place to place one sees significant differences in the crops grown and the proportion of land being irrigated. Throughout the region the process of change is continuous. Crop choice, irrigation methods, and amount of land irrigated vary in the High Plains. Diversity exists, therefore, both in the present patterns and in the occurrence of change, making irrigated agriculture a dynamic and spatially varied human endeavor.

The diversity is best visualized by flying in a small plane several hundred feet above the land. Rectangular field patterns formed by furrow irrigation contrast with large circles resulting from center pivot irrigation; both differ from the cultivated dryland fields and areas in pasture. Virtually all land is in some form of agricultural use. Often, only one of the four patterns prevails although a few areas maintain all four activities in a relatively short linear distance. The observer in the plane, by carefully choosing the season to fly, would note white cotton bolls in Texas, amber wheat fields in Kansas, and sturdy green stalks of corn in Nebraska. What could not be seen from the airplane would be the rapid change and decline of irrigated agriculture.

The development of irrigated agriculture since 1959 in the High Plains is a study of change (Table 1.3). Irrigated acres peaked in the 1978 census year when just under 13 million acres were harvested. The number declined by nearly 20 percent in the following nine years. The actual greatest acreage probably occurred two or three years after the 1978 agricultural census. The High Plains Study used an estimate of 15 million acres for 1980 (High Plains Associates 1982). All states reached their maximum number of irrigated acres during the census year of 1978. In addition to the subsequent decline there has also been a shift to the north in the relative proportion of irrigated acres. Texas and New Mexico contributed their highest proportion in 1959 and their lowest in 1987. Texas declined from well over half of the regional total to just above one-quarter. Nebraska, Kansas, and Colorado had their greatest proportion of the regional irrigated acres in 1987, although Kansas and Colorado experienced very modest increases from the previous census. Nebraska became more and more important, expanding its proportion from 28.5 percent in 1969 to 39.1 percent in 1978 and to a strong plurality of 47.8 percent in 1987. Oklahoma was relatively most important in 1969. All six states saw a decline in irrigated acres after 1978, with Texas experiencing the greatest loss and Nebraska the least.

A certain proportion of harvested acres were irrigated in each of the High Plains states (Table 1.4). In interpreting these data it should be kept in mind that the total number of acres harvested varied among the census years, largely in response to federal agricultural programs. The total acreage harvested in 1987 was relatively low for all six states. Both the

Table 1.3. Total Irrigated Area by State in the High Plains

	1959		1969		1978		1987		(%)	(%)
State	Acres	Regional Percentage	Acres	Regional Percentage	Acres	Regional Percentage	Acres	Regional Percentage	Change 1959–1987	Change 1978–1987
Nebraska	1,937,036	28.1	2,620,382	28.5	5,046,815	39.1	4,967,607	47.8	+156.5	−1.6
Texas	3,921,189	56.9	4,379,471	47.6	4,496,514	34.8	2,616,446	25.2	−33.3	−41.8
Kansas	548,642	8.0	1,195,548	13.0	1,956,087	15.1	1,607,301	15.5	+193.0	−17.8
Colorado	253,186	3.7	492,147	5.3	890,241	6.9	746,975	7.2	+195.0	−16.1
Oklahoma	53,342	0.8	259,647	2.8	264,155	2.0	246,367	2.4	+461.9	−6.7
New Mexico	226,435	3.3	253,456	2.8	269,519	2.1	209,728	2.0	−7.4	−22.2
Total	6,886,488		9,200,651		12,923,331		10,394,424		+50.9	−19.6

Source: U.S. Census of Agriculture, 1959, 1969, 1978, and 1987.

Aerial view of center pivot irrigation in Finney County, Kansas. From the air the circles of irrigated crops form the most prominent feature in many areas of the High Plains.

number of acres harvested and the percentage of land irrigated declined between 1978 and 1987.

A north-south division emerges again. Both Texas and New Mexico had a significant proportion of their harvested acres in irrigation as early as 1959. Although the percentage of land irrigated was higher for 1969 and 1978 in these two states, their 1987 percentages were almost the same as for 1959. Texas and New Mexico accounted for over 60 percent of the irrigated acres in the High Plains in 1959 but had just slightly above 27

Table 1.4. Percentage of Cultivated Land Irrigated in the High Plains

State	1959	1969	1978	1987
Nebraska	14.5	25.4	42.1	44.3
Texas	43.1	56.3	53.5	42.7
Kansas	8.5	20.9	31.4	26.7
Colorado	9.2	20.3	30.2	33.9
Oklahoma	2.5	14.3	14.1	14.9
New Mexico	36.2	45.8	37.4	36.9
Total, High Plains	20.0	31.0	40.2	37.4

Sources: Calculated from data in U.S. Census of Agriculture, 1959, 1969, 1978, and 1987.

From the ground level the most visible feature of the settled landscape remains the grain elevator. Hansford County, Texas.

percent of the total in 1987. The other four states had relatively limited irrigation in 1959 but expanded rapidly in subsequent years, with all but Kansas, which peaked in 1978, having their highest proportion of irrigated acres in 1987. Nebraska became the regional leader, increasing its proportion of the acres irrigated from about 28 percent in 1959 to almost 50 percent in 1987. Also reflecting the northward shift of irrigation, the share for Kansas nearly doubled from 8 percent to over 15 percent.

There have been substantial changes in the number of irrigated acres for specific crops as well. The leading crop for 1969, 1978, and 1987 has been corn (Table 1.5; individual crop data is not available for 1959). Corn also increased its proportion from a little less than one-third in 1969 to over one-half in 1987. The highest acreage for corn and cotton occurred in 1978. The highest relative and absolute levels for grain sorghum occurred in 1969 and for wheat in 1987. In recent years the proportion of total harvested acres accounted for by the four major crops has approached 90 percent, with a gradual shift toward wheat and away from cotton. Except for the relative expansion in the number of acres planted to corn (nearly all of which has come from sustained high-production levels in Nebraska), the movement has been toward wheat, a less moisture-intensive crop that requires less irrigation water to thrive. The acres devoted to other crops declined both absolutely and relatively between 1978 and 1987. Some

Table 1.5. Irrigated Acres by Crop, 1969–1987

	1969		1978		1987	
	Acres	Percentage	Acres	Percentage	Acres	Percentage
Corn	2,847,959	31.0	6,202,354	48.0	5,218,367	50.2
Wheat	1,097,772	11.9	1,297,412	10.0	1,582,013	15.2
Sorghum	2,637,332	28.7	1,494,947	11.6	1,114,551	10.7
Cotton	1,392,681	15.1	1,926,154	14.9	1,073,220	10.3
Other	1,224,907	13.3	2,002,404	15.4	1,193,222	13.6
Total	9,200,651		12,923,331		10,394,424	

Source: Calculated from U.S. Census of Agriculture for 1969, 1978, and 1987.

specialty crops have increased, such as vegetables in the southern reaches of the High Plains and potatoes in the north; alfalfa, which has a high water demand, has decreased throughout the region. Other minor crops include soybeans and pinto beans.

A substantial difference occurs in the share of water for each crop irrigated in the individual states (Table 1.6). In the north irrigation makes possible a westward extension of the corn belt. There is a relatively strong cotton belt in Texas and an intermediate wheat belt (Figure 1.7). Corn is the dominant crop in both Nebraska and Colorado. Nearly half the irrigated land in Oklahoma is in wheat, which is also the leading crop for about one-third of the irrigated land in Kansas and New Mexico. Cotton prevails in the Texas High Plains, where it dominates from Lubbock south. The 1969 agricultural census showed grain sorghum to be second only to corn among irrigated crops in the region, but grain sorghum has declined significantly and now is most important in Kansas and Oklahoma in terms of its share of irrigated acres. The sharpest reduction in grain sorghum occurred in Texas, with significant declines also in New Mexico and Oklahoma. The share of irrigated land devoted to wheat has expanded most rapidly in Oklahoma, Colorado, and Kansas.

Table 1.6. Percentages of Irrigated Acres by Crop, 1987

State	Corn	Wheat	Sorghum	Cotton	Other
Nebraska	77.1	2.1	1.8	0.0	19.0
Texas	15.5	23.4	15.7	40.2	5.2
Kansas	33.7	34.8	21.8	0.0	9.7
Colorado	56.1	15.6	3.7	0.0	24.6
Oklahoma	14.2	48.4	21.5	0.0	15.9
New Mexico	14.0	31.8	18.8	9.0	26.4
Total, High Plains	50.2	15.2	10.7	10.3	13.6

Source: U.S. Census of Agriculture for 1987.

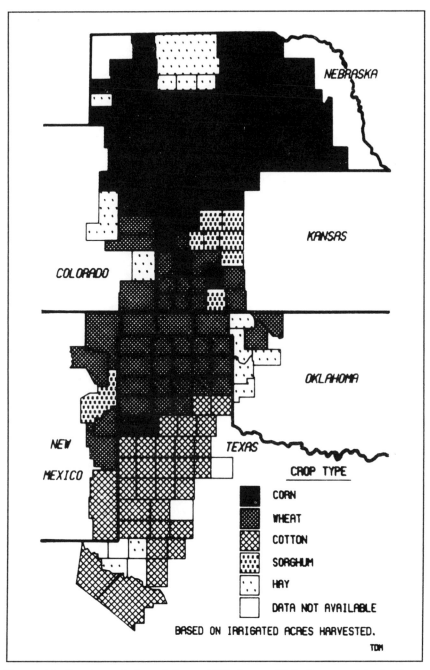

Figure 1.7. Dominant Irrigated Crop, 1987. *Source:* U.S. Census of Agriculture, 1987

REFERENCES

Albrecht, Don E., and Steve H. Murdock. 1985. *The Consequences of Irrigation Development in the Great Plains.* Technical Report 85–1. College Station: Texas Agricultural Experiment Station.

Baltensperger, Bradley H. 1985. *Nebraska: A Geography.* Boulder, Colo.: Westview Press.

Bittinger, Morton W., and Elizabeth B. Green. 1980. *You Never Miss the Water Till . . . (The Ogallala Story).* Littleton, Co.: Water Resources Publication.

Bleed, Ann, and Charles Flowerday. 1989. "Introduction." In Bleed and Flowerday, eds., *An Atlas of the Sandhills.* Lincoln: Conservation and Survey Division, University of Nebraska.

Brunn, Stanley D., and Donald J. Zeigler. 1981. "Human Settlements in Sparsely Populated Areas: A Conceptual Overview with Special Reference to the U.S." In Richard E. Lonsdale and John H. Holmes, eds., *Settlement Systems in Sparsely Populated Regions: The United States and Australia.* New York: Pergamon Press, 14–52.

Dale, Robert F. 1967. "The Climate of the Great Plains." In Carle C. Zimmerman and Seth Russell, eds., *Symposium on the Great Plains of North America.* Fargo: North Dakota Institute for Regional Studies, 35–39.

Fenneman, Nevin M. 1931. *Physiography of the Western United States.* New York: McGraw-Hill.

Flora, Cornelia B., and Jan Flora. 1988. "Public Policy, Farm Size, and Community Well-Being in Farming-Dependent Counties of the Plains." In Louis E. Swanson, ed., *Agriculture and Community Change in the U.S.* Boulder, Colo.: Westview Press, 76–129.

Green, Donald E. 1973. *Land of the Underground Rain: Irrigation on the Texas High Plains, 1910–1970.* Austin: University of Texas Press, 1973.

Gutentag, Edwin D., Frederick J. Heimes, Noel C. Krothe, Richard R. Luckey, and John B. Weeks. 1984. *Geohydrology of the High Plains Aquifer in Parts of Colorado, Kansas, Nebraska, New Mexico, Oklahoma, South Dakota, Texas and Wyoming.* USGS Professional Paper 1400–B. Washington, D.C.: Government Printing Office.

High Plains Associates. 1982. *Six-State High Plains–Ogallala Aquifer Regional Resources Study–Summary.* Austin, Texas.

Holmes, John H. 1981. "Lands of Distant Promise." In Richard E. Lonsdale and John H. Holmes, eds., *Settlement Systems in Sparsely Populated Regions.* New York: Pergamon Press, 1–13.

Kraenzel, Carl Frederick. 1955. *The Great Plains in Transition.* Norman: University of Oklahoma Press.

Kromm, David E., and Stephen E. White. 1981. *Public Perception of Groundwater Depletion in Southwestern Kansas.* Manhattan: Kansas Water Resources Research Institute.

———. 1985. *Conserving the Ogallala: What Next?* Manhattan: Kansas State University.

———. 1987. "Interstate Groundwater Management Preference Differences." *Journal of Geography* 86: 5–11.

Mather, E. Cotton. 1972. "The American Great Plains." *Annals of the Association of American Geographers* 62: 237–57.

Popper, Deborah E., and Frank J. Popper. 1987. "The Great Plains: From Dust to Dust: A Daring Proposal for Dealing with an Inevitable Disaster." *Planning* 53, 6: 12–18.

————. 1988. "The Fate of the Plains." *High Country News* 20, 18: 15–19.

Reisner, Marc. 1986. *Cadillac Desert: The American West and Its Disappearing Water.* New York: Viking Press.

Rosenberg, Norman J. 1987. "Climate of the Great Plains Region of the United States." *Great Plains Quarterly* 7: 22–32.

Shannon, Fred A. 1940. *An Appraisal of Walter Prescott Webb's The Great Plains: A Study in Institutions and Environment (Critiques of Research in the Social Sciences: 3).* New York: Social Science Research Council.

Strahler, Arthur N., and Alan H. Strahler. 1987. *Modern Physical Geography.* 3d ed. New York: John Wiley and Sons.

Sweeten, John M., and Wayne R. Jordan. 1987. *Irrigation Water Management for the Texas High Plains: A Research Summary.* Texas Water Resources Institute. Technical Report 139. College Station: Texas A & M University.

Taylor, Jonathan G., Mary W. Downton, and Thomas R. Stewart. 1988. "Adapting to Environmental Change: Perceptions and Farming Practices in the Ogallala Aquifer Region." In Emily E. Whitehead et al., eds., *Arid Lands: Today and Tomorrow.* Boulder, Colo.: Westview Press, 665–84.

U.S. Bureau of the Census. 1991. *1990 Population Totals.* Form: D–69. Washington, D.C.: Government Printing Office.

Webb, Walter Prescott. 1931. *The Great Plains.* New York: Ginn and Co.

Weeks, John B., and Ren Jen Sun. 1986. "High Plains Regional Aquifer Study." In Ren Jen Sun, ed. *Regional Aquifer-System Analysis Program of the U.S. Geological Survey Summary of Projects, 1978–84.* U.S. Geological Survey Circular 1002. Washington, D.C.: Government Printing Office.

————. 1987. *Regional Aquifer-System Analysis Program of the U.S. Geological Survey–Bibliography, 1978–86.* Water Resources Investigations Report 87–4138. Denver: U.S. Geological Survey.

CHAPTER TWO

A History of Irrigation Technology Used to Exploit the Ogallala Aquifer

Donald E. Green

In James Michener's historical novel *Texas*, cotton farmer Sherwood Cobb decides to sell his large farm in the rich blackland prairie soil near Waxahachie and to move his family west to the High Plains. There he plans to buy thousands of acres of flat land, to sink irrigation wells, and, like his southern-plantation forebears, to raise cotton. The fortunes of his ancestors had been produced by chattel slaves, but Cobb would seek his fortune through another type of exploitation: by pumping (mining is perhaps more descriptive of the effect) groundwater from one of the world's vast aquifers. Cobb oversimplified the phenomenon as he enthusiastically explained it to his wife, Mary Nell: "Think of it as a vast underground lake. Bigger than most European countries. Dig deep and you invariably find water. It's called the Ogallala Aquifer, after this little town in Nebraska where it was discovered. Fingers probe out everywhere to collect immense runoffs, and the aquifer delivers it right to our farm" (Michener 1985, 969). Cobb obviously knew nothing of the fossil origins or of the limited recharge capacity of the Ogallala, but his attitude was common among early irrigators, who viewed the thick groundwater formation as an inexhaustible albeit reluctant goose awaiting only the technology capable of extracting the golden egg (Green 1973, 165–69).

When farmers first began to tap the Ogallala during the droughts of the late nineteenth century, the only technology available was the American-style windmill first patented by a New Englander named Daniel Halladay in 1854. The demand later in the century for these "wind engines" on the newly settled Great Plains was satisfied by scores of windmill-manufacturing companies and their salesmen (Baker 1985). By the 1890s, windmills were being used in conjunction with small earthen reservoirs by farmers desperate to irrigate a few acres of truck farms, orchards, or both. Some farmers even resorted to building their own "jumbo" or "battle-ax" windmills. Dr. W. J. Workman of western Kansas claimed in 1895 that he had constructed the largest jumbo ever built for irrigation. Shaped like the horizontal paddle wheel on the stern of a steamboat, Workman's mill was 21 feet in diameter. An observer in 1897 noted that homemade mills were scattered throughout the Platte River valley of Nebraska (Sageser 1967, 107–18; Green 1973, 40–42).

One of the greatest advantages of the windmill was its cheapness. At the turn of the century many models sold for under $100 (not including the cost of drilling or digging the well and erecting a tower). Jumbos and battle-axes could be built for only a few dollars, especially when constructed on the farm (Green 1973, 41; Baker 1985, 76, 260–61).Windmill irrigation, however, had three important drawbacks: Windmills of that period were designed primarily for shallow depths of less than 80 feet; the machines could produce enough water for only a few acres; and the wind was not always a dependable source of energy, especially during the heat of summer when water was most needed. One farmer complained, "I know that Kansas had the reputation of being a windy state, but I have found, when it comes to making use of the wind, it is not there" (Longstreth 1895, 370).

Machines capable of lifting the water to the surface in quantities large enough to satisfy the thirst of Great Plains farmers for extensive commercial irrigation did not appear on the scene until about the turn of the century. The initial step in developing this technology occurred in 1875, when an improved centrifugal pump with diffusion vanes surrounding the impeller was patented in England. With this pump, water was sucked into the center of a circular chamber encasing the impeller and discharged through a pipe at the edge of the chamber by centrifugal force. The centrifugal pump, depending upon its size, could deliver large volumes of water, hundreds of gallons or more per minute. A large 10-inch pump (the measurement refers to the diameter of the discharge pipe) could pull 2,000 gallons per minute from a thick aquifer. Unlike the windmill's much smaller piston pump, which required a well of only a few inches in diameter, the centrifugal pump had to be set in a hand-dug pit not more than 20 feet or so above the water level of the well.

By 1900 two types of centrifugal pumps were in use—the horizontal and the vertical. The horizontal, named for its horizontal impeller-shaft, was used in shallower wells. The power was supplied either by an electric motor in the pit joined directly to the pump or by an internal combustion or steam engine at the surface connected to the impeller-shaft by a long, wide belt. An inclined trench had to be dug from the engine to the pump in order to accommodate the belt.The vertical centrifugal pump, usually set below the water level, was used for deeper wells, those below 25 feet. It had a long, vertical shaft aligned with shaft-bearings at various elevations within a wooden framework that reached to the surface. The most serious problem facing irrigators using the vertical pump was the difficulty of perfectly aligning the shaft to protect the life of the bearings.

Irrigators were operating the early centrifugal pumps in a number of areas of the American West before 1900. In 1885 a centrifugal pump powered by a steam engine was in use near Eaton, Colorado, and Kansas farmers had the pumps by 1896 in the area of Garden City. By the turn of the century, centrifugal pumps could be found in the Sacramento Valley of California and in the valleys of Arizona (Green 1973, 44–47).

These early pumps were suited only for relatively shallow groundwater areas such as river valleys, however. Exploitation of the Ogallala required a pump that could be set in deep-drilled wells. The need for such a "pitless pump" was apparent in the California fruit and vegetable industry and in the Gulf Coast rice belt. Inventive minds in both regions at the turn of the century were independently at work, designing a large volume, deep-well pump.

As early as 1897, P. K. Wood of Los Angeles invented an inefficient screw pump consisting of propeller-like impellers within a pipe. In 1901 Byron Jackson of San Francisco built a deep-well, vertical centrifugal pump with its shaft prealigned in a tubular housing for the Pabst Brewing Company of Milwaukee. Power was supplied to the Jackson pump by an electric motor. Elwood Mead, later head of the Bureau of Reclamation, worked as consulting engineer on the project. Jackson, however, did not put his pump into production for several years.

Installation in deep wells of the kind of large volume pump designed by Byron Jackson required a different technology for drilling wells. The most common drilling method at the time, and probably still the most common for boring shallow, low-production water wells, was the "spudder," which literally punched a small-diameter hole in the ground by raising and dropping a steel bit. A rig capable of drilling a hole with a large diameter was needed for the new type of pump.

LAYNE'S "PITLESS" PUMP

The first inventor to put a "pitless" pump into production was a welldriller named Mahlon E. Layne. As early as 1886 Layne was drilling large-diameter wells in South Dakota, using augurs of 18 to 36 inches in diameter turned by a horse walking in a circle. His wells were designed for his patented well screen, placed at the bottom of wells plagued by fine sand. Layne's screen allowed the fine sand to pass through the perforations while gradually packing coarse gravel around the outside. This process would eventually keep the fine sand, now blocked by the gravel, out of the well. For more than a decade Layne drilled wells for municipalities and railroads as well as for farmers in South Dakota, Nebraska, Minnesota, Wisconsin, and Iowa.

Layne continued to improve his rigs. Eventually six horses were required to turn his augur. In 1896 Layne built a rotary drill, similar to the rigs then being used in the Louisiana oil fields, and bought his first steam engine to furnish the power. When the vast Spindletop oil boom erupted east of Houston, Layne moved to Beaumont, Texas, hoping to use his screen for petroleum production. After only limited success in the oil fields, Layne and a young engineer named O. P. Woodburn turned to the nearby rice fields of the Gulf Coast. In 1902 the two men dug four pit-wells for a rice planter near Pierce, Texas. The pits were 8 to 10 feet square and 30 to 40 feet deep. At the bottom of each pit Layne and Woodburn then drilled wells, some 16 to 24 inches in diameter and approximately 100 feet deep, to draw upon the deeper strata of water. They cased the well as they drilled and installed a Layne Keystone Screen at the bottom (Green 1973, 49–50).

The drillers installed horizontal centrifugal pumps in three of the wells and a vertical centrifugal pump in the deepest well. All were powered by Fairbanks-Morse internal-combustion engines. Layne used rope as belting. The rope fit into grooved pulleys and extended from the oil-burning engines over idlers and down into the pits. Fifty-pound iron weights, dangling at the top of the pits, maintained the tension on the ropes. In later life, O. P. Woodburn recalled the nightmare of servicing those pumps: "Imagine getting down into the pit to oil the pump with the mess of rope running at the velocity of the outside diameter of the 54" fly wheel with 6 or 8 50# [pound] weights dancing on the tightener above your head. BAD DREAMS" (Green 1973, 51).

According to Woodburn, during summer 1902 when Layne and he were crawling out of those dangerous pits, Layne "got me off to the side of a building, sketched a pit on the wall with a pump at the bottom and shaft running to the top." The shaft was prealigned, enclosed in a pipe, and flanged onto the pump. The pump was to be installed in a large diameter steel casing set in a drilled well. Bearings would be lubricated by oilers at the surface, and the pump could also be raised or lowered from there. In 1903 Layne constructed his first crude pitless pump and installed it in a rice field near El Campo.

In 1904 Mahlon E. Layne formed a partnership with Woodburn and a salesman named P. D. Bowler. Two years later Layne patented the pump, and in 1907 he created the Layne and Bowler Company with its headquarters at Houston. The company did a booming business in the rice fields and at times could not keep up with the demand for the pump (Green 1973, 51–52). A Texas planter, one R. D. Ratliff of Ganado, put his enthusiasm for the pump to verse in 1908 when he wrote to Layne and Bowler:

> That old fashion Pump!
>   That old wooden pit,
> When I dream of them now
>   I most have a fit.
>
> But then in my dreams,
>   I realize at last
> That the old Pumping outfit
>   is a thing of the past.
>
> My soul fills with joy
>   And my heart gives a jump
> When I remember with pleasure
>   My "Layne [steel] Pit and Pump." (Green 1973, 52)

The pitless pump appeared to answer many an irrigator's prayers, but it also required a suitable power plant before it could be used to exploit the Ogallala Aquifer. Although steam engines were used to power some pumps in California, Arizona, and other parts of the West, one engineer

Boosterism was important when European settlement for farming began and remains so today. Seminole, Texas.

concluded after experiments in Arizona: "It will be seen that the expense of raising water by steam power is very great indeed, and that as a general proposition such water is too costly for constant use in ordinary farming operations" (Mead 1901, 66, 69).

NEW POWER SOURCES

Electric power, still in its infancy, held some promise. In a few areas near municipalities, where pump irrigation was concentrated, power companies actively solicited farmers to link electric motors to their pumps. In a few instances, electrical generating plants were built for the specific purpose of supplying power for irrigation plants. For example, the United States Sugar and Land Company used a central power plant near Garden City, Kansas, to supply energy to fourteen pumps in the Arkansas valley in 1909. That same year a group of farmers in the vicinity of Portales, New Mexico, formed an irrigation cooperative and contracted with the Westinghouse Company to construct a central power plant and to run electrical distributing lines to their wells. As collateral, Westinghouse held mortgages on the farmland. Neither project enjoyed success because the cost of electrical generation exceeded reasonable profits made on crops.

In the early years of European settlement, the High Plains was primarily a cattle area, with the animals grazing the nutritious native grasses. Although ranching continues, most animals today are confined in large feedyards. Gray County, Kansas.

The United States Sugar and Land Company project simply faded away. The Portales fiasco led to bankruptcy for the New Mexico farmers, and the Westinghouse power plant was sold to the city of Tulsa, Oklahoma (Green 1973, 53–55; Sorensen 1968, 88; Green 1990, 37–39).

By 1910 the internal-combustion engine appeared to be the cheapest power source for irrigation pumping plants. A German inventor named Nikolaus August Otto and an American, George Brayton, working independently, invented the first successful four-cycle internal-combustion engines in 1876. Otto's engine was powered by illuminating gas, but Brayton's engine, exhibited at the Centennial Exposition in Philadelphia, burned gasoline. Relatively expensive, gasoline at that time was used primarily as a cleaning agent and as a solvent.

Adapting the internal-combustion engine to a cheaper fuel occurred in 1890, when the English engineer Herbert Ackroyd-Stuart invented the low-compression oil-burning engine. Hornsby and Company of England first marketed the Hornsby-Ackroyd in 1894, and an American company was licensed to manufacture the engine the following year. Within a few years such companies as Primm, Charter, Bessemer, Van Sevrein, Fairbanks-Morse, Herr, and others were manufacturing their own oil-burning engines and marketing them throughout the nation.

The oil-burning engine had two desirable features: a simple design and cheap fuel. Most of the engines had only one large cylinder, with horsepower ranging from 5 to 70. There was no electrical system to bother with. The fuel was ignited by a "hot bulb" or "hot plug" in the head of the cylinder that in turn reheated the bulb or plug for the next ignition. Initially, the engine was started by heating the bulb or plug with an alcohol or gasoline torch. The operator then pushed the cylinder forward either by rotating the flywheel by hand or by opening a valve to a compressed-air tank that forced air into the cylinder head until the oil was injected. When the fuel splashed against a hot piece of metal (the "spoon" or "lip") extending into the cylinder head from the "hot bulb," it vaporized into gas, which was ignited by the bulb (Green 1973, 55–76). This early irrigation unit could be identified from a distance by the squat derrick, the small, frame building enclosing the engine that abutted onto the derrick, the loud arrhythmic pop-chug-chug-chug-pop of the engine, and the blue smoke belching from the vertical exhaust with each ignition. Some engines even blew an occasional smoke ring into the atmosphere.

By the outbreak of World War I, several hundred pumping plants were sucking from the Ogallala across the southern High Plains. Most were in the so-called "shallow water belt" stretching in a rough triangle from Hereford to Lubbock, Texas, to Portales, New Mexico. Western Kansas, Scott County in particular, also boasted a few of the pumping plants. D. L. McDonald drilled the first wells on the Texas Plains in 1909

The manufacturing sectors of the regional economy largely provide inputs for agriculture or process primary commodities. Above is a fertilizer plant in Ford County, Kansas, and below is a meat-packing facility near Holcomb, Kansas.

and 1910 near Hereford, after he had examined a pumping plant that had been installed near Portales in 1909. As early as 1911 J. W. Lough was using a Layne pumping plant near Scott City, Kansas, to churn 1,600 gallons of water per minute to the surface (Green 1973, 59–61; Green 1990, 39–40).

ENTHUSIASM AND REALITY

Local boosters showed unbridled enthusiasm over the possibilities for turning the semiarid pastures of the High Plains into a vast oasis of irrigated farms. One T. J. Molinari of Portales boasted that the aquifer contained "oceans of water"; another New Mexico booster added that the region needed only "the magic of the pump" (Green 1990, 36). After J. C. Mohler, assistant secretary to the Kansas State Board of Agriculture, had made a cursory investigation of the wells in western Kansas, he wrote, "These large, deep wells, with the centrifugal pumps and powerful cheap oil-engines, are the means by which the underground waters will be utilized to irrigate the lands of this great territory" (Green 1973, 60–61).

Superlatives flowed from the pen of Zenas E. Black, the secretary of the Commercial Club of Plainview, Texas. In a 1914 article, Black first coined the phrase "The Land of the Underground Rain" in the title and asserted, "The centrifugal pump has lifted the shallow water portions of the Texas plains from bondage to the erratic cloud. In this work it has been assisted by the crude oil and distillate burning engine. The perfection of the above agencies has been the greatest boon that inventors have given the world during the past ten years" (Black 1914, 13; Green 1973, 61).

The enthusiasm of local boosters whitewashed the disadvantages of the early pumping plants. First, costs were beyond the reach of the average farmer. Shallow wells no more than 35 feet deep using the cheaper vertical or horizontal centrifugal pumps could cost as much as $2,300, including labor for digging the well, the pump, and the engine. But the installation of a pitless pump in a deeper well of 125 to 175 feet could range from $4,000 to $6,000 for a turnkey job. In 1913 a 70-horsepower Bessemer engine installed at the well site could cost as much as $1,900. Well-drillers using the new rotary rigs adapted from the Louisiana and Texas oil fields charged from four to five dollars per foot for drilling a 28- to 30-inch-diameter well to accommodate the pump. The Layne pump retailed for about $500. Additional costs, including lumber and labor for constructing a derrick over the drilling site and an engine-house, a concrete base for the engine, expenses for freight, drayage, an air compressor and air tanks, an oil-storage tank and other incidentals, could push the total to another $1,000 or so (Green 1973, 56, 59–60, 113–15).

The early engine was also plagued with mechanical problems. In that

With farm consolidation, many small towns in the High Plains have almost disap-peared from the map. Meadville, Nebraska.

prepower farming era, most farmers had little or no experience repairing internal-combustion engines. Very few owned automobiles before the unveiling of Henry Ford's cheap Model T, first produced on the innova-tive assembly line in 1913. The farm tractor did not arrive on the scene until World War I when labor shortages in British agriculture, caused by the slaughter of the war, forced engineers in Great Britain to produce experi-mental models that were readily copied in the United States. Irrigator Roland Loyd, who farmed near Hereford, Texas, filled his diary with comments about the mechanical difficulties he had with his Bessemer engine. On one occasion, he "worked about half of afternoon trying to start pumping outfit" before he "gave it up as bad job and cut weeds rest of afternoon." Loyd was fortunate, however; a mechanic called "Bes-semer" Smith residing in Hereford specialized in repairing Bessemer oil-burning engines (Loyd 1914, June 20, August 10; Green 1973, 106–7).

Although farmers did not require a mechanic to adjust the long, broad leather belts that connected the pulleys of their pumps to the flywheels of their engines, the need to make frequent adjustments forced the irrigator to remain near the pumping plant; nor did he leave the pump running at night. If the summer temperature soared, the belt expanded and slipped on the pulley. Nightfall often brought cooler temperatures on the High Plains and a tightening of the belt. Thus the farmer had to shorten or lengthen the belt to avoid excessive wear on the pump-shaft bearings or slippage on the pulley, which could burn and weaken the belt (Loyd 1914, June 29, July 21, July 30, August 1; Green 1973, 107–8).

Mechanical difficulties and high costs for the pumping plants were only two of the reasons the early movement to exploit the Ogallala Aquifer failed. Other factors included the lack of markets for irrigated crops, the absence of credit to finance the installation of pumping plants, and an adequate amount of rainfall during the 1920s, which literally dampened any enthusiasm for irrigation. Indeed, the early efforts to exploit the aquifer were not really the farmers' but the boosters', led by local businessmen and land speculators. Yet a few of the old pumps remained in operation, symbols for the future (Green 1973, 101–18).

MODERN PUMPING PLANTS

The modern pumping plant on the High Plains today had its origin during those twin disasters, the Great Depression and the Dust Bowl. Through New Deal government-guaranteed financing, many of the new plants began springing up on the Texas Plains in 1934, when a tobacco-chewing, financially stressed banker from Lockney, Artemus "Artie" Baker, used several government programs and credit from pump and engine manufacturers to install turnkey operations for about $2,000. The farmers who made the plunge into irrigation and debt did so only because they were desperate. As Baker said in later years, "A man who had money wouldn't buy an irrigation well; you had to find a 'poor devil' to buy one." Baker's green Ford with its tobacco-stained driver's side became a familiar sight on the dusty roads of Hale County as he made his sales pitch to farmers (as often to the wife as to the husband). Within a year or so after Artie Baker began to sell farmers on the idea of irrigation, pump companies such as Peerless, Layne and Bowler, Johnston, Byron Jackson, and some local machinery companies began to extend credit to farmers for turnkey jobs (Green 1973, 136–41).

The new plants used a more efficient pump (now called a deep-well turbine pump) developed during the 1920s, probably for municipal water-supply systems. The pump was only about 8- to 10-inches in diameter, with closed, multistage impellers turning inside "bowls." It revolved at much higher revolutions per minute (rpm) than the old pump and was also cheaper to install because it required a well much smaller in diameter than the old pitless pump. The new pump was powered by high-speed multicylindered engines, made for industrial purposes, or by automobile engines, both of which developed considerably more rpm than the old 250-rpm oil burners. By 1935 cheap, rebuilt automobile engines manufactured by Ford, Chevrolet, Buick, Pierce Arrow, Studebaker, and others were much in evidence in the fields of the High Plains. In 1938 a new Ford V-8 engine could be purchased for $310, and a 6-cylinder Chevrolet power plant cost $235 (Green 1973, 125–27).

Just as important as the new pump and engine was the new invention linking the two. When geologist/hydrologist Charles L. Baker of the University of Texas investigated the Ogallala Aquifer on the Texas Plains in 1915 he wrote, "Some system of direct connection should be devised in order to get more efficiency" (Baker 1915, 95). As early as 1916, perhaps a year earlier, George E. Green of Plainview, Texas, who had dug or drilled and installed many of the early irrigation wells in Hale County, adapted the basic design of an automobile differential to connect pump and engine. Green called the adaptation with its right-angle meshed gears a "geared-head"; locals later shortened it to "gear-head." He installed the first of his gear-heads, run by a 45-horse-power 4-cylinder Twin City engine in 1917, but the invention did not come into general use until the 1930s. Green, incidentally, was never able to procure a patent on the device, perhaps because of its easily copied simplicity of design. No one ever secured a patent on the gear-head, and by the 1930s other manufacturers such as the Johnson Gear and Manufacturing Company of Berkeley, California, and the Amarillo Machine Shop of Amarillo, Texas, were manufacturing and marketing the device.

The new pumping plants had many advantages. Not only were they more efficient; they were more dependable. Farmers began running their units twenty-four hours a day, significantly increasing their irrigated acreage. In 1919 the average pump watered 72 acres; the new plant by 1937 was irrigating 139 acres. These pumps were also cheaper: The older plants had cost $4,000 to $6,000 installed, but a turnkey job for a 180-foot well using the new pumping plants was about $2,000. That included $835 for the pump, $585 for drilling and casing, $270 for the gear-head, and $310 for the engine. Operating costs were also lower. An acre-foot of water using the older technology ranged from $5.00 to $6.25; costs for the newer plants ran from $3.30, using a Chevrolet 6-cylinder engine, to $4.50, with a Ford V-8 power plant (Green 1973, 127–30).

As exploitation of the Ogallala expanded north from the Texas Plains after World War II, new technology brought about more changes in irrigation practices. Fuel costs were lowered when farmers switched from gasoline to liquified-petroleum, butane/propane gas, or natural gas piped in from the nearby gas fields of the Texas and Oklahoma panhandles and southwestern Kansas. By the late 1950s cheap natural gas, much of it brought to the pumping plants by gas lines laid and financed by farmer-cooperatives, powered most of the pumps.

WATER-DELIVERY SYSTEMS

Significant changes in water-delivery systems also occurred. Rubber, plastic, or aluminum siphon tubes replaced the old labor-intensive method of keeping a laborer with a spade in the field to slice out or fill up sections of the ditch as water was moved from row to row. Underground concrete pipe replaced the ditches, resulting in significant savings in water previously lost to evaporation or soakage. Gated aluminum pipe then transferred the water from the underground pipe via riser valves, easily recognizable from the road by the old tires encircling them as markers so that farmers would not accidentally demolish them with a tractor or a pickup truck (Green 1973, 152–55).

Aluminum pipe was used not only for running water down the rows by gravity, but also in a new method in applying water—sprinkler irrigation. American aluminum companies such as Alcoa and Kaiser had greatly expanded production during World War II to meet the new demand for the lightweight metal in aircraft. In efforts to open up new markets after the war, the companies began manufacturing aluminum pipe. At first, production amounted to only a trickle, with 250 miles of pipe turned out in 1946, but as demand increased, the miles of pipe grew to 7,500 in 1952. Sprinkler irrigation itself was not new; it had existed for decades in orchard and truck farming, where steel galvanized pipe had been permanently set on posts.

But aluminum pipe resulted in the advent of widespread portable sprinkler irrigation, using pipe of 20 to 40 feet in length with quick-locking/quickly detachable coupling devices that could be moved across a field by one person, set by set. W. H. Stout of Portland, Oregon, held the patent to the most popular coupler of the early 1950s, the so-called Stout coupling. Actually, some experiments using steel pipe equipped with fast-coupling devices were carried out in the 1930s, but the pipe was simply too heavy to be carried by one worker. Aluminum pipe was not only lighter than steel; it was also cheaper. Just as important, the shiny new pipe made it possible to irrigate sandy or rolling land, thus setting the stage for expanding the exploitation of the Ogallala into regions previously thought to be unirrigable ("Portable Sprinkler" 1950, 97–98, 132, 134; "Aluminum Pipe" 1953, 132–34; Holman 1957, 76–79).

Early portable irrigation required moving the sets every twelve to twenty-four hours; depending on the total length of pipe, one to two hours might be needed to complete the move. In efforts to save labor costs, inventors experimented with ways to cut the time. W. H. Stout, who held the patent on one of the two basic couplers, invented and began manufacturing the Wheel-Move in 1950, a device in which the pipe passed through the hubs of steel wheels set at intervals to keep the pipe off the ground. Moves could then be made much faster, especially by several workers pushing the wheeled pipe to its next set ("Portable Sprinkler" 1950, 98).

INTRODUCTION OF THE CENTER PIVOT SYSTEM

Wheel-Move and its many imitators were soon surpassed by the most significant development in artificial watering since Mahlon Layne patented his pitless pump—the invention of center pivot irrigation. The center pivot was the creation of Frank Zybach, who patented his first model in 1949 when he was farming near Strasburg, Colorado. Suspending the pipe only a couple of feet, the system was originally designed to water sugar beets, which offered a rather limited market in areas already serviced by ditch-flow gravity irrigation. Zybach moved to Columbus, Nebraska, around 1950, where he formed a partnership with A. E. Trobridge, who supplied much of the capital for adapting the system to watering row crops. Another patent was secured in 1952. The next year, Zybach and Trobridge sold the rights to produce and sell the system to Valmont Industries of Valley, Nebraska, which marketed the center pivot under the brand name "Valley." Valley systems, with wires extending from aluminum pipes suspended some 8 feet from the ground and connected to A-frame towers mounted on tandem wheels, began to appear conspicuously on the landscapes of the High Plains from Texas to Nebraska. Airplane passengers flying over the region began to ask their stewardesses about those mysterious green circles, which dotted the landscape by the 1970s.

The early center pivot systems were connected by swivel, either to a well drilled in the center of a quarter-section (160 acres) or to underground pipe laid to the section's center. Diesel engines usually supplied the power. Hydraulic power slowly pivoted Zybach's invention in a circle around the pump and over the field, pushing it over uneven ground and even over hills. The system bled water from the aluminum pipes to power a cylinder and piston at each wheel. The piston used a "Trojan" bar, which acted as a ratchet on the wheels.

Since the initial appearance of the Valley system many other makes of center pivots have been developed, but only a few large brand names remain. Pivots use hydraulic power or, more commonly, electric motors with gear boxes. Most are mounted on pneumatic rubber tires rather than on steel wheels. The earlier systems revolving in perfect circles could not irrigate the corners of the field, so only about 133 of the 160 acres could be watered; a few systems now use a hinged unit that waters the corners. All have in common the virtually complete automation of the irrigation system. Except for repairs, the only labor required is in starting and servicing the engine and pump.

Development of the center pivot made it possible for irrigation to expand into the extensive Sandhills of Nebraska, which overlie much of the Ogallala Aquifer. The sudden surge of agricultural commodity prices in 1974 apparently stimulated the rapid development of the systems in Nebraska. In 1973 fewer than 3,000 circle systems were in the state; within six years the state counted 15,000 center pivots, most of which were pumping from the Ogallala. The systems were expensive and employed a high level of energy; by 1976 a center pivot could cost as much as $50,000 installed and it consumed 50 gallons of diesel fuel per acre each year in applying a total of 22 inches of water per season.

The advent of portable sprinkler irrigation has been a mixed blessing for the Ogallala. In the older irrigated areas of the southern High Plains, now plagued with increasingly weaker sources of water as a result of more than half a century of mining the Ogallala, sprinkler systems have conserved water by using the systems to apply only the minimum amount of water to crops and by hanging the sprinkler heads below the aluminum pipe on flexible hoses to reduce water loss through evaporation and drift. But the center pivots have opened to irrigation the Nebraska Sandhills, a fragile ecosystem of sand dunes only a few thousand years old and one of nature's most productive grazing/hay lands (Splinter 1976, 90–99; Aucoin 1979, 17–20, 38–40; Green 1973, 206–8).

THE LEGACY OF IRRIGATION

To many farmers on the High Plains who made the decision to install pumping plants, irrigation technology has brought relative prosperity and an enhanced standard of living. Yet dependence on these new systems has also created a kind of secular faith that technology is infinitely capable of solving future problems involving overdraft of the Ogallala and pollution of the aquifer caused by chemical fertilizers and pesticides.

When many farmers on the southern Texas Plains were faced with exhaustion of the Ogallala they turned to expensive and massive engineering schemes for importing water from such faraway places as the Mississippi and Missouri rivers and even from Canada. At a symposium in which I participated in 1974, one chamber of commerce representative from a Texas town proposed that the long chain of outer islands along the Texas Gulf Coast be enclosed. The resulting reservoir could be used to impound the waters of Texas rivers, which would then be pumped back uphill to the High Plains. This unbridled faith in technology was expressed by W. D. Rogers in 1976 when he was mayor of Lubbock, Texas:

"The history of this country is that as the need arose for anything, somebody was there with the right tool to take care of it. This is the way this country was built" (Green 1973, 230). Today, this optimism about the efficiency of technology to produce water for the High Plains appears not only to be naive, but in view of growing environmental concerns it is also destructive.

The development of irrigation technology in the region during the twentieth century provides us with a key to the origins of this attitude. The appearance of the centrifugal pitless pump, the hot-ball engine, and the rotary well-drilling rig demonstrated that the Ogallala held massive amounts of water that could be exploited for croplands. The technology then evolved into a cheaper, smaller, and more efficient pumping plant, thanks to the invention of cheap 6- and 8-cylinder automobile engines, the closed impeller pump, and the pump gear-head. The labor-efficient center pivot sprinkler system appeared as a kind of capstone in the evolution of pump-irrigation. With this historical perspective in mind, it is easy to understand why the people of the Ogallala look to technology for the answers to problems of both the present and the future.

REFERENCES

"Aluminum Pipe." 1953. *Business Week.* May 9, 132–34.

Aucoin, J. 1979. "The Irrigation Revolution and Its Environmental Consequences." *Environment* 21: 17–20, 38–40.

Baker, C. 1915. *Geology and Underground Waters of the Northern Llano Estacado.* Austin: University of Texas Bulletin No. 57.

Baker, T. L. 1985. *Field Guide to American Windmills.* Norman: University of Oklahoma Press.

Black, Z. E. 1914. The Land of the Underground Rain. *Earth* 11: 13–14.

Green, D. E. 1973. *Land of the Underground Rain: Irrigation on the Texas High Plains, 1910–1970.* Austin: University of Texas Press.

———. 1990. "Land of the Underground Rain in Eastern New Mexico." *Panhandle-Plains Historical Review* 58: 34–44.

Holman, R. L. 1957. "Man-Made Rain." *American Mercury* 85: 76–79.

Longstreth, C. H. 1895. "Fruit and Vegetable Growing under Irrigation." *Ninth Biennial Report of the Kansas State Board of Agriculture* 14: 370.

Loyd, R. 1914. Diary. Lubbock: Southwest Collection, Texas Tech University.

Mead, E. 1901. *Report of Irrigation Investigations for 1901.* U.S. Department of Agriculture Experiment Stations Bulletin No. 119. Washington, D.C.: Government Printing Office.

Michener, J. 1985. *Texas.* New York: Random House.

"Portable Sprinkler Irrigation." 1950. *Fortune* (June): 97–98, 132, 134.

Sageser, A. B. 1967. "Windmill and Pump Irrigation on the Great Plains." *Nebraska History* 48: 107–18.

Sorensen, C. 1968. "A History of Irrigation in the Arkansas River Valley in Kansas, 1880–1910." Master's thesis, University of Kansas.

Splinter, W. E. 1976. "Center-Pivot Irrigation." *Scientific American.* 234: 90–99.

CHAPTER THREE

Groundwater Problems

David E. Kromm and Stephen E. White

Many of the groundwater problems associated with the High Plains are no more serious than those elsewhere in the United States, but the overwhelming dependence on groundwater as the source for all water uses makes any problem more threatening. The lack of alternative water sources from rivers, lakes, or precipitation makes groundwater critical in the region and heightens the severity of any reduction in quality or quantity. In an area of few natural resources and limited economic opportunity, an integrated agribusiness economy based on groundwater defines regional potentials. Problems with groundwater mean problems with the economic base and the balance between humans and the environment.

There is much variability in the groundwater resource and its use, and no single issue affects all counties in the High Plains. Some areas enjoy seemingly endless saturated thickness, yet others have limited groundwater in natural storage. Water quality ranges from that pure enough to drink without filtration to that with high levels of dissolved solids. Human activity has compounded this natural diversity by depleting much of the groundwater in some areas and contaminating it in others. Great differences also obtain in groundwater-related natural habitat, streamflow, and wetlands. People perceive problems differently from place to place as well, so that similar problems are viewed in distinct ways by residents living in widely separated areas of the High Plains. One finds a diverse mosaic of environmental conditions and human perceptions.

We shall examine the nationally recognized problem of groundwater depletion first. Grigg (1985) writes that the Ogallala Aquifer "has become a famous name in U.S. agriculture and water policy discussions. The reason is the concern that has been generated by the overuse of the aquifer and the projected decline in the agricultural basis for the economy in a six-state region" (Grigg 1985, 284). This specific concern led to the High Plains Study which examined the impact of groundwater decline on the economy, on energy, and on water resources and which selected groundwater management policies (High Plains Study Council 1982). This project, along with numerous newspaper, magazine, radio, and television reports on the depleting Ogallala, made groundwater decline in the High Plains almost a household word in the early 1980s.

By the mid-1980s the problem of water quality, the second issue, became widely-known. Contaminated domestic and municipal wells, blue babies, increasing cancer rates, and diseased livestock were being reported by the scientific community and the press. Fear of poisoned water grew in many locales in the High Plains. Some worried that although they might not run out of water, they still might not be able to drink it or to water their cattle with what remained. The vulnerability of this groundwater-dependent region was clearly demonstrated.

Other groundwater problems receive somewhat less attention. Streamflow has been dramatically reduced in many areas because the infusion of groundwater has been stopped. On classroom wall maps and in atlases, the blue band representing the Arkansas River in southwest Kansas suggests to school children everywhere a grand river with water recreation and aesthetic appeal. For long stretches the reality is a dried-up river bed almost devoid of vegetation; riparian trees and other plants along the river have died. Depletion has destroyed much of the water-supported habitat for fish and mammals in the High Plains, and in many areas the water ecosystem is gone. As streamflow declines, problems of sedimentation and concentration of pollutants worsens. Other factors examined are population change, economic restructuring, and social disruption.

Finally, we shall consider the variations in perception of the High Plains and its water problems. People in different walks of life and from different areas see things differently. These variations reflect the actual range of conditions existing in the region and the distinct ways that people with specific backgrounds and from particular places view events. Policies designed to protect groundwater will succeed best where the population affected agrees with the seriousness of the problem and the need for restrictions. The kinds of policies considered also reflect the institutional setting. In Texas, groundwater rights are associated with property rights; elsewhere in the High Plains state governments exert control and grant permits for private use. Local groundwater or natural-resource districts exist in some of the states and enjoy widely varied powers. Priorities regarding groundwater also vary among the states and counties of the High Plains.

GROUNDWATER DEPLETION

Since the mid-1970s the depletion of the Ogallala Aquifer has captured nationwide attention. Media accounts referred to the "mining" of a virtually nonrenewable resource. For example, the annual volume of water pumped (23 million acre-feet) during 1978 exceeded the flow in the Colorado River. Federal and state governments also took notice. In 1976 Congress appropriated over $6 million for the High Plains Study to examine the future economic impact on agribusiness resulting from continued groundwater depletion. States began to encourage greater restrictions on use of groundwater; several of them organized administrative units for the effective management of controlled groundwater depletion. Approximately 30 percent of all irrigation water in the United States is pumped in the High Plains; thus it is not surprising that systematic mining of the water has become a national concern (Weeks 1986).

At the national level, the question has been, Is the Ogallala going dry? Within the High Plains, perhaps the more important question is, Where is the Ogallala going dry? In some areas depletion has already eliminated irrigation, in other locations the conversion to dryland farming has begun, and in many areas the potential for depletion is in the distant future. The High Plains aquifer contains about 3.25 billion acre-feet of usable water (Weeks 1986). Put in perspective, this is enough water to fill Lake Huron or to cover the state of Colorado to a depth of 45 feet (Colorado Department of Agriculture 1983). About 166 million acre-feet of water was mined throughout the entire region between the time irrigation first evolved in the late 1800s and 1980. This represents only 5 percent of the total drainable water that could be put to beneficial use with present technology (USGS 1983). Although the aggregate level of depletion may appear small for the entire region, localized declines in water levels have been significant because many areas have a relatively shallow zone of saturation. Only 5 percent of the region is underlain with a saturated thickness exceeding 600 feet; 46 percent of the area has less than 100 feet (Weeks 1986).

As groundwater depletion reduces the saturated thickness of the aquifer, well yields can change dramatically. Well yields decrease in relation to declining water levels according to an inverse-square relationship (Sweeten and Jordan 1987). For example, a 50 percent reduction in saturated thickness could mean that a well will yield only 25 percent of its initial capacity. Generally, if the saturated thickness is less than 35 feet, the remaining water is not economically recoverable (Colorado Department of Agriculture 1983).

The impact of reduced saturated thickness on irrigation has been most dramatic in Texas. Total acre-feet pumped in the Texas portion of the High Plains aquifer declined from 8.1 million acre-feet in 1974 to just 5.0 million acre-feet in 1984. Decreased pumpage has resulted from increased pumping lifts, higher energy costs, and lower well yields that in turn are the direct result of groundwater depletion. Generally, a well producing 750 gallons per minute can effectively irrigate 160 acres with a center pivot system. Wells producing 250 gallons per minute, however, can effectively irrigate only about 40 acres (Gutentag et al. 1984). Although more than one well can be used to operate a center pivot system, the energy costs may become prohibitive as depletion continues. In those parts of Texas where the saturated thickness has declined by at least 50 percent, the average number of acres irrigated per well dropped from 118 in 1958 to just 62 in 1980 (Luckey et al. 1988). The predevelopment volume of water stored in the aquifer had declined 23 percent in Texas by 1980 (USGS 1983).

The High Plains regional aquifer underlies approximately 174,000 square miles. About 16,000 square miles had experienced water-level declines of more than 50 feet as of 1980, and 50,000 square miles had had declines greater than 10 feet (Luckey et al. 1988). Just as irrigation expansion spread from south to north within the High Plains region, the depletion of groundwater has followed a similar pattern. The southern plains have experienced widespread depletion, the central plains in Colorado and Kansas have witnessed moderate declines, and the northern plains have had only localized depletion problems (Figure 3.1).

Most of the areas showing declines greater than 50 feet are south of the Canadian River in Texas and New Mexico. The maximum decline of almost 200 feet was registered in Floyd County, Texas (Luckey et al. 1988). By 1980 Kansas had used 8 percent of its predevelopment water and had experienced significant declines in the southwestern portion of the state, most notably in Grant County, which has had declines of more than 100 feet (Bittinger and Green 1980). Nebraska irrigators, however, have used less than 1 percent of the groundwater available to them before irrigation development. Although groundwater levels have declined by more than 30 feet in Chase and Box Butte counties, they have actually risen along the Platte River in Gosper, Phelps, Kearney, and in portions of Dawson counties (Nebraska Conservation and Survey Division 1986). The rises are due to aquifer recharge from canal irrigation that uses water directly from the Platte.

The impact of groundwater depletion on irrigated agriculture is highly variable from place to place. In Texas, many more farmers have returned to dryland farming than have farmers in Kansas or Nebraska. Between 1974 and 1984 furrow irrigation declined 40 percent in Texas. Sprinkler irrigation declined only 3 percent, suggesting a tendency to locate capital-intensive sprinkler systems over portions of the aquifer that have a greater saturated thickness. In contrast, very little irrigated land in Nebraska has been shifted to dryland farming, and in some areas sprinkler systems are being added.

Throughout most of the High Plains, natural recharge is insignificant

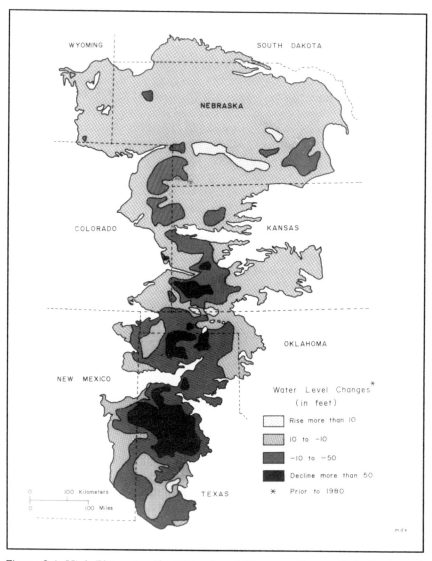

Figure 3.1. High Plains Aquifer Water-Level Changes. *Source:* U.S. Geological Survey

when compared to the volume of water pumped for irrigation. Ground-water depletion is inevitable for most locations, at least over the long term. The estimated mean recharge for the entire High Plains aquifer is just .6 inch per year. Recharge varies from .02 inches per year in parts of

Texas to more than 6 inches per year in sandhill areas. Approximately 19 percent of the High Plains aquifer is covered by sand dunes (Weeks 1986). The major area includes the Sandhills region of Nebraska, but significant dune areas are also found along the Arkansas River in southwestern Kansas. Unfortunately, areas where recharge is greatest often correspond to locations where irrigation development is controversial because of problems with soil stabilization and ecological concerns.

The average specific yield for the High Plains aquifer is about .15, meaning that only 15 percent of all the water available in the aquifer can be recovered with irrigation pumps while the rest remains unused and retained in the dewatered zone. Problems with groundwater depletion could be forestalled if this nonrecoverable water could be forced into the saturated zone. One experimental means involves the injection of air into the unsaturated zone, breaking down capillary action and permitting the movement of water down to the saturated zone. Air-injection experiments have shown positive results for very localized areas; however, the widespread applicability of this technology has not yet proven effective.

If U.S. Geological Survey (USGS) projections of future groundwater pumpage prove correct, the southern High Plains will experience extreme consequences from depletion before 2020 (Luckey et al. 1988). Three management scenarios were projected: (1) a baseline strategy assuming continuation of 1980 trends, (2) voluntary adoption of new techniques to decrease irrigation-water use, and (3) mandatory decreases in water use. If one assumes that the second option is the most realistic one for the southern High Plains, the projections suggest that between 1980 and 2020 approximately 109 million acre-feet will be pumped. If this occurs, more than 50 percent of the southern High Plains will have less than 25 feet of saturated thickness. By 2020 well yields will have dropped to 250 gallons per minute for 80 percent of the area, not enough water to permit the operation of most center pivot systems. The depletion problem is most severe in Texas. The central (southwestern Kansas, southeastern Colorado, and Oklahoma) and northern (northwestern Kansas, Nebraska, and northeastern Colorado) portions of the High Plains will fare much better.

Although more water will be pumped according to option two, depletion will be a smaller problem. The projections indicate that 178 million acre-feet will be pumped in the central region, and 360 million acre-feet will be mined in the northern sections. However, the average saturated thickness in 2020 will be 100 feet for the central High Plains and 217 feet for the northern High Plains. Importantly, extreme local variation in groundwater depletion will occur, and we may see specific portions of

Wind and water erosion may occur where soils are thin in the High Plains, especially if the land is not irrigated, as in Gaines County, Texas (top). Soil and water conservation districts assist farmers in resource management, as shown in adjacent Dawson County, Texas (bottom).

the central and northern plains in circumstances similar to those that will be plaguing most Texas irrigators.

WATER QUALITY

The usefulness of water depends on its quality as well as on its quantity. Materials dissolved or suspended in water can render it unfit for many uses (*Progress Report on the Sandhills Area Study* 1984, 47). State and federal agencies have established standards to protect groundwater, with the highest criteria set for drinking water. Municipalities and other governmental offices routinely test water samples to ensure that satisfactory quality is being maintained. Compliance with drinking-water standards provides adequate protection for all other uses. Because farm and town groundwater supplies have been found to be contaminated in the High Plains, water sampling programs have been instituted throughout the region.

In its natural state, water from the High Plains aquifer is generally of high quality and is suitable for domestic use, stock watering, and irrigation without filtration or treatment. In some places, however, the concentration of dissolved solids, fluoride, chloride, and sulfate exceed recommended limits for drinking water (Weeks 1986, 34). Numerous small, shallower aquifers are also of good quality and are frequently the water source for farmsteads, other rural residences, rural towns, and municipalities. Yet in the past twenty years, serious questions regarding water quality have arisen in several areas of the High Plains along with the fear that much of the water supply is threatened by pollution.

A 1987 survey conducted among state water administrators indicates that problems with groundwater quality in the High Plains are about as serious as those for the nation as a whole. A total of fourteen issues on groundwater quality were listed, and the water administrators scored those they considered to be severe in their state with a two. The mean number for the forty-seven responding states was 12.8; the mean for the five responding High Plains states was a slightly higher 14.0. Kansas scored highest in the region with a 17, well below the high of 25 for Pennsylvania; and Oklahoma scored lowest at 11 (*Groundwater Survey* 1987, 4–5). Since the responses were for individual states, the specific incidences of perceived problems for the High Plains area as a whole cannot be determined.

The potential for groundwater contamination is greatest where significant recharge occurs because polluted water can then be introduced into an aquifer more easily. The high recharge in the Nebraska Sandhills makes this area especially vulnerable to contamination. Recharge water is

Breaking the sandsage prairie for cultivation can lead to blowouts. Lamb County, Texas.

most likely to be polluted by agricultural chemicals and by animal or human waste. Shallow wells in two counties have shown high concentrations of contaminants related to agricultural chemicals. Moreover, natural filtration is limited in the Sandhills. Bleed noted that "the lack of a thick topsoil and much vegetation, together with rapid infiltration rates, means that contaminants have less time to be removed by chemical or biological processes before they reach the groundwater" (Bleed 1989, 82).

Natural intrusion of minerals or salts into aquifers is not a serious problem in the High Plains; human activity causes most groundwater contamination. Landfills produce leachate, a liquid effluent containing soluble and suspended contaminants that can percolate down to shallow aquifers. Bacterial contamination occurs in poorly constructed wells, especially those near septic systems. Underground storage tanks sometimes leak. The petroleum and natural gas industry affects local areas because of faulty well-casings, allowing leakage into aquifers, and because of disposal of brines in ponds that eventually infiltrate groundwater. Liquid wastes, such as saline water from petroleum and natural-gas extraction, are injected into deep wells and can enter groundwater through leaks in well-casings. Abandoned water wells provide a direct link between surface pollutants and aquifers (Studer 1989, 33–39).

Nitrogen fertilizers are a major source of groundwater contamination in the High Plains. The nitrogen is added to the soil and eventually converted to nitrate or is available in nitrate form in some fertilizers. The nitrates that are not used by the plants are leached down into the ground. In coarser soils the leached nitrogen moves more quickly and in greater abundance. If the sandy soils overlay a shallow aquifer, groundwater contamination probably will occur. Control of fertilizers and water application through fertilization and irrigation scheduling can significantly reduce the excessive leaching of nitrates. Economic losses and potential health hazards can result from over fertilizing crops at appropriate times during the growing season. Proper management slows down and reduces the amount of nitrate that reaches the groundwater. Some nitrates have entered groundwater through chemigation, the application of agricultural chemicals via irrigation water. Contamination can occur when a well-casing or a valve leaks or when chemicals backflow into the groundwater. Other sources of nitrate that might contaminate a local or a domestic groundwater supply include feedlots and barnyards, septic-tank discharges, and the spreading of animal, human, or industrial wastes on the land (Studer 1989, 26–31).

The primary health hazard from groundwater contamination is methemoglobinemia, essentially the deprivation of oxygen to the brain. Known as "blue-baby disease," methemoglobinemia usually affects children because their digestive systems do not absorb the nitrates before they enter the lower gastrointestinal tract. Bacteria in the lower tract convert the nitrates to nitrites, which cause methemoglobinemia. Nitrates and nitrites, once recycled back into the gastrointestinal tract, may undergo further transformations to form nitrosamines and nitrosamides, which are carcinogens (Kies 1981, 5–8). Nitrates are also toxic for livestock, especially cattle and hogs.

The limit for nitrates in drinking water is 10 mg/l nitrate-nitrogen and was established to protect infants from acute nitrate poisoning. The standard does not take into account carcinogenic (cancer-causing) or teratogenic (fetal malformation) effects (Studer 1989, 26–27). Municipalities and domestic wells throughout the High Plains states have tested above the limit, resulting in expensive replacement water systems and filtration. Shallow wells have a particularly high incidence of nitrate poisoning, but contamination also occurs in deep wells where there is heavy irrigation and fertilization of sandy soils.

OTHER CONSEQUENCES

Since 1950 irrigated agriculture has increasingly reshaped both the physical and the cultural landscape throughout the High Plains. Expansion of irrigation has forced many changes—both good and bad—upon the region. In addition to increased grain production and protection from drought, irrigation has brought about groundwater depletion, decreased streamflow, loss of vegetative cover, localized problems in water quality, dramatic changes in population redistribution, and economic restructuring. Much research has focused on understanding the consequences of groundwater depletion on agricultural production, on the economic viability of the High Plains (High Plains Study Council 1982), and on its geologic characteristics, but relatively little work has been done on the social, demographic, and ecological impact of irrigation development. A few examples of widely ranging irrigation-based impacts follow.

In an analysis of 294 nonmetropolitan High Plains counties, Albrecht and Murdock (1985) found that counties without irrigation development were the most likely to have experienced severe declines in population between 1940 and 1980. In counties using medium irrigation the population remained relatively constant, and counties with high irrigation experienced population increases. This suggests that a map of irrigation expansion would closely resemble a map of population growth. During the 1970s irrigation expansion in southwestern Kansas resulted in significant population gains for several counties that had not experienced population increases since 1930 or before (Self and White 1986). Still to be examined are the effects of the changing population of the region on the sustainability of small towns.

Irrigated agriculture has increased feedgrain production, allowing the expansion of feedlots that in turn have encouraged the movement of the beef-packing industry to the High Plains. Multiple effects associated with these economic changes have resulted in rapid population growth for some communities. For example, Garden City, Kansas, witnessed the opening of two large processing plants, Iowa Beef Products (IBP) in nearby Holcomb and Val-Agri, which was bought out and expanded by Montford. Between 1980 and 1986, Garden City's population increased over 27 percent, from 23,825 to 30,300 residents (Broadway 1991). School enrollments increased 37 percent and the number of eating establishments increased by more than 50 percent during the same period. The ethnic composition also changed; about three thousand Vietnamese came to Garden City, where most adults found work in the beef-packing plants. This proved to be a particular challenge to a school system attempting a bilingual education for an increasing minority population.

By 1987 IBP had employed more than 2,600 workers in Holcomb, had a payroll that totaled more than $42 million, and had bought more than $1 billion worth of cattle from area feedlots (Blankenship 1988). Although these are impressive economic statistics, Broadway (1991) has concluded that Finney County also experienced many of the socially disruptive effects associated with boomtown growth, such as housing shortages, increased child abuse, violent crime, alcoholism, and a highly transient population. Similar conditions are expected in Lexington, Nebraska, with the recent construction of another huge packing plant (Broadway 1991).

A major negative environmental result of intense irrigation development is the decline of stream base flows and the subsequent disruption of the riparian ecosystem (Kansas Water Office 1984). Though many parts of the High Plains have only intermittent streams, more than 700 miles of once permanently flowing rivers in Kansas no longer flow (Layher 1986). Perhaps the most notable dewatered stream in the United States is the Arkansas River, which is generally dry from west of Garden City to several miles east of Dodge City. Streamflow depletion results partly from the reduction of base flow as groundwater movement from adjacent aquifers declines and water-conservation practices on cultivated lands prevent runoff.

In 1980 the Kansas Legislature passed a law to protect streamflow from the encroachment of new appropriation rights by establishing minimum desirable streamflows. These standards are meant to "preserve, maintain, or enhance base flows for instream water uses relative to water quality, fishing, wildlife, aquatic life, recreation, general aesthetics, and domestic uses and for the protection of existing water rights" (Kansas Water Office 1988). This legislation may help to save rivers in eastern Kansas, but it has come much too late to benefit those rivers in the western part of the state that have either died or are terminally ill.

The elimination of base flow is also a major concern in the Sandhills of Nebraska (Dreeszen 1984), where the viability of over one thousand lakes depends on the future level of irrigation expansion and on the degree to which the saturated thickness of the aquifer is reduced. An additional concern in the Sandhills centers on the potential development of irrigation on 3.7 million acres of soils that are classified as highly erodible and another 16 million acres deemed fragile and best left to grazing (Johnson 1984). An examination of 254 abandoned center pivot sites in Nebraska during 1985 revealed that about 20 percent of the 32,807 acres formerly irrigated were eroding at twice the rate acceptable to the Soil Conservation Service (Nebraska Water Resources Center 1986).

The elimination of windbreaks and hedgerows is inevitable in areas where center pivot systems are installed. They require large, unimpeded open spaces, generally a quarter section or larger, since they cannot negotiate tall obstacles. Dilaura (1988) studied Gray and Clark counties in Kansas and found that the greatest reductions in windbreaks correlated with heavy concentrations of center pivot irrigation development. Between 1961 and 1981, 31 percent of the windbreaks were eliminated in Clark County (a low-irrigation county), but 59 percent had been removed in Gray

County (a high-irrigation county); the reduction was highest in those areas within Gray County where center pivots were operated.

Another important consequence of irrigation expansion has been farm debt. An initial investment of about sixty thousand dollars is required for the installation of a well, a center pivot, and the auxiliary equipment to run it and does not include interest, taxes, insurance, seed, fertilizer, and chemical costs (Center for Rural Affairs 1988). Much center pivot expansion occurred during the 1970s when interest rates were high. Because center pivots are capital intensive they cannot be affordably idled. Thus, although they have made irrigators immune to drought, center pivots have increased these farmers' vulnerability to low crop prices. In 1986 only 6 percent of all farmland in Nebraska was irrigated with center pivot systems; however, one-third of all land taken by lenders to settle farm debts was irrigated with center pivots (Center for Rural Affairs 1988).

The large financial investments and risks imposed by center pivot irrigation combined with the need for large parcels of land to make irrigation profitable have encouraged corporate ownership (albeit many are family corporations) and absentee landlords. During the mid-1970s in Nebraska about one-third of the wells were registered to nonfarm operators, most of whom were either absentee or corporate investors (Evans et al. 1976). Absentee ownership affects small farming communities negatively because the profits reaped from irrigated agriculture are more likely to be reinvested outside the producing areas.

Irrigation has transformed not only agricultural production in the High Plains but also has brought about other significant changes, directly and indirectly. These range from physical changes such as groundwater depletion and streamflow decline to demographic changes (boomtown growth), social disruption, heavy debt, and increased outside control. Significantly, we know much less about the physical, social, economic, and ecological changes than we do about the impact of irrigation on agriculture.

PERCEPTION OF REGIONAL WATER PROBLEMS

Attitudes about the degree to which groundwater depletion is a problem differ from place to place and generally correspond to the severity of the decline. In 1985 Kromm and White completed a study of the response to groundwater depletion in the High Plains. Residents of fourteen counties in six states were surveyed, with 956 persons completing the questionnaire (Figure 3.2). Two questions dealt with perceived problems in the home county of the respondent; the first asked about the seriousness of

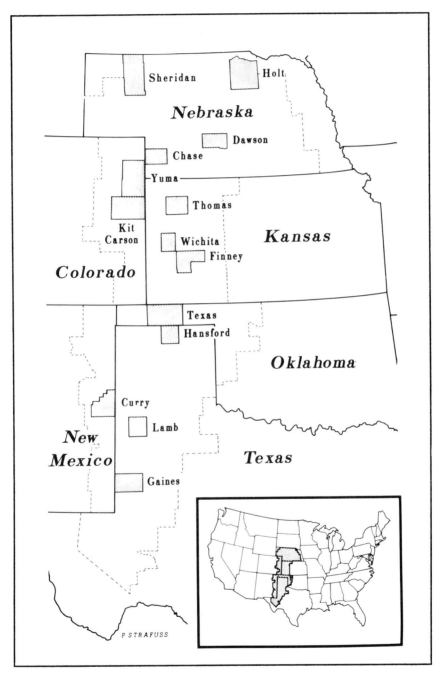

Figure 3.2. High Plains Study Area

fifteen different problems, and the second elicited views on the seriousness of thirteen possible groundwater problems. Respondents were
asked to evaluate each problem on a 5-point scale, with 1 labeled "not
serious" or "no problem," 3 labeled "serious" or "a problem," and 5
labeled "very serious" or "a major problem." To simplify the analysis, 1
and 2 ratings were combined into a "not serious" or "not a problem"
category, and 4 and 5 ratings were combined into a "very serious" or
"major problem" category (Tables 3.1 and 3.2). The issues judged most
serious would be those with a mean score of 3.00 or above.

Groundwater depletion had a high mean score of 3.74 and was rated
as either serious or very serious by 84 percent of the respondents. Over
half saw it as very serious. Only low crop prices and cost of fuel for
irrigation, both highly important economic concerns, were rated as more
serious problems in the county. Streamflow depletion, which is closely
linked to groundwater decline, was seen as serious by two-thirds of those
responding. Two other water-associated problems, loss of wildlife habitat
and groundwater pollution, were seen as serious by slightly over half the
respondents, ranking ahead of such issues as poor transportation links,
soil erosion, and unemployment (Kromm and White 1985, 3).

The seriousness with which these problems were viewed varied by
state, and regional differences in attitude tended to correspond to the
degree of groundwater depletion and groundwater availability. Groundwater depletion has been greatest in those states where respondents

Table 3.1. Serious Problems in Respondent's Home County

Problem	Mean*	Not Serious (%)	Serious (%)	Very Serious (%)
Low crop prices	3.98	13	20	67
Cost of fuel for irrigation	3.89	12	26	63
Groundwater depletion	3.74	16	27	57
Cost of fuel for tractors	3.48	19	35	46
Streamflow depletion	3.28	33	21	46
High price of cropland	3.20	29	31	40
Low rainfall	3.06	36	32	32
Lack of industry	2.99	38	27	35
Loss of wildlife habitat	2.77	48	22	30
Groundwater pollution	2.75	49	21	30
Poor recreational facilities	2.64	52	23	25
Poor transportation links	2.63	52	24	24
Soil erosion	2.55	50	35	15
Inadequate shopping opportunities	2.42	60	19	21
Unemployment	2.42	60	25	15

*In the mean range, 1= Not Serious, 3 = Serious, 5 = Very Serious.

ranked it as a very serious problem: Kansas (70.3 percent), Texas (68 percent), and New Mexico (67.9 percent). Kansans (70.7 percent) ranked streamflow depletion first, reflecting their concern over the disappearance of water in stretches of the Arkansas River and the substantial decline of flow in the Republican and Cimarron rivers. Streamflow decline has not been perceived as a problem in the High Plains of Colorado (29.1 percent), where most streams were intermittent before irrigation development, or in Nebraska (35.0 percent), where streamflows have yet to decline significantly. Groundwater pollution is probably highest in Nebraska, though not necessarily in the state's four counties studied, and was seen as a very serious problem by a significantly greater proportion of respondents from that state than it was by those from Kansas, New Mexico, and Texas (Kromm and White 1987, 7).

The relative seriousness perceived for different groundwater problems was also analyzed (Kromm and White 1985, 3). Depletion and the cost of fuel for pump engines each had a high mean score of 3.79, and well over half the respondents noted both as major problems. The cost of fuel for pump engines depends mostly on the depth to water, which determines the amount of energy needed to lift the water, and the total price of the energy source. Depletion increases the depth to the water table, thereby directly influencing fuel cost. Two other groundwater problems viewed as relatively serious were the effects of water conservation and the cost of irrigation equipment. The poor quality of water ranked last, with only 8 percent perceiving it as a major problem (Kromm and White 1985, 3). This apparent lack of concern about water quality can be attributed to

Table 3.2. Groundwater Problems in Respondent's Home County

Problem	Mean*	Not a Problem (%)	A Problem (%)	A Major Problem (%)
Depletion of resource	3.79	15	27	59
Cost of fuel for pump engines	3.79	14	28	58
Lack of water conservation	3.41	25	28	47
Cost of irrigation equipment	3.29	25	33	42
Cost of well drilling	3.01	35	32	34
Domestic wells going dry	2.99	38	26	36
Uneven distribution of groundwater	2.89	41	26	33
Limit on spacing of wells	2.67	62	23	15
Great depth to water table	2.69	47	27	26
Unequal allocation of water	2.34	59	24	18
Poor soils for irrigation	2.38	59	21	21
Land subsidence	2.28	59	31	11
Poor quality of water	1.64	85	8	8

*In the mean range, 1 = Not a Problem, 3 = Problem, 5 = A Major Problem.

the relatively high quality of the High Plains aquifer in all fourteen counties studied. In some local areas more shallow-water sources may have become contaminated, but the problem is not widespread.

Again, additional differences by state generally corresponded to the actual variations in depletion. The three states with the highest depletion marked that problem as significantly serious (Kansas, 72.8 percent, Texas, 72.7 percent, and New Mexico, 68.4 percent), but only 36.4 percent of those responding from Nebraska ranked it as very serious. With the abundant groundwater reserves beneath the Sandhills, Nebraskans responded with the lowest percentage indicating very serious problems for eight of the thirteen issues listed. Respondents from Nebraska gave the highest percentage rating to poor soils for irrigation, which is consistent with the sandier, lighter soils in much of the state. No significant regional differences appeared in response to the lack of water conservation among the six states; about half the respondents in each state saw it as a major problem (Kromm and White 1987, 8).

The variation in perceived seriousness of different regional and groundwater problems calls into question Walter Prescott Webb's observation that deficiency in water is "the key to what may be called the Plains civilization" (Webb 1931, 17). One could argue, of course, that the High Plains of 1985 was much different from the High Plains of the 1930s because of widespread irrigation. Instead of relying only on the volume of rainfall and surface waters noted by Webb, contemporary farmers who irrigate use what Green calls "underground rain" (Green 1973), the vast groundwater reservoir. As the High Plains aquifer is far from uniform in its areal extent, its depth below the surface, or its saturated thickness throughout the region, its use creates greater diversity in outlook and in economic activity than existed before its development. The seriousness with which the general public views groundwater depletion suggests the comment that "the scarcity of moisture is the subject that furnishes the greatest amount of thought and talk" (Webb 1931, 322) remains largely true. From what we have heard in the coffee shops and cafes throughout the High Plains, only the economic issues of farming receive more attention. Yet these economic concerns are connected to groundwater and irrigation and higher fixed costs, making farming in the High Plains even more vulnerable to instability (Kraenzel 1955, 163).

AN OVERVIEW

Ironically, while our nation's farmers are confronting agricultural surpluses, low crop prices, reduced land values, and foreclosures, we are systematically mining a virtually nonrenewable resource to produce more in a time of plenty. At the national scale it might seem prudent to conserve High Plains groundwater for future generations, but at the individual or local level, irrigated agriculture is often perceived as necessary for survival. In many cases, farmers may decide to irrigate not only to protect themselves from drought and to increase yields but also because their neighbors are pumping from an aquifer with a relatively short life expectancy. They may have to decide whether to take advantage of the availability of water now or perhaps forego the opportunity to irrigate forever since the declining aquifer makes the water more costly each year. Likewise, the decision to revert to dryland farming often has little to do with the perceived need to conserve water but instead results from the economic reality that continued irrigation is simply less cost-effective.

Undoubtedly, irrigation has proven extremely profitable for many farmers. Production has increased, regional economic gains from the multiplier effects of agribusiness have been impressive in some areas, and generally, counties in high-irrigation areas have fared better economically and experienced population gains that have not occurred in predominantly dryland areas. Irrigation has also imposed significant costs on the region, however. Resource exploitation has severely reduced the irrigation potential of the future in some locations, problems of water quality have started to emerge, streamflows have declined, wetlands and riparian vegetation have disappeared, windbreaks and shelterbelts have been taken out, absentee ownership has increased, and some irrigators have been forced out of farming because of intense competition from larger operators.

These positive and negative consequences are not uniformly distributed across the High Plains. The physical, economic, demographic, managerial, and legal contexts vary greatly from place to place. Importantly, the awareness of and attitudes about groundwater problems and their impact are not homogeneous. Our earlier research has documented the ways in which irrigators rely on different sources of information for water-conservation management (Kromm and White 1987, 1986, 1991). Irrigators in one state may have a great deal of confidence in an administrative level of groundwater management that may be viewed as entirely inappropriate in another state. Moreover, the adjustments that irrigators have adopted to conserve water (and to save money) can be quite different, depending on the particular place.

For convenience, we often talk about the "groundwater problem" at an aggregate level; yet we must keep in proper perspective the complex range of interrelationships between irrigation and the physical and cultural landscapes throughout the High Plains. From our research experiences, we believe that general solutions are much less likely to be as effective as active local management.

REFERENCES

Albrecht, Don E., and Steve H. Murdock. 1985. *The Consequences of Irrigation Development in the Great Plains.* Technical Report no. 85–1. College Station: Texas Agricultural Experiment Station.

Bittinger, Morton W., and Elizabeth B. Green. 1980. *You Never Miss the Water Till . . . (The Ogallala Story).* Littleton, Colo.: Water Resources Publication.

Blankenship, Ted. 1988. "Beef May Be State's Top Industry." *Kansas Business News* (January): 25–27.

Bleed, Ann. 1989. "Groundwater." In Ann Bleed and Charles Flowerday, eds., *An Atlas of the Sandhills.* Lincoln: Conservation and Survey Division, University of Nebraska, 67–82.

Broadway, Michael J. 1991. "Economic Development Programs in the Great Plains: The Example of Nebraska." *Great Plains Research* 1: 324–44.

Center for Rural Affairs. 1988. *Beneath the Wheels of Fortune: The Economic and Environmental Impacts of Center Pivot Irrigation Development on Antelope County, Nebraska.* Walthill, Nebr.: Center for Rural Affairs.

Colorado Department of Agriculture. 1983. *Colorado High Plains Summary Report.* Denver: Colorado High Plains Committee.

Dilaura, Roxanne L. 1988. "Factors Influencing the Changing Patterns of Field Windbreaks in Southwestern Kansas," Master's thesis, Kansas State University.

Dreeszen, Vince. 1984. "Overview of Nebraska and the Sand Hills." In *The Sandhills of Nebraska—Yesterday, Today and Tomorrow.* Lincoln: Nebraska Water Resources Center, Water Resources Seminar Series.

Evans, Bert, Allen J. Heine, Kenneth Mesner, and Robert Warrick. 1976. *Wheels of Fortune: A Report on the Impact of Center Pivot Irrigation on the Ownership of Land in Nebraska.* Walthill, Nebr.: Center for Rural Affairs.

Green, Donald E. 1973. *Land of the Underground Rain: Irrigation on the Texas High Plains, 1910–1970.* Austin: University of Texas Press.

Grigg, Niel S. 1985. *Water Resources Planning.* New York: McGraw-Hill.

Groundwater Survey. 1987. Washington, D.C.: Interstate Conference on Water Policy.

Gutentag, Edwin D., Frederick J. Heimes, Noel C. Krothe, Richard R. Luckey, and John B. Weeks. 1984. *Geohydrology of the High Plains Aquifer in Parts of Colorado, Kansas, Nebraska, New Mexico, Oklahoma, South Dakota, Texas, and Wyoming.* USGS Professional Paper, 1400–B. Washington, D.C.: Government Printing Office.

Hergert, Gary W., and George W. Rehm. 1981. "Nitrogen in Our Environment." In *Living with Nitrate.* Lincoln: Nebraska Cooperative Extension Service, 3–4.

High Plains Study Council. 1982. *A Summary of Results of the Ogallala Aquifer Regional Study, with Recommendations to the Secretary of Commerce and Congress.* Washington, D.C.: U.S. Department of Commerce.

Johnson, Clinton. 1984. "SCS Study of the Sandhills." In *The Sandhills of Nebraska—"Yesterday, Today, and Tomorrow.* Lincoln: Nebraska Water Resources Center, Water Resources Seminar Series.

Kansas Rural Center, Whiting. 1987. *Rural Papers.* No. 56.

Kansas Water Office, Topeka. 1984. *Demand Reduction Techniques for Agricultural Water Use.* State Water Plan Background Paper no. 6.

———. 1988. *Kansas Water Plan Executive Summary.*

Kies, Constance. 1981. "Nitrates, Nitrites, N-Nitroso Compounds and Nutrition." In *Living with Nitrate.* Lincoln: Nebraska Cooperative Extension Service, 5–9.

Kraenzel, Carl Frederick. 1955. *The Great Plains in Transition*. Norman: University of Oklahoma Press.

Kromm, David E., and Stephen E. White. 1985. *Conserving the Ogallala: What Next?* Manhattan: Kansas State University.

―――. 1986. "Variability in Adjustment Preferences to Groundwater in the American High Plains." *Water Resources Bulletin* 22: 791–801.

―――. 1987. "Interstate Groundwater Management Preference Differences." *Journal of Geography* 86: 5–11.

―――. 1991. "Reliance on Sources of Information for Water-saving Practices by Irrigators in the High Plains of the U.S.A." *Journal of Rural Studies* 7: 411–21.

Layher, Bill. 1986. "The Four Deadly Sins." *Kansas Wildlife* 43, 6: 32–35.

Luckey, Richard R., Edwin D. Gutentag, Frederick J. Heimes, and John B. Weeks. 1988. *Effects of Future Groundwater Pumpage on the High Plains Aquifer in Parts of Colorado, Kansas, Nebraska, New Mexico, Oklahoma, South Dakota, Texas and Wyoming*. USGS Professional Paper, 1400–E. Washington, D.C.: Government Printing Office.

Nebraska Conservation and Survey Division. 1986. *The Groundwater Atlas of Nebraska*. Lincoln: University of Nebraska.

Progress Report on the Sandhills Area Study. 1984. Lincoln: Nebraska Natural Resources Commission.

Self, Huber, and Stephen E. White. 1986. "One Hundred and Twenty Years of Population Change in Kansas." *Transactions of the Kansas Academy of Science* 89, 1–2; 10–22.

Studer, Vic. 1989. *Groundwater in Kansas: Current Perspectives, New Initiatives*. Whiting: Kansas Rural Center.

Sweeten, John M., and Wayne R. Jordan. 1987. *Irrigation Water Management for the Texas High Plains: A Research Summary*. Texas Water Resources Institute. Technical Report no. 139. College Station: Texas A & M University.

U.S. Geological Survey. 1983. *The High Plains Regional Aquifer*. Water Fact Sheet. Reston, Va.: USGS.

Webb, Walter Prescott. 1931. *The Great Plains*. New York: Ginn and Co.

Weeks, John B. 1986. "High Plains Regional Aquifer-System Study." *Regional Aquifer-System Program*. USGS Circular 1002. Washington, D.C.: Government Printing Office, 30–49.

Weeks, John B., and Ren Jen Sun. 1987. *Regional Aquifer-System Analysis Program of the U.S. Geological Survey —Bibliography, 1978–86*. Water Resources Investigations Report 87–4138. Denver: U.S. Geological Survey.

CHAPTER FOUR

The Legal Context
for Groundwater Use

Otis W. Templer

The right to pump and use groundwater in the High Plains states is dependent on the legal framework that has gradually evolved in each state over the past century or so. Most jurisdictions apply different rules of law to surface water in streams, atmospheric moisture, surface runoff or diffused surface water, and underground water—all evidence of a failure to recognize the interconnected nature of water moving in the hydrologic cycle. The result is a veritable hodgepodge of unrelated and often competing water rights. The water law concerning these various classes of water developed as the ability evolved to use each class effectively. Thus, the law of surface water rights is much more detailed and voluminous than that pertaining to groundwater, which in turn is much more voluminous than that concerning atmospheric moisture.

A massive common aquifer, the Ogallala formation, underlies the largely semiarid High Plains states of Texas, New Mexico, Oklahoma, Colorado, Kansas, and Nebraska. Even though they share this common resource in a similar environment, the groundwater law in these states could hardly be more diverse. In each state the legal institutions that control the ownership and allocation of groundwater are usually a complex blend of early common-law principles expressed in court decisions. Common law prevailed until the state legislatures developed statutory frameworks, which often modified or supplanted the preexisting legal principles. Further, administrative policies of state and local agencies have provided still more specific regulation. The allocation of water resources is generally controlled by the states, and essentially no body of federal regulation oversees the use, management, and conservation of groundwater except as it relates to interstate diversion and to the regulation of interstate commerce.

From the perspective of a geographer/lawyer I shall discuss the groundwater law of the six High Plains states, focusing on key court decisions that have interpreted the common law and on a growing body of legislative statutes and administrative regulations. Generalizations about water-law systems are difficult, can be misleading, and of necessity many specifics must be omitted. Nonetheless, this study should make evident the more significant differences and similarities among the several states.

TEXAS GROUNDWATER LAW

Texas courts generally divide subsurface water into two legal classes: (1) water flowing in well-defined underground streams and (2) percolating groundwater (Hutchins 1961). It is extremely difficult to prove the existence of water in definite underground streams, and the law concerning it is not well established. If proven, the water would probably be subjected to the same rules as surface streams, with the same kinds of public and private rights attaching. However, Texas courts presume that all groundwater is percolating (Templer 1976).

Corwin Johnson (1982a), a leading water-law scholar, has observed that Texas groundwater law is striking in its "paucity" when compared to surface water law and in its "uniqueness" when compared to the groundwater law of other western states, including the five other High Plains states. Many western states once recognized the common law or "English" rule, which gives the overlying landowner the right to capture and use percolating groundwater beneath the land. Currently, only Texas and some eastern states still retain the common-law rule; the other High Plains states have developed greatly contrasting and diverse groundwater-law systems.

The common-law rule was firmly established shortly after the turn of this century by the Texas Supreme Court in *Houston & T. C. Ry. Co. v. East* (1904). Under this rule, the overlying landowner may, in the absence of malice or wanton conduct, capture and use the water beneath the land, whatever the impact may be in depriving adjoining or more distant water users of underground or surface water supply (Templer 1976, 1978, 1989a, 1989b). This landmark case involved a groundwater dispute in Denison, north of Dallas, in the humid eastern half of Texas. The defendant railroad company dug a large well on its property and pumped about 25,000 gallons per day (gpd) to supply its locomotives and shops, a minuscule amount by today's standards. As a result, the plaintiff's shallow well on adjacent land went dry, and he sued the railroad. In deciding in favor of the railroad, the court relied on an 1843 English case, *Acton v. Blundell*, and an 1861 Ohio case, *Frazier v. Brown*, which was quoted with approval in *East*:

> as between proprietors of adjoining land, the law recognizes no correlative rights in respect to underground water percolating, oozing,

or filtrating through the earth; and this mainly from considerations of public policy: 1) because the existence, origin, movement, and course of such waters . . . are so secret, occult, and concealed that any attempt to administer any set of legal rules in respect to them would be involved in hopeless uncertainty, and would therefore, be practically impossible.

In the *East* case, it was concluded that

the owner of the land is the absolute owner of the soil and percolating water, which is a part of and not different from the soil.

Since that time, the rule has not been modified to any great extent though it has been elaborated and clarified in a few subsequent court decisions (Tex. Water Dev. Bd. 1968), and it is now established that

1. landowners can dispose of their groundwater rights by sale as with any other type of property;

2. groundwater can be used on the land from which it is pumped or away from that land;

3. and, by firm presumption, all groundwater is percolating, unless clear proof exists to the contrary of the presence of a well-defined understream, a very difficult burden of proof that has never been sustained in Texas cases.

A half-century after the *East* decision, the Texas Supreme Court considered another important groundwater case, *Corpus Christi v. Pleasanton* (1955). During the prolonged South Texas drought of the early 1950s, the city of Corpus Christi purchased groundwater produced from the Carrizo-Wilcox formation in Atascosa County. The discharge from four large artesian wells, approximately 10 million gpd, was allowed to flow down the dry bed of the Nueces River for over 100 miles to Lake Corpus Christi and the city water-intake plant. This unrestricted flow diminished the underground water supply of adjacent landowners and nearby towns. Evidence indicated that as much as three-fourths of the water was lost to evaporation and seepage before reaching its final destination. Plaintiffs contended that this was wasteful use under statutes controlling waste of artesian groundwater, but the court upheld the common-law rule (Templer 1976).

More recently, the Texas Supreme Court had another occasion to examine the common-law rule in *Friendswood Development Company v. Smith-Southwest Industries, Inc.* (1981). This decision also reaffirmed the basic doctrine of *East,* but it was admitted in the opinion that "some aspects of the English or common law rule are harsh and outmoded." *Friendswood* was a suit for damages by landowners who alleged that surface subsidence of their lands was caused by the defendants' pumping of groundwater for industrial purposes. The court did decide, however, that in future cases of land subsidence caused by withdrawals of groundwater, liability would be imposed for damages resulting from negligent pumping (Johnson 1982b; Kenyon 1979). In the *Friendswood* case, the court took great care to limit its decision to cases of damage resulting from surface subsidence, a significant problem only along portions of the Texas Gulf Coast (Graf 1982b). In sum, groundwater law as developed by Texas courts has undergone only minor modification, remaining almost static for nearly nine decades.

Underground Water Conservation Districts

The need for some form of groundwater management has long been recognized in Texas, and in 1913 the newly created Texas Board of Water Engineers pointed out the desirability of regulation. Not until the 1930s, however, when irrigation using groundwater in the state was rapidly expanding, did this need become more widely recognized. Demands for regulation to prevent overdevelopment and waste were made repeatedly, and legislation that might have accomplished these objectives was unsuccessfully introduced in 1937, 1939, 1941, and 1947 (Templer 1976). Finally, in 1949 a statute passed (*Texas Water Code* 1981, chap. 52); providing for the establishment of local underground water conservation districts (UWCDs). Green (1973) and Rayner and McMillion (1960) explored the difficulties of passing this law and the history of the early districts' formation.

These local districts exercise virtually the only control over landowner rights, though the validity of private groundwater rights is specifically acknowledged in the statute. In addition to the districts formed under this general law, special legislation has created other entities, some with powers and responsibilities considerably different from those of general-law districts (Templer 1978, 1983a).

Since the passage of the 1949 UWCD statute, the most significant revision of Texas groundwater law occurred in 1985. The legislation was part of a comprehensive water package designed to implement the 1984 revised Texas Water Plan, and it addressed many long-standing surface- and groundwater problems as well as bay and estuary protection. The 1985 groundwater legislation applies only to general-law UWCDs and not to districts created by special legislation. Its most significant provisions are as follows:

1. It eliminates the requirement that UWCD boundaries coincide with those of an aquifer or an aquifer subdivision, allowing other factors such as political boundaries to be considered.

2. As had long been recommended by local district advocates (Graf 1985), it expands the powers of general-law UWCDs to sell and distribute surface or groundwater and to exercise the power of eminent domain in some instances. Further, it expands the jurisdiction of UWCDs to smaller wells, including those capable of producing 25,000 gpd or more.

3. Most important, it authorizes the state to designate "areas with critical groundwater problems" and to push for creation of UWCDs in these areas. The Texas Water Commission (TWC) is empowered to establish a regional advisory committee, prepare a report on regional groundwater problems, recommend creation of a UWCD, hold local hearings, and eventually order an election in which local voters decide whether to establish a UWCD (Templer 1987).

The reforms of the 1985 legislation demonstrate that the state of Texas remains committed to the local district approach to groundwater management. Until recently, only a few districts had been formed under the 1949 statute or by special legislation. Prior to 1985 twelve UWCDs had been created, and most of these older, larger, multicounty districts were formed under the general law, commonly acknowledged to be a lengthy and cumbersome procedure. The pace for creating the districts accelerated in 1985, probably in partial response to the new legislation. Two new UWCDs were created in 1985, including one that replaced a smaller, preexisting district; three were created in 1986 and six in 1987, for a total of twenty-two districts in 1988. All but two of the new districts consist of one county or less in size, and most conform to county rather than to aquifer boundaries. Except for one, all the new UWCDs were created by special legislation, and in a few instances groundwater management powers have been conferred on preexisting surface water districts. In 1989 the rate of district formation increased even more rapidly. The Seventy-first Legislature, which convened in 1989, considered the creation of eighteen more UWCDs, thirteen of which eventually received legislative approval. Thus there may be thirty-five UWCDs in Texas if local confirmation elections for each of the new districts are successful, as expected (Templer 1989b). Most of the districts, old and new, lie west of San Antonio in Bexar County. Though the number of UWCDs has increased, several areas with heavy groundwater withdrawals are not yet included within a district. In 1973, for the second time, voters in seven south Plains counties overlying an intensively developed portion of the Ogallala Aquifer rejected the creation of a proposed UWCD (Templer 1976). Some long-established UWCDs are relatively inactive, for example, the small Dallam County UWCD No. 1 in the northwest Panhandle (Templer 1983a).

General-law districts have comprehensive statutory powers to make and to enforce conservation rules. Typically, however, the most significantly enforced rules are those controlling off-farm waste of groundwater (Graf 1982a, 1982b). None of the general-law districts, such as those overlying the Ogallala Aquifer of the Texas High Plains, has attempted to control on-farm waste or has attempted direct control of groundwater production. Several of these districts do have well-regarded programs for demonstration, research, and education that strongly promote groundwater conservation (Templer 1983a, 1983b, 1985).

The more numerous special-law UWCDs have widely varying powers; for example, those of the Edwards UWCD, which overlies the Edwards limestone aquifer in south-central Texas, are very limited when compared with other districts. Only the Harris-Galveston Coastal Subsidence District regulates groundwater production from wells through use of permit fees based on the quantity of water extracted (Templer 1983a), though at least two new UWCDs have reported plans for imposing pumpage controls (Templer 1989b).

In 1986, and in response to the new 1985 legislation, the TWC designated seventeen areas with critical groundwater problems. In these areas groundwater is extensively used for irrigation or for municipal or industrial purposes; all are now experiencing or will soon have overdraft problems, complicated in some instances by subsidence or by salt-water contamination or both. As yet, however, none of the critical-area designations has resulted in a UWCD. Some critics view the 1985 legislation as just a tentative first step toward more effective groundwater management, especially since it contains only the most limited of the proposals considered for inclusion in the comprehensive water package. Kramer (1986) described the groundwater management provisions as "the lengthiest, but perhaps the least meaningful, part of the 1985 water package." Among the perceived weaknesses of the new provisions, first, there are many exemptions of different kinds of wells from the provisions. Any new UWCDs created must issue permits to existing wells within their jurisdictions, thus "automatically grandfathering existing overpumpage and depletion problems." Second, voters in designated critical areas may or may not create new UWCDs, and there is no assurance that districts will operate effectively even if formed (Kramer 1986).

The major leverage given the TWC to assure the creation of new UWCDs in designated critical areas is a provision that would deny state financial assistance for water projects to those political subdivisions where voters have rejected UWCDs. A bill before the current legislature would give the TWC the authority to assume management jurisdiction over critical areas where the creation of a UWCD is voted down. A new Water Districts and River Authorities Committee created by the legislature has also recommended that the TWC be given authority to impose minimum criteria for groundwater regulation by UWCDs. Such a provision should help ensure that local districts remain active and reasonably effective.

The gradual depletion of some nonrenewable aquifers, such as the Ogallala formation, is only one of several diverse groundwater management problems affecting different areas of the state. The gradual groundwater-depletion problems of the Ogallala of the Texas High Plains have yet to generate much concern, either at the local or at the state level. Movement of groundwater under unconfined conditions in the Ogallala is relatively slow, and thus ownership of the surface generally means control of a reasonably definable amount of water (Stagner 1988). Most residents appear to be satisfied with the limited controls and the research/education programs of the existing UWCDs. Of course, these districts have always contended that local regulation already achieves a desirable level of groundwater conservation without impeding economic development or compromising private property rights and that the local UWCD system is the only desirable management strategy (Graf 1982a, 1982b; Wyatt 1982). The vast majority of irrigation farmers in west Texas share this view (Shelley 1983).

For over eight decades in Texas, largely unregulated private rights to groundwater have become firmly entrenched. Over thirty years ago, Hutchins (1958) noted that Texas court decisions had welded the absolute-ownership doctrine into a rule of property that would be most difficult to overturn. Notwithstanding recognition of the "absolute ownership" of percolating groundwater, Johnson (1982a) contended that Texas landowners lack effective groundwater rights because each has the right to pump at will from a common source, a point with which Thomas (1972) agreed:

> "A landlord is clearly lord of his land, and he cannot be denied the right to drill a well in it and extract water therefrom. If he stops the flow of a neighbor's spring or dries up his well, the neighbor has no recourse; if his neighbor gets the jump on him he is the loser. In the world of absolute rights it is not easy to protect private interests from themselves or for themselves.

Countless proposals for revising and reforming Texas groundwater law have been put forth, ranging in scope from imposing a statewide appropriation system for groundwater to more stringent regional or local regulation; all of these proposals are based on relevant constitutional, statutory, or case-law precedents (Booth 1974; Castleberry 1975; Cisneros 1980; Hobby 1974; Johnson 1982a, 1982b; Patterson 1982; Smith 1977; Snyder 1973; Stagner 1988). Realistically, however, even the most fervent advocates of stricter regulation admit the improbability of achieving sweeping change. It is most unlikely that a court decision will overturn the basic tenets of groundwater law in Texas, nor is it likely that the legislature will impose sweeping change. More likely, as in the past, special legislation will be directed toward solving the specific problems of particular areas, a piecemeal approach on an emergency basis, long after the particular problem has become serious. Those who advocate a "radical redefinition of Texas groundwater law . . . which will move the State into the mainstream of water management in the West" (Stagner 1988) cannot reasonably expect to achieve such sweeping goals, given the gradual historical evolution of Texas groundwater law.

NEW MEXICO GROUNDWATER LAW

Some evidence indicates that New Mexico courts first followed the absolute-ownership doctrine of the English common law, as did a number of other western states. Modification of the doctrine ensued, however, because of numerous conflicts over the use of underground water that occurred in the 1920s. Thus New Mexico can be distinguished from the other western states in that early in its history of groundwater use the state legislature discovered the need for changing the law. New Mexico's prior appropriation permit system of groundwater law was enacted in 1927, and it became the first of the High Plains/Ogallala Aquifer states to establish state control over groundwater development. Though this initial law was declared unconstitutional because of a technical error, the New Mexico Supreme Court did uphold the principles and intent of the act. In 1931, new legislation corrected the law's technical defects and the constitutionality of groundwater appropriation by the state was upheld in 1950. Despite numerous amendments and additions to the 1931 act, it still provides the basis for current groundwater law in New Mexico (Aiken 1984; DuMars 1982; Smith 1988).

Given the authority to issue permits for groundwater development in designated basins, the New Mexico state engineer's office has developed regulations intended to cope with the problem of groundwater depletion. Only groundwater within declared basins is subject to state control, and no permit or license is required to appropriate waters outside such basins. In 1985 the New Mexico Water Code was amended, prohibiting the issuance of a groundwater permit if it is found to be "contrary to the conservation of water or detrimental to the public welfare of the state" (Smith 1988). Recently, thirty-one designated basins have been declared by the state engineer, encompassing almost 85,000 square miles. Because these basins include over 90 percent of the usable groundwater supplies

Aerial spray or "crop-dusting" airplane in Curry County, New Mexico.

in New Mexico, the permit requirement is virtually statewide (Aiken 1984). Two designated underground water basins cover portions of the Ogallala Aquifer on the Llano Estacado of eastern New Mexico.

For aquifers having a significant hydrologic relationship to a stream, a situation rarely pertaining to the Ogallala, the state engineer estimates the pumping effect of the proposed well on streamflow and requires the groundwater appropriator to purchase and retire sufficient surface water rights to compensate for the well's effect. This procedure generally applies to artesian aquifers, which are treated differently from unconfined aquifers. Where large amounts of groundwater are in storage but little recharge occurs, as with the Ogallala Aquifer, maintaining economical pumping depths for irrigators serves as the limiting factor. When annual water-table decline exceeds 2.5 feet within a 9- to 25-square-mile area (depending on aquifer transmissivity), no new groundwater appropriations are allowed. For aquifers with less total storage, maintaining domestic water supplies dictates the limits; the test that applies restricts depletion to 66 percent in forty years. When this depletion rate is exceeded within a 9- to 25-square-mile area, no new permits will be issued. Permits are routinely granted for small wells devoted to providing water for livestock and domestic purposes, however. The state engineer can revoke groundwater permits if the holder does not put the water to beneficial use within four years and fails to proceed with development within one year after receiving notice from the state engineer. Such forfeited rights revert to the state, and the water is subject to further appropriation.

Since the early 1980s New Mexico has been involved in an ongoing dispute with the city of El Paso, Texas, which has long been interested in developing a municipal water supply from groundwater basins in southern New Mexico. As a result of the 1982 U.S. Supreme Court decision in *Sporhase v. Nebraska*, which declared groundwater an article of commerce, in 1983 a federal district court struck down New Mexico's statutory prohibition on the export of groundwater as an unconstitutional restriction on interstate commerce. Subsequently, the New Mexico Legislature passed a new law establishing a permit system for the appropriation of groundwater to be transported out of the state. The law includes a requirement that the permit not be contrary to the conservation of water within the state and not be otherwise detrimental to the public welfare of New Mexico's citizens. In 1984 a New Mexico federal district court upheld the transportation-permit requirement, finding that "if applied in a manner which does not burden interstate commerce, the regulation of groundwater appropriation for the purpose of promoting conservation is constitutionally permissible" (Smith 1988). The courts broadly define public welfare to include health, safety, and recreation as well as aesthetic, environmental, and economic interests, though considerable disagreement still continues over the proper interpretation of conservation and public welfare. This ongoing and as yet unresolved dispute is not relevant to the Texas–New Mexico High Plains border, but in the future it could have a significant impact on possible interstate transportation of Ogallala groundwater from New Mexico to Texas (see Banks 1981; Clark 1982; Fischer 1974).

In sum, New Mexico's groundwater law has a lengthier legislative history and stricter state control policies than the other High Plains/ Ogallala Aquifer states, and it attempts to restrict groundwater development through an administratively established depletion policy. Still, the state does not impose withdrawal limitations on existing users, except through adjudication of groundwater appropriations in artesian conservancy districts; moreover, its policies protect existing users at the expense of potential users rather than requiring present and potential users to share shortages (Aiken 1984).

OKLAHOMA GROUNDWATER LAW

From 1890 until 1937 Oklahoma followed English common-law doctrine of absolute ownership for groundwater. Unlike Texas, Oklahoma does not distinguish between percolating groundwater and water flowing in underground streams. In 1937, in *Canada v. City of Shawnee*, Oklahoma courts adopted the doctrine of reasonable use, also known as the American rule. The state enacted statutory appropriation laws in 1949 that declared a policy of groundwater conservation based on a permit system requiring the Oklahoma Water Resources Board to make a determination of the annual yield of each groundwater basin measured by the average annual recharge. The legislation prohibited the issuance of permits that would result in overdrafting, recognized the existence of prior rights, and established a judicial method for adjudicating these rights (Smith 1988).

In 1972 the 1949 law was repealed and a more comprehensive groundwater code was enacted establishing a permit requirement for all groundwater withdrawals except for domestic uses and regulating well spacing. The new law vested primary responsibility for the management of groundwater in the Oklahoma Water Resources Board. The board establishes groundwater allocations after it has conducted a hydrologic survey of the particular groundwater basin or subbasin and then determines the allocations according to the basin's maximum annual yield. The board considers the area of land overlying the aquifer, the quantity of water in storage, the natural recharge and total discharge, the aquifer's transmissivity, and the likelihood of groundwater pollution from natural sources, among other factors. Each landowner overlying an aquifer is entitled to an equal allocation, except for instances in which grandfather clauses give prestatutory users higher allocations (Aiken 1984; Smith 1988).

Groundwater allocations are subject to a minimum twenty-year aquifer life from July 1, 1973, and administrative provisions ensure continued domestic use beyond the minimum aquifer life. In establishing the maximum annual yield for each aquifer, the board excludes overlying land where the aquifer has a saturated thickness of less than 15 feet, and withdrawals of prestatutory users are subtracted. State allocations of groundwater are enforced through a required annual water-use report. The board may require well-metering only if a majority of landowners in the designated basin request it, however, thus weakening enforcement.

Oklahoma law also provides for the organization of irrigation districts upon the petition of landowners irrigating from a common source or sources. Irrigation districts have broad powers, including the ability to establish equitable rules and regulations for the distribution and use of water among landowners within the district. Similar powers are given to conservancy districts, which have dealt mostly with surface-water development. Though relations between the Oklahoma Water Resources Board and local irrigation districts have been adversarial at times, most of the substantive decision-making power concerning groundwater management still rests with the board.

In most basins where hydrologic surveys are currently underway, irrigators receive a 2-acre-foot temporary allocation, which later may be reduced in their regular permit allocation. Those with reduced allocations are reportedly reducing their irrigated acreage, and some in western

Oklahoma are abandoning irrigation altogether because of increased pumping costs. By enacting the 1972 groundwater law, the state has sanctioned the eventual depletion of the Ogallala Aquifer in Oklahoma. Through adoption of permit allocations based on a minimum twenty-year life for each aquifer, the state legislature has opted for an orderly exhaustion of the state's groundwater resources.

The Oklahoma approach to groundwater management is based largely on state control and pro rata withdrawal reductions, except for prestatutory uses. According to Aiken (1984), despite having been implemented too late to have a lasting effect on conserving groundwater supply, Oklahoma's groundwater allocation policies are the most equitable of any High Plains state and are recommended as a model for other states. Yet it should be noted that Oklahoma water law does not establish priorities for the possible beneficial uses of groundwater. In 1978 the Oklahoma Supreme Court upheld the Water Resources Board's contention that all beneficial uses share the same priority. Some see this as a failure of the system, especially in western Oklahoma where rapid depletion of groundwater is occurring, and predict that the legislature will soon act to remedy this situation (Smith 1988).

COLORADO GROUNDWATER LAW

Though Colorado was one of the first western states to develop a body of prior-appropriation law for surface water, it enacted laws dealing with groundwater much more recently. The first legislative step concerning groundwater came in 1953 and consisted only of a requirement for the filing of well logs and the authorization of groundwater studies; at the same time the state engineer assumed that the position had no authority to regulate wells. Conflicts began in the 1960s when many wells were drilled in the alluvial valleys of rivers flowing onto the Great Plains, where ground and surface water often interconnect; competition arose between junior groundwater users and senior holders of surface-water rights (Smith 1988).

In 1965 the state repealed its earlier legislation, replacing it with the Colorado Groundwater Management Act, which subjected groundwater, including percolating groundwater, to a form of appropriation designed to obtain reasonable use and maximum economic development of groundwater resources. The state engineer then attempted to shut down the Arkansas River valley wells, which were the worst offenders in depleting streamflow. The Colorado Supreme Court, in *Fellhauer v. People*, ruled against the state, finding this exercise of authority to be arbitrary and capricious, but the court did uphold the general power of the state

Wray is a farm service center in the High Plains of eastern Colorado.

engineer to cap wells interfering with senior rights, and it set forth standards that if followed would result in valid regulation of groundwater pumping (Hillhouse 1975; Smith, 1988).

Colorado divides groundwater into three classes: tributary groundwater, designated groundwater basins, and confined groundwater. In tributary groundwater basins, which are hydrologically connected to streams, extractions are regulated by the state engineer to minimize the effects of groundwater withdrawals on holders of senior surface water rights (Smith 1988). Colorado's major tributary groundwater systems are those interconnected with the South Platte and Arkansas rivers. The major confined groundwater basin extends along the foot of the Front Range from north of Denver south to Colorado Springs.

Colorado groundwater law requires state restriction of groundwater development in designated basins, which are not interconnected with surface water sources, but only within a 3-mile radius of the proposed well. This approach does not unnecessarily preclude additional development in areas with less groundwater development or more abundant groundwater supplies. Groundwater depletion, such as is occurring in the Ogallala Aquifer, is dealt with principally through designated basins. Statutes authorize the establishment of designated basins by the Colorado Groundwater Commission, which is authorized to restrict withdrawals by junior appropriators for the benefit of senior appropriators. Water is not available for appropriation in a designated basin if its withdrawal is "materially in excess of the reasonable anticipated average rate of future recharge" (Aiken 1984).

Designated basins restrict all wells of 50 gallons per minute (gpm) or greater in capacity and deny all applications for new appropriations if, in addition to existing withdrawals, the proposed withdrawals will deplete groundwater within a 3-mile radius of the proposed well more than 40 percent in twenty-five years from the permit application date. Requirements for a half-mile well spacing and flow meters have also been established in designated basins. In the two designated basins on the High Plains, the commission has set annual groundwater allocations at 2.5 acre-feet per irrigated acre for the northern basin and 3.5 acre-feet for the southern basin. Outside the designated basins, appropriation of nontributary groundwater is restricted by a test to assure a 100-year minimum useful aquifer life (Aiken 1984; Smith 1988).

Groundwater management districts may be established in designated basins by petition and referendum. A district, after consultation with the commission and a public hearing, may regulate groundwater withdrawals and well spacing. Ten districts have been formed, most in the northern High Plains designated basin. Most districts have adopted regulations limiting withdrawals. Methods include requiring a public hearing and district approval to export groundwater from the district, half-mile well spacing for high-capacity wells, and a 2.5 acre-foot groundwater allocation (Aiken 1984).

Thus, Colorado employs state restriction of groundwater development in its essentially nonrecharging groundwater basins based on administratively established depletion policies that will result in eventual exhaustion of the resource. These policies establish withdrawal limitations on existing users and protect them at the expense of potential users instead of requiring shortages to be shared by both present and potential users. The major shortcoming of these policies is the failure to require gradual reductions in groundwater withdrawal, possibly allowing greater development of the resource or prolonged aquifer life (Aiken 1984). Some observers believe that potential conflicts between current and future groundwater users will be mitigated, largely because Colorado water rights are transferable to a much greater extent than those in most other states (Smith 1988).

KANSAS GROUNDWATER LAW

As one legal scholar described the evolution of Kansas water law: "Our entire water law is similar to the homesteader's house— it just grew as demand dictated" (Windscheffel 1978). In 1881 in *Emporia v. Soden* the Kansas Supreme Court followed the English common-law doctrine and found groundwater to be the private property of the overlying land-owner. As late as 1944 the Kansas Supreme Court reaffirmed the common-law doctrine in *State ex rel. Peterson v. State Board of Agriculture*, finding that the state was without authority to hold hearings on an application to appropriate groundwater or to regulate those appropriations. Kansas imposed only a duty not to pollute groundwater and prohibitions against diminishing underground streamflow (Smith 1988). As early as 1886 Kansas had passed legislation making its surface waters subject to appropriation. In 1927 authority for administering water rights was transferred from the Kansas Water Commission to the Division of Water Resources of the State Board of Agriculture, where it remains today. Following the *Peterson* decision, the Kansas governor appointed a committee to evaluate state water law and to make recommendations for changes (Smith 1988).

From these recommendations came the Kansas Water Appropriation Act of 1945, which subjected underground water to state regulation. The state continues to rely on these appropriation permit statutes, the constitutionality of which has been affirmed. This permit system is administered by the chief engineer of the Division of Water Resources. The 1945 act and subsequent amendments give significant powers over the management of groundwater to the chief engineer, without whose approval no one can appropriate water or acquire water rights in Kansas. Domestic uses, meaning water for household purposes or for irrigation of up to two acres, are exempt from the permit requirement. Other provisions give the chief engineer authority to require groundwater users to install measuring devices in pumps and to report the readings. (Smith 1988).

Kansas groundwater depletion policies reflect a political conflict between state and local groundwater control. Although groundwater allocation is generally a state responsibility, authority relating to groundwater depletion is shared between the Kansas chief engineer and local groundwater management districts. In 1968 the Kansas Legislature passed measures allowing the creation of groundwater management districts (GMDs); the action proved inadequate because of confusion over who could take the necessary steps to create a district. In 1972 this law was repealed and reenacted as the Kansas Ground Water Management District Act, which reflects the preference of groundwater users and landowners for control of groundwater management at the local level (Kromm and White 1981). Smith (1988) observed that legislators were not averse to sharing groundwater management with local entities, thus taking some pressure and responsibility off the state for the solution of groundwater-depletion problems in western Kansas. In fact, depletion of groundwater reserves is the main issue facing the GMDs, which are attempting to slow depletion so as to avoid unnecessary disruptions of the predominantly agricultural economy and to provide a smooth transition for those farmers forced into dry-land farming. The districts can be organized by local water users and may charge up to sixty cents per acre-foot for groundwater withdrawals. They may propose groundwater development policies that subject new development to depletion guidelines; these policies are adopted and enforced by the chief engineer however, rather than by the districts. Since passage of the 1972 act, five districts have been organized, three of which cover portions of the High Plains/Ogallala Aquifer. The GMDs have established well-spacing regulations and depletion guidelines used by the chief engineer in evaluating appropriation applications.

The chief engineer may also regulate groundwater withdrawals, including those of existing users and of new users, but this authority has not yet been exercised. In areas not regulated by a GMD, the chief engineer manages groundwater either on a safe-yield basis, where groundwater basins have adequate recharge, or by allowing the mining of basins where there is little or no recharge (Smith 1988). On a personal motion, the chief engineer can establish special groundwater regulations in control areas of intensive groundwater use outside a district or within a district at its request or at the request of its local water users. Designation criteria include excessive groundwater declines and withdrawals approaching or exceeding recharge. In control areas of intensive groundwater use the chief engineer may close the area to further appropriation, restrict withdrawals of junior or of any appropriators, and require rotation of pumping. In one such control area, well-metering requirements, a well-drilling moratorium, and water-use reporting requirements were decreed (Aiken 1984). The depletion rates established by either the GMDs or the chief engineer range from 1 percent a year to 40 percent over a twenty-five-year period (Smith 1988).

In Kansas, state-level policymakers have apparently decided that most groundwater management decisions should be made on the local level whenever local entities request that authority. Change of this policy would be difficult because farmers constitute one of the most powerful interest groups in the state. The shortcomings of a purely local groundwater management approach have been ameliorated to some extent by expansion of the chief engineer's authority. Yet the extent to which this administrative discretion will be used to reduce the adverse effects of groundwater depletion remains unclear. The state's groundwater management policy has been primarily to limit new developments through district-initiated depletion policies with the chief engineer developing moratoriums, thus protecting existing users at the expense of future users. In sum, Kansas faces the same legal problems in implementing a policy of gradually reducing groundwater appropriations as do other western states that apply the appropriation doctrine.

NEBRASKA GROUNDWATER LAW

Historically, the development of Nebraska groundwater law evolved largely from a series of court decisions, with only limited and infrequent legislative action. The lack of legislative involvement can be explained in part because Nebraska has a wealth of groundwater, which has postponed the conflicts prompting groundwater management legislation in many other states, and because the political power of the irrigation lobby and the rugged individualism of Nebraska's farmers have played an important role in delaying and preventing centralized control of groundwater (Aiken 1980).

In 1933 in *Olson v. City of Wahoo*, the Nebraska Supreme Court established what has become known as the Nebraska rule of reasonable use:

> The owner of land is entitled to appropriate the subterranean waters found under his land, but he cannot extract and appropriate them in excess of a reasonable and beneficial use upon the land which he owns, especially if such is injurious to others who have substantial rights to the waters, and if the natural underground supply is insufficient for all owners, each is entitled to a reasonable proportion of the whole.

In 1981 the Nebraska Supreme Court confirmed the essence of the Nebraska rule in *State ex rel. Douglas v. Sporhase* but further declared that groundwater in Nebraska was public property. Later, in *Sporhase v. Nebraska*, the United States Supreme Court overturned the decision because it found that a Nebraska statute requiring a permit for transporting groundwater out of the state was unconstitutional and a burden on interstate commerce. It did not, however, address the declaration of public ownership of groundwater by the Nebraska court. The Nebraska court decision suggests to some observers that groundwater remains public property even after capture, indicating that the legislature could regulate use as well as withdrawals (Smith 1988). Both the Nebraska Constitution and its water statutes recognize preferential use of the state's waters. Domestic use has preference over all other uses, and agricultural use has priority over manufacturing and industrial use.

Although the legislature has played a small role in groundwater management, in 1957 it created the Department of Water Resources,

Among the natural hazards experienced in the High Plains is hail. This field was damaged by hail in Holt County, Nebraska.

which maintains water-well registrations. In 1969 legislation reorganized 150 single-purpose water districts into 24 natural resource districts (NRDs), which are concerned with the planning and management of soil, water, and wildlife. In response to increasing concerns over groundwater depletion, Nebraska enacted the Ground Water Management Act in 1975, which was amended and recodified in 1982 as the Ground Water Management and Protection Act. This was not an attempt to establish comprehensive control of groundwater under any one state agency; instead, without specifically stating that private property rights over groundwater are precluded, the statute set up an administrative control system with various agencies having duties. Its purpose was to empower NRDs to request establishment of control areas if the groundwater supply was determined to be inadequate to meet present or reasonably foreseeable needs of beneficial use. Thus, groundwater management remains largely a subregional responsibility. NRDs can be set up at the local level, and they have broad powers in resource planning and development (Aiken 1980, 1984; Smith 1988).

Groundwater control areas may be designated by the state director of Water Resources at the request of local districts if water development and use have caused or are likely to cause an inadequate groundwater supply to meet present or reasonably foreseeable needs or if groundwater pollution is likely to occur. With state approval, districts in control areas may restrict total withdrawals, prohibit well drilling, restrict well spacing, require rotation of pumping, and require irrigation scheduling to prevent agricultural chemicals from percolating into aquifers. Three ground-water control areas have been established by the state director. Local districts have imposed well-spacing requirements in two control areas, and well-metering and withdrawal limitations have been imposed in the other (Aiken 1984).

In 1982, legislation gave NRDs the power to establish management areas, which, unlike control areas, do not require state approval but do require a management plan, including establishment of a groundwater reservoir-life goal. Districts then may adopt regulations such as limiting withdrawals, requiring rotation in pumping, and restricting well spacing. No groundwater management areas have yet been established in Nebraska. This same legislation officially adopted the Nebraska rule of reasonable use as the state standard. In 1984, legislation required all NRDs to prepare groundwater management plans by January 1, 1986. These plans had to identify an aquifer-life goal and any regulations needed to implement it. Most of the plans submitted by the NRDs have received approval by the director of the Department of Water Resources (Smith 1988).

Thus, Nebraska has set up local controls over groundwater, not unlike those of Texas, with two important distinctions: Membership in natural resource districts is not voluntary, and local NRDs are subject to state control. Nebraska vests the capacity for management of various aspects of groundwater in six state-level agencies. Most of Nebraska is both fortunate and unique in currently having ample groundwater supplies to provide it with a larger margin for managerial error than the other Ogallala Aquifer states. Unlike Texas, it has time to implement more stringent controls if the local management approach should prove to be inadequate, and the required preparation of groundwater management plans statewide may be the first step in that direction.

Water law is quite specific and does not lend itself well to sweeping generalizations or to comparisons among states. Many, if not most, of the subtle nuances of the groundwater law of each state have been omitted. Groundwater-law systems in this region run the gamut of degrees of state control, from the long-established prior appropriation system of New Mexico to the relatively unaltered strict common-law rule of Texas, surely providing excellent examples that could be used to refute determinist theories. Still, all the states are moving at different rates toward more rigorous management and control of groundwater. Many legal scholars have extolled the virtues of the prior appropriation system in comparison to what they deem to be the outmoded strict common-law rule. Still, we have no definitive proof or evidence that one system is superior to the other in encouraging the more efficient use and conservation of groundwater from nonrenewable aquifers such as the Ogallala. Possibly the local district approach that pertains in Texas, Kansas, and Nebraska is just as effective in encouraging farmers to conserve groundwater and in preserving the regional economy as are the more rigidly managed systems of New Mexico or Colorado. Even in the states with prior-appropriation rules, nonrenewable groundwater is usually managed in such a way that it will eventually be depleted. When this will occur probably depends more on the adequacy of groundwater reserves than on specific legal doctrines or management approaches.

Certainly, once a legal system becomes firmly established that recognizes private property rights over groundwater or that favors local control, it is most difficult to replace or to modernize it. Irrigation farmers in Texas, Kansas, and Nebraska have political power, and the imposition of more stringent state control over groundwater faces many political obstacles. The opinions of legal scholars favoring one system or another that would significantly change the local status quo will probably not be very convincing to local groundwater users whose wishes must certainly be considered. In those states where local control is the preferred management system, the most significant changes will probably continue to be through special legislation directed toward particular local problems, a system long favored in Texas, rather than through sweeping change.

REFERENCES

Aiken, J. David. 1980. "Nebraska Groundwater Law and Administration." *Nebraska Law Review* 59, 317:860–1000.
———. 1984. "Depleting the Ogallala: High Plains Ground Water Management Policies." In George W. Whetstone, ed., *Proceedings of the Ogallala Aquifer Symposium II*, 451–64. Lubbock: Water Resources Center, Texas Tech University.
———. 1986. *Nebraska Water Law Update*. Lincoln: Cooperative Extension Service, University of Nebraska–Lincoln.
Aucoin, J. 1980. *Water in Nebraska: Use, Politics, Policies*. Lincoln: University of Nebraska Press.
Banks, H. O. 1981. "Management of Interstate Aquifer Systems." *Journal of Water Resources Planning and Management Division* 107, 2:563–77.
Barnes, J. R., 1956. "Hydrologic Aspects of Ground Water Control." In *Proceedings, Water Law Conference, 1956*, 134–45. Austin: University of Texas School of Law.
Barnett, Philip M. 1984. "Mixing Water and the Commerce Clause: The Problems of Practice, Precedent, and Policy in Sporhase v. Nebraska." *Natural Resources Journal* 24, 1:161–94.

Booth, Frank R. 1974. Alternative Ground Water Laws for Texas. In *Proceedings, 1974 Water for Texas Conference, Ground Water Management—Current Issues,* 29–60. College Station: Water Resources Institute, Texas A&M University.

Broadhurst, W. L., 1954. "Ground Water Hydrology." In *Proceedings, Water Law Conferences, 1952–1954,* 5–10. Austin: University of Texas School of Law.

"Buried Treasure." 1982. *Texas Water Resources* 8, 3:1–3.

Canada v. City of Shawnee. 1937. 64 P2d 694, Okla. Sup. Ct.

Castleberry, James N., Jr. 1975. "A Proposal for Adoption of a Legal Doctrine of Ground Water Interrelationship in Texas." *St. Mary's Law Journal* 7, 3:503–14.

Chalmers, John R. 1974. *Southwestern Groundwater Law: A Textual and Bibliographic Interpretation.* Arid Lands Resource Information Paper No. 4. Tucson: Office of Arid Lands Studies, University of Arizona.

Cisneros, George D. 1980. "Texas Underground Water Law: The Need for Conservation and Protection of a Limited Resource." *Texas Tech Law Review* 11, 3:637–53.

Clark, Robert E. 1972. "Western Ground-Water Law." In Robert E. Clark, ed., *Waters and Water Rights.* Vol. 5, 407–46. Indianapolis: Allen Smith Co.

———. 1982. "Overview of Groundwater Law and Institutions in United States Border States." *Natural Resources Journal* 22, 4:1007–15.

Corpus Christi v. Pleasanton. 1955. 276 SW2d 798, Tex. Sup. Ct.

"Court Orders Tailwater Waste Stopped." 1984. *Cross-Section* 30, 12:1,4.

DeYoung, Tim. 1984. *Preferences for Managing New Mexican Water.* Las Cruces: New Mexico Water Resources Research Institute.

"Districts Make a Difference." 1978. *Texas Water Resources* 4, 8:1–4.

DuMars, Charles T. 1982. "New Mexico Water Law: An Overview and Discussion of Current Issues." *Natural Resources Journal* 22, 4:1045–64.

Emporia v. Soden. 1881. 25 Kan. 558, Kan. Sup. Ct.

Fellhauer v. People. 1968. 157 Colo. 320, 447 P2d 986, Colo. Sup. Ct.

Fischer, Ward H. 1974. "Management of Interstate Groundwater." *Natural Resources Lawyer* 7:528–45.

Fricke, Carl A. P., and Darryl T. Pederson. 1979. "Ground-Water Management in Nebraska." *Ground Water* 17, 6:544–49.

Friendswood Development Company v. Smith-Southwest Industries, Inc. 1978. 576 SW2d 21, Tex. Sup. Ct.

Graf, Don. 1982a. "The Case for Local Regulation." *Cross-Section* 28, 12:1–4.

———. 1982b. "Groundwater Management under Current Texas Laws." In *Environmental Law: Texas Water Resources, 1982,* El–E20. Austin: State Bar of Texas.

———. 1984. "Legal Aspects of Groundwater Management in the Ogallala Area." In George W. Whetstone, ed., *Proceedings of the Ogallala Aquifer Symposium II,* 465–80. Lubbock: Water Resources Center, Texas Tech University.

———. 1985. "Additional Legislative Powers Needed by Underground Water Conservation Districts in the Ogallala Area." In E. T. Smerdon and W. R. Jordan, eds., *Issues in Groundwater Management* 243–46. Austin: Center for Research in Water Resources, University of Texas.

Green, Donald E. 1973. *Land of the Underground Rain: Irrigation on the Texas High Plains, 1910–1970.* Austin: University of Texas Press.

Greenhill, Joe R., and Thomas G. Gee. 1955. "Ownership of Ground Water In Texas: The *East* Case Reconsidered." *Texas Law Review* 33, 5:620–30.

Guyton, William F. 1974. "Technological Limitations to Ground Water Management." In *Proceedings, 1974 Water for Texas Conference, Ground Water*

Management —Current Issues, 113—20. College Station: Texas Water Resources Institute, Texas A&M University.

Hannay, Felicity. 1981. "Recent Developments in Colorado Groundwater Law." *Denver Law Journal* 58:801–23.

Harnsberger, Richard, J. Oeltjen, and R. Fischer. 1973. "Groundwater: From Windmills to Comprehensive Public Management." *Nebraska Law Review* 52:179–92.

Harnsberger, Richard, and Norman Thorson. 1984. *Nebraska Water Law and Administration.* St. Paul, Minn.: Butterworth Legal Publishers.

Harrison, David L., and Gustave Sanstrom, Jr. 1971. "The Groundwater Surface Water Conflict and Recent Colorado Water Legislation." *University of Colorado Law Review* 43:9.

Hillhouse, William A. 1975. "Integrating Ground and Surface Water in an Appropriation State." *Rocky Mountain Mineral Law Institute* 20:691.

Hobby, Lt. Gov. William P. 1974. "Ground Water Issues Facing Texas." In *Proceedings, 1974 Water for Texas Conference, Ground Water Management —Current Issues,* 11–13, College Station: Texas Water Resources Institute, Texas A&M University.

Houston & T. C. Ry. Co. v. East. 1904. 98 Tex. 146, 81 SW 279, Tex. Sup. Ct.

Hutchins, Wells A. 1958. "Ground Water Legislation." *Rocky Mountain Law Review* 30:416–40.

———. 1961. *The Texas Law of Water Rights:* Austin: Texas Board of Water Engineers.

———. 1974. *Water Rights in the Nineteen Western States.* Vol. 2. Miscellaneous Publication No. 1206. Washington, D.C.: Natural Resource Economics Division, Economic Research Service, U.S. Department of Agriculture.

Jenkins, Edward D. 1983. "Ground-Water Management in Western Kansas." *Journal of Hydraulic Engineering* 109:1314.

Johnson, Corwin W. 1982a. "Reform of Texas Groundwater Law." In *Proceedings, 1982 Water for Texas Conference, Water Issues for Today, for Tomorrow,* 71–77. College Station: Texas Water Resources Institute, Texas A&M University.

———. 1982b. "Texas Groundwater Law: A Survey and Some Proposals." *Natural Resources Journal* 22, 4:1017–30.

Kenyon, Terry F. 1979. "*Friendswood Development Company v. Smith-Southwest Industries, Inc.:* There May Be Hope for Sinking Landowners." *Baylor Law Review* 31, 1:108–20.

Klein, M. 1978. "Groundwater Management in Nebraska without a Legislative Solution: Is There an Alternative?" *Nebraska Law Review* 57:78–90.

Kramer, Kenneth W. 1986. "The Texas Water Package: The Beginning of a New Era or 'Business as Usual'?" *State Bar of Texas, Environmental Law Journal* 16, 3:57-63.

Kromm, David E., and Stephen E. White. 1981. *Public Perception of Groundwater Depletion in Southwestern Kansas.* Manhattan: Kansas Water Resources Research Institute.

"The Local Institution for Ground Water Basin Management, 1971." *Cross-Section* 22, 10:3.

Longo, Peter J., and Robert D. Miewald. 1989. "Institutions in Water Policy: The Case of Nebraska." *Natural Resources Journal* 29, 3:751-62.

Olson v. City of Wahoo. 1933. 124 Neb. 802, 248 NW 304, Neb. Sup. Ct.

Patterson, Kirk. 1982. "Legislative Alternatives for Groundwater Management in

Texas." In *Environmental Law: Texas Water Resources, 1982*, D1-D20. Austin: State Bar of Texas.

"Pumping beyond Our Means." 1983. *Texas Water Resources* 9, 2:1–3.

Rayner, Frank A., and Leslie G. McMillion. 1960. *Underground Water Conservation Districts in Texas*. Austin: Texas Board of Water Engineers.

"Right to Capture Law Threatened by Edwards Water Shortage." 1988. *Cross-Section* 34, 10:1,4.

Shelley, Fred M. 1983. "Groundwater Supply Depletion in West Texas: The Farmer's Perspective." *Texas Business Review* 57, 6:279–83.

Sloan, Richard F. 1979. "Groundwater Resource Management in Kansas." *Kansas Water News* 22:3.

Smith, Garland F. 1977. "The Valley Water Suit and Its Impact on Texas Water Policy: Some Practical Advice for the Future." *Texas Tech Law Review* 8, 3:631–36.

Smith, Zachary A. 1984. "Centralized Decisionmaking in the Administration of Groundwater Rights: The Experience of Arizona, California and New Mexico and Suggestions for the Future." *Natural Resources Journal* 24, 3:641–88.

———. 1985. *Groundwater Policy in the Southwest*. El Paso: Texas Western Press.

———. 1988. *Groundwater in the West*. San Diego, Calif.: Academic Press.

Smith, Zachary A., ed. 1989. *Water and the Future of the Southwest*. Albuquerque: University of New Mexico Press.

Snyder, Stephen E. 1973. "Groundwater Management: A Proposal for Texas." *Texas Law Review* 51, 2:289–317.

Sporhase v. Nebraska. 1982. 458 U.S. 981, U.S. Sup. Ct.

Stagner, S. 1988. "Trends and Developments in Texas Groundwater Policy." *State Bar of Texas, Environmental Law Journal* 18, 3:77–82.

State ex rel. Douglas v. Sporhase. 1981. 208 Neb. 708, 305 NW2d 618, Neb. Sup. Ct.

State ex rel. Peterson v. State Board of Agriculture. 1944. 158 Kan. 603, 149 P2d 604, Kan. Sup. Ct.

Templer, Otis V. 1973. "Water Law and the Hydrologic Cycle: A Texas Example." *Water Resources Bulletin* 9, 2:272–83.

———. 1974. "The Llano Estacado: A Geographic Overview." In Donald W. Whisenhunt, ed. *Land of the Underground Rain: Water Usage on the High Plains*, 12–22. Portales: Eastern New Mexico State University.

———. 1976. *Institutional Constraints and Conjunctive Management of Water Resources in West Texas*. WRC–76–1. Lubbock: Water Resources Center, Texas Tech University.

———. 1978. "Texas Groundwater Law: Inflexible Institutions and Resource Realities." *Ecumene* 10, 1:6–15.

———. 1980. "Conjunctive Management of Water Resources in the Context of Texas Water Law." *Water Resources Bulletin* 16, 2:305–11.

———. 1983a. Groundwater Management Institutions in Texas. In Randall J. Charbeneau, ed., *Regional and State Water Resources Planning and Management*, 43–52. Washington, D.C.: American Water Resources Association.

———. 1983b. "Groundwater Management Institutions on the Texas High Plains." Paper presented at the annual meeting of the Association of American Geographers. Denver, Colorado.

———. 1983c. "Legal Constraints on Water Resource Management in Texas." *Environmental Professional* 5, 1:72–83.

———. 1985. "Water Conservation in a Semi-Arid Agricultural Region: The Texas High Plains." In Templer, ed., *Forum of the Association for Arid Lands Studies*.

Vol. 1, 31–38. Lubbock: International Center for Arid and Semi-Arid Land Studies, Texas Tech University.

———. 1986. "Water Resources on the Llano Estacado." *ICASALS Newsletter* (Special Sesquicentennial Issue) 19, 3:1–2.

———. 1987. "The 1985 Water Legislation and Groundwater Management in Texas." In James E. Jonish, ed., *Forum of the Association for Arid Lands Studies*. Vol. 3, 3–10. Lubbock: International Center for Arid and Semi-Arid Land Studies, Texas Tech University.

———. 1988. "Water Rights Issues." In Duane D. Baumann and Yacov Y. Haimes, eds., *The Role of the Social and Behavioral Sciences in Water Resource Management*, 216–37. New York: American Society of Civil Engineers for the Universities' Council on Water Resources.

———. 1989a. "Adjusting to Groundwater Depletion: The Case of Texas and Lessons for the Future of the Southwest." In Zachary A. Smith, ed., *Water and the Future of the Southwest*. ch. 14, 247–68. Albuquerque: University of New Mexico Press.

———. 1989b. "Managing Groundwater in Texas: The Changing Pace of Regulation." In Frederick E. Davis, ed., *Water: Laws and Management*. Proceedings of the 25th AWRA Conference, 4B7–4B16. Bethesda, Md: American Water Resources Association.

Texas Water Code Annotated. 1981. St. Paul, Minn.: West Publishing Co.

Texas Water Development Board. 1968. *Laws and Programs Pertaining to Texas Land and Water Resources*. Report No. 89. Austin: Texas Water Development Board.

Thomas, H. E. 1972. "Water-Management Problems Related to Ground Water Rights in the Southwest." *Water Resources Bulletin* 8, 1:110–17.

Thompson, Clifford. 1983. "Chronic Tailwater Waste Violators Warned." *Cross-Section* 29, 6:1–2.

Tyler, Roger. 1976. "Underground Water Regulation in Texas." *Texas Bar Journal* 39:533.

Utton, Albert E. 1983. "The El Paso Case: Reconciling *Sporhase* and *Vermejo*. *Natural Resources Journal* 23:ix–xv.

Waddle, Bill J. 1974. "Approaches to Ground Water Management." In *Proceedings, 1974 Water for Texas Conference, Ground Water Management—Current Issues*, 23–26. College Station: Texas Water Resources Institute, Texas A&M University.

Wickersham, Ginia. 1980. "Groundwater Management in the High Plains." *Ground Water* 18:286.

Wilkinson, Charles F. 1985. "Western Water Law in Transition." *Colorado Law Review* 56:317.

Williams, Jean. 1972. "Ground Water Management Potentials." *Water for Texas* 2, 6:4–6.

Windscheffel, Arno. 1978. "Kansas Water Rights: More Recent Developments." *Journal of the Kansas Bar Association* (Fall):223.

Wyatt, A. Wayne. 1982. "Institute Aspects of Groundwater Management." In *Proceedings, 1982 Water for Texas Conference, Water Issues for Today, for Tomorrow*, 67–69. College Station: Texas Water Resources Institute, Texas A&M University.

CHAPTER FIVE

Groundwater Management Institutions

Rebecca S. Roberts

"Too little, too late." Thus Aiken (1984) depicted groundwater manage-ment efforts in the High Plains; many other observers agree. They view with alarm the rapid depletion rates in parts of the Ogallala Aquifer. The conceptual model most often underlying these assessments is the "Tragedy of the Commons" (Hardin 1968), which predicts excessive rates of depletion under common property institutions, and the related economic theory of negative externalities (Randall 1981), which attri-butes overuse of natural resources to the condition of open access to the resource. Open access can come about either by the institution of com-mon property or by the fugitive (flowing) character of the resource; both conditions may be relevant to groundwater use. Open access encour-ages a "free for all" to acquire the resource and in particular discourages saving the resource for the future, because what one user saves another user grabs. Observers note that groundwater management programs in the High Plains emphasize local control and voluntarism, exercise weak regulatory powers, and are subservient to farmers' perceived interests. At issue is whether current institutions deal adequately with the common-property characteristics of groundwater rights presented by the fugitive nature of groundwater.

Recent research raises questions about the validity of this predomi-nant view. Do groundwater property rights actually create the condi-tions of open access necessary for the remorseless development of the tragedy? Are existing management institutions as weak as their form suggests? What are the implications of alternative answers to these questions for defining the management problem and reappraising the institutions? I shall explore these institutional issues in part by examin-ing the existing groundwater management programs in the High Plains and the attitudes underlying local political support for these programs and by considering the consequences for the appraisal of management systems.

A SURVEY OF GROUNDWATER MANAGEMENT
INSTITUTIONS IN THE HIGH PLAINS

The focus for groundwater management in all six High Plains states is the local active management area (AMA) (Figure 5.1). In Nebraska, natural resource districts (NRDs) define the AMAs, there called groundwater control areas (GCAs); in Colorado and Kansas the term is groundwater management districts (GMDs); in New Mexico, declared underground water basins (UWBs); and in Texas, underground water conservation districts (UWCDs). Oklahoma does not organize districts but divides the

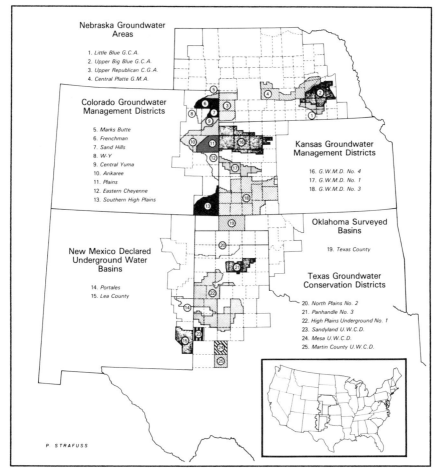

Figure 5.1. High Plains Groundwater Management Areas

state's groundwater resources into basins that are the focus for analysis and water apportionment. For example, the state has surveyed ground-water resources in Texas County in the Oklahoma Panhandle and established permanent allocations. This is not to say that all management programs are equally active; they are not. It does, however, point to the active management area as a common, significant institution for groundwater management in the High Plains.

Active management areas do not form a uniform patchwork across the High Plains. Numerous small districts are jumbled together in Colorado's northern plains, and large expanses of Nebraska, Kansas, and Texas have no AMAs. Comparing the distribution of AMAs to the distributions of groundwater resources and depletion is informative (see Table 5.1 and Figure 5.1; also Figure 1.2 and Figure 3.1). AMAs tend to be concentrated where groundwater resources are great enough to be worth protecting and where continued irrigation is threatened by depletion. Thus, areas with very little water—for example, areas with less than 50 feet of saturated thickness—are typically outside management area boundaries. At the opposite extreme, large parts of Nebraska, where over 400 feet of recharging saturated thickness can be found, are also not actively managed through groundwater control areas. AMAs are concentrated in those regions of all six states with intermediate saturated thickness and substantial depletion. The activity of these management bodies likewise correlates with the threat to irrigation. Texas High Plains UWCD No. 1, with smaller saturated thicknesses and higher depletion rates, shows a higher profile and is more active in many respects than either North Plains UWCD No. 2 or Panhandle UWCD No. 3. The most restrictive of the Kansas districts, Northwest Kansas GMD No. 4, is threatened by a relatively shallow saturated thickness base.

Approaches to groundwater management vary among active management areas on several key points that highlight both their similarities and their differences, including the extent of local control over AMA policies, the range of regulatory powers authorized by legislation, and the regulatory powers actually exercised (see Tables 5.2 and 5.3).

Local Control

Local rather than state control distinguishes groundwater management in much of the High Plains (Table 5.2). In fact, the reliance on local voluntarism for both adoption and enforcement of regulations has engendered considerable suspicion as to its effectiveness in reducing groundwater use (Templer 1983, 1985; Aiken 1984; Emel and Maddock 1986; Johnson 1982, 1986; Roberts and Gros; Tarlock 1985). Can irrigators regulate themselves?

Table 5.1. Groundwater Resources by Management District

Active Management Area		1980 Saturated Thickness	Saturated Thickness Decline Predevelopment to 1980 (%)
Texas			
High Plains UWCD	No.1	0-200	10->50
North Plains GWCD	No.2	100-400	Minimal to 50
Panhandle GWCD	No.3	100-400	10-25
Martin County UWCD		0-100	10->50
Sandyland UWCD		0-100	10-25
Mesa UWCD		0-100	+25-25
New Mexico			
Portales UWB		0-150	10-50
Lea County UWB		100-200	Minimal-25
Oklahoma			
Texas County		100->400	Minimal-50
Colorado			
Northern High Plains Districts:			
Sand Hills, Central Yuma		200-400	Minimal-10
Arikaree		0-100	Minimal-25
Plains		0-200	Minimal-25
Others		0-200	Minimal-25
Southern High Plains		0-100	Minimal
Kansas			
Western GMD No. 1		0-100	25->50
Southwest GMD No. 3		100->400	Minimal->50
Northwest GMD No. 4		0-200	Minimal-25
Nebraska			
Upper Republican GCA		100-400	Minimal-25
Upper Big Blue GCA		100-400	Minimal-25
Little Blue GCA		100-400	Minimal-25
Central Platte GMA		200-600	Minimal

Sources: Luckey et al. 1981, "Water-Level," Atlas, HA-562, USGS; Weeks and Gutentag 1981, "Bedrock," Atlas, HA-648, USGS.

Local control is firmly established in Texas, Nebraska, and Kansas. Texas represents the extreme; all powers to regulate groundwater are vested in districts formed at the discretion of local voters and these districts are under their control. In Nebraska, locally controlled natural-resource districts have the power to request establishment of groundwater control areas and to develop regulations for control areas, both

Table 5.2. Regulatory Powers for Groundwater Management

State	Localization of Regulatory Power	Regulatory Powers Authorized (selected)
Texas	Local districts by local petition and referendum	Well spacing Regulate withdrawals Make and enforce reasonable rules for conserving, preserving, protecting Develop comprehensive plans Eminent domain Construct supply works Buy and sell water Research
New Mexico	State engineer in designated underground water basins	Grant appropriation permits Set standards for appropriation (including depletion timetable, well spacing and so on)
Oklahoma	Oklahoma Water Resources Board	Determine acreage allocation to ensure 20-year aquifer life Well spacing Metering on request of landowners Prohibit waste
Kansas	Local groundwater management districts by recommendation to the Kansas chief engineer	Well spacing Regulate withdrawals Establish rules and regulations to implement standards and policies Require metering Levy water-user charges Eminent domain Buy and sell land and water rights Build supply works Research and demonstration
Colorado	State Ground Water Commission in designated basins; local groundwater management districts may enforce stricter regulations	Well spacing Regulate withdrawals Establish other reasonable rules and regulations for consuming, preserving Adopt devices, procedures, measures, or methods Develop comprehensive plans Require metering and flow regulation Construct supply works
Nebraska	Local natural resources districts in control areas under approval of state director of Water Resources	Well spacing Regulate withdrawals Establish other reasonable rules and regulations Require metering and reports of use Prohibit tailwater runoff Close areas to new wells Require rotation pumping Issue cease-and-desist orders

Sources: Respective state legislation and state/local water management officials

Headquarters of the Central Platte Natural Resource District in Grand Island, Nebraska.

subject to the approval of the state director of Water Resources. Initiative therefore resides locally, but with the presence of a state veto. The chief engineer of Kansas exercises regulatory power over groundwater but routinely follows management plans and rules and regulations developed by voluntarily formed, locally controlled groundwater management districts. In fact, these districts were specifically developed to promote local control.

New Mexico and Oklahoma are the chief exceptions to such local control. The New Mexico state engineer and the Oklahoma Water Resources Board hold the power to grant water rights permits in groundwater basins. Local input is not organized through any formal institution but occurs as individuals or private groups challenge water rights actions by the state. Colorado mixes the two approaches. The Ground Water Commission, a state body, exercises regulatory power over permits and use in designated groundwater basins. Locally controlled districts can be established by local petition and referendum; districts may then assume some of the regulatory powers of the state, subject to its approval. Colorado districts in the High Plains, however, have been slow to develop their own policies and regulations.

Authorized Powers

The regulatory powers over groundwater use authorized by state enabling legislation are considerable throughout the High Plains (see Table

Table 5.3. Existing Groundwater Management Programs

State and Management Area	Regulations			Approach to Conservation[1]
	Well spacing	Withdrawals	Other	
Texas				
High Plains UWCD No. 1	600–1320 ft. depending on well diameter	none	Tailwater control	Active: education, demonstrations, publicity, technical assistance, member services
North Plains GWCD No. 2	600–1320 ft. depending on well diameter	none	Tailwater control	Moderate: member services, research, demonstrations, education
Panhandle GWCD No. 3	600–1320 ft. depending on well-diameter; Well-density regulations by well capacity	none	Tailwater control	Moderate: education, member services
Martin County UWCD	Yet to be adopted		Active groundwater quality program	Moderate
Sandyland UWCD	Yet to be adopted		—	Moderate: education, technical assistance
Mesa UWCD (under organization)	—	—	—	—
New Mexico				
Portales UWB	600 ft.	Permits denied if depletion >66% over 40 yrs. within 36–100 sq.-mi. template	Basin fully appropriated	Rely on other agencies
Lea county UWB	600 ft. rule of thumb	Permits denied if depletion >66% over 40 yrs. within 900 sq.-mi. template	—	Rely on other agencies
Oklahoma				
Texas County	none	New wells permitted at 2 acre-feet/year	Reporting of water use	Rely on other agencies
Kansas				
Western Kansas GMD No. 1	1300–2640 ft. depending on depletion	New wells restricted where would result in >1% depletion per year or >50% depletion, 2 acre-ft. limit	Cloud seeding; Tailwater control; Supplemental wells prohibited	Limited: newsletter, water-user services

	Spacing	Well restrictions	Control measures	Education/enforcement
Southwest Kansas GMD No. 3	1300–2300 ft. depending on capacity	New wells restricted where would result in 40% depletion over 25 years, 2 acre-ft. limit	Metering pending Tailwater control Most areas completely appropriated Supplemental wells prohibited	Moderate: newsletter, research, demonstrations
Northwest Kansas GMD No. 4	1400–2800 ft. depending on capacity	New wells restricted where would result in >1% depletion year, 2 acre-ft. limit Strategies to implement safe yield under discussion	Moratorium on new wells Long-term safe-yield goal to be implemented Tailwater control Metering on new wells Supplemental wells prohibited Aggressive enforcement	Moderate: active enforcement preferred
Colorado				
Northern High Plains DB	2640 ft.	Permits denied if depletion >40% over 25 yrs. within 3-mile radius, 2.5 acre-feet/yr. 3.5 acre-feet/yr.	—	Rely on other agencies
Southern High Plains DB	2640 ft.		—	Rely on other agencies
Nebraska				
Upper Republican GCA	3300 ft.	15 acre-inches/yr.	Control irrigated acreage Metering and reporting Supplemental wells prohibited	Active: education, demonstrations, cost-sharing, newsletter
Upper Big Blue GCA	1000 ft.	16 acre-inches/yr. pending trigger point	Metering pending trigger	Moderate: education, demonstrations, cost-sharing, newsletter
Little Blue GCA	600 ft.	Pending trigger point	Metering pending trigger	Limited: newsletter, limited demonstrations
Central Platte GMA	600 ft.	None	Acreage limits pending trigger Active groundwater quality program	Limited: newsletter

[1]Categorizations are approximate only.
Source: State and local groundwater management documents and officials.

5.2). The powers to control well spacing and groundwater withdrawals exist in all states, either through direct regulation or through the process of water rights permits. Sometimes a goal to guide regulation of withdrawals is legislatively provided, as in Oklahoma where legislation specifies a twenty-year depletion period, but most often such decisions are left to management officials or to districts. There is a wide variety of additional specific delegations of power. For example, Kansas authorizes groundwater management districts to buy and sell land and water rights, exercise eminent domain, levy water-user charges, require metering of wells, engage in research and development, and build supply works. Other states have similar lists of specific powers. General language also confers broad powers in most states; Texas, for example, authorizes districts to "make and enforce reasonable rules for conserving, preserving, protecting," water (Texas Water Code 1989, annot. sec. 52.151). In sum, management authorities have considerable powers to manage groundwater resources; state legislative authority differs more in detail and form than in substance.

Management Programs in Practice

The powers actually exercised are considerably less than those authorized. Nonetheless, states and districts are gradually extending their management activities; some programs are actively assertive (Table 5.3). Well spacing is regulated in all active management areas except Oklahoma. The minimum permitted distance between wells ranges from 600 feet (one-eighth mile) to 3,300 feet (five-eighths mile). That the smallest and largest distances are found in the same state, Nebraska, attests to the importance of local control and to the wide latitude provided by state legislation.

Withdrawals are regulated in most active management areas; the Texas districts and all the control areas in Nebraska apart from the Upper Republican GCA are exceptions. The goal for all the AMAs that manage withdrawals is planned depletion. Such a goal recognizes that recharge rates are so small that a sustainable yield is not consistent with any practical use of the aquifer. The anticipated depletion timetable varies, however. We need a closer analysis of standards to evaluate how much of a constraint on withdrawals this goal actually poses.

Districts in New Mexico, Oklahoma, Kansas, and Colorado have established depletion timetables. These range from the most restrictive —one percent of saturated thickness per year in northwest and western Kansas GMDs—to the most liberal—a twenty-year lifetime in Oklahoma. The New Mexico UWBs, the Colorado Northern High Plains Designated Basin, and the Southwest Kansas GMD No. 3 combine a depletion rate and a time period that fall between these two extremes. The timetables for other states and districts are implicit in their allocation guidelines.

Northwest Kansas GMD No. 4 is taking the most radical approach of any AMA to depletion scheduling. Its current timetable limits withdrawals to 1 percent per year, but it is initiating a safe-yield depletion goal. The intent is not to maintain a large-scale irrigation economy in the indefinite future; that is impossible. Rather, the district will take measures to curb water use actively in the coming years so that overdraft stops while water still remains in the aquifer to manage. Plans to implement such a goal are being developed and will pose a substantial challenge both to officers and irrigators within the locally controlled district.

Strategies for depletion goals differ greatly. Two questions are central to this variation: Must existing irrigators share water shortfalls with potential irrigators, and to what extent is water-use efficiency encouraged?

Kansas, New Mexico, and Colorado protect prior appropriators by limiting the number of users when supplies become short. Permits are granted for beneficial use as long as water is available under the respective depletion timetable criterion; the basin is then closed to new users. The Portales (New Mexico) UWB and the Southwest Kansas GMD No. 3 are essentially closed to new wells, for example. Protections granted to prior appropriators do not include the right to the full quantity of the original permit as water levels decline according to the depletion timetable. They do mean that the number of acres or users is restricted to achieve the designated lifetime.

In contrast, Nebraska, Oklahoma, and Texas require long-time water pumpers to share the declining water supply with junior pumpers. In all cases, the general principle dictates that all existing and potential users share a limited supply of water equally. In the clearest example of management that is restrictive but based on sharing, the Upper Republican NRD (Nebraska) places no restrictions on the number of pumpers in its GCA but limits both old and new users to an average of 15 inches of water per acre per year. Other Nebraska districts are following this lead but have not reached depletion levels or rates that trigger allocation. Oklahoma and Texas also rely on sharing but put fewer limits on withdrawal. Oklahoma writes permits for both old and new users in Texas County for 2 feet per acre per year. Withdrawals are not limited in Texas except by requirements for density or spacing so that all users share shortfalls.

The second issue that affects implementation of goals is the extent to which water-use efficiency is explicitly encouraged. Some states specify a "duty" of water, or a fixed allocation per acre. In Texas County, Oklahoma, the duty of water is 2 feet per acre per year; in the Colorado High Plains basins it varies between 2.5 and 3.5 acre-feet per acre; in Nebraska's Upper Republican GCA the per-acre allocation is 15 inches. Only in the Upper Republican GCA is the per-acre allocation small enough to encourage efficient water transportation and application technologies. Gross waste would be restricted in all cases, but 2 feet of water per acre per year provides enough water to grow corn with row-water technology—one of the highest water-use crops with one of the least-efficient technologies. With a fixed duty of water, little incentive exists for irrigators to aspire to greater efficiency. In contrast, New Mexico and Kansas write permits for a specific withdrawal rate per well. If irrigators can achieve greater efficiencies, they can irrigate more acres with a given quantity of water. Implementation of the safe-yield goal in Northwest Kansas GMD No. 4 will create the strongest incentives for farmers to improve efficiencies; only through efficiency upgrades will they be able to extend the time they can pump before a pumpage-reduction trigger mandates reduced water use (Bossert 1990).

Management programs in the High Plains also attempt to encourage water-use efficiency through a variety of active and creative voluntary technical conservation programs. Such programs are concentrated where districts are locally controlled—in Texas, Nebraska, Kansas—and therefore are responsive to local preferences. States exerting central control tend to rely on other agencies, such as the federal Soil Conservation Service or the state Agricultural Extension Service, to provide these programs. Locally controlled AMAs often enthusiastically promote conservation awareness and technical measures that individual farmers may take to conserve water. They also maintain active demonstration programs and participate in cooperative research with the land-grant university systems to develop new technologies. The intent is not only to reduce water use but, perhaps even more important, to increase the productivity of water. Lacewell and Lee (1988) viewed such improvements in net income to farmers as especially valuable in enabling them to make the coming transition to dryland farming.

The Texas High Plains UWCD No. 1, for example, relies primarily on its programs for conservation education and technical assistance to achieve water-management goals. It has developed a conservation-education program adopted by most local school districts and has helped to establish norms of tailwater management. By publicizing water-loss rates between well and application point, it has encouraged farmers to replace open ditches with underground pipe, to replace furrow irrigation with sprinklers or surge valves, and to convert sprinklers to low-energy precision application (LEPA) systems. The LEPA sprinkler systems distribute water directly to the furrows through drop tubes and low-pressure emitters to achieve application efficiencies of up to 98 percent (Lacewell and Lee 1988). High Plains UWCD No. 1 encourages and dem-

Corner unit on a center pivot system in Platte County, Nebraska. A corner system permits irrigation of most of the land not reached with a conventional system, which irrigates a circle within a square quarter-section.

onstrates technologies such as furrow diking to reduce runoff and soil/ plant moisture measurement to improve irrigation scheduling for efficient water use. The district reports that water-application rates declined from 2 acre-feet per acre per year to 1 acre-foot between the early 1950s and the 1980s (Templer 1985).

In summary, control over well spacing is almost universally an accepted management tool. Formal constraints on withdrawals exist for most but not all active-management areas. The effectiveness of the various approaches has been unclear. Most conclusions rely on legal case studies of formal regulations; empirical analysis to supplement the case-study analyses is lacking. Texas, without allocation limits and by relying primarily on education, has been considered as providing almost no control; in contrast, New Mexico has long been regarded as having the only program with substantial control over water use. This latter judgment is no longer obvious. Kansas, Nebraska, and Colorado have now established goals similar to those of New Mexico. True, these states did so forty years later than New Mexico, but irrigation developed later in the north. The Kansas GMDs and Nebraska's Upper Republican NRD, in particular, have made substantial headway in the 1980s. Their formal controls now rival or exceed those of New Mexico. Locally controlled districts throughout the High Plains show initiative and energy in developing programs to encourage voluntary technical water conservation through education and demonstration.

Attitudes toward Groundwater Management Institutions

Attitudes toward groundwater management in the High Plains help to explain the pattern of its actual practice. Surveys have documented people's attitudes toward groundwater management among High Plains and Texas general populations (Kromm and White 1985, 1986, 1987; Baird 1976), High Plains and Texas irrigators (Kromm and White 1985, 1986, 1990; Shelley 1983; Taylor et al. 1985), and northern High Plains groundwater management officials (Keller et al. 1981). The results of these studies tell a remarkably consistent story.

People, especially irrigators, are aware of problems of depletion (Shelley 1983; Taylor et al. 1985). They are more concerned in areas where depletion is advanced enough that irrigators are experiencing its effects financially (Taylor et al. 1985). But in all cases, they view other problems such as hail and the economic situation facing farmers as more important. They even consider other aquifer-related problems—the cost of energy to lift water or the cost of irrigation equipment—as more significant than aquifer depletion.

Residents and irrigators prefer that the power to manage groundwater be vested locally. They choose local groundwater management districts over state or federal management by a plurality throughout the High Plains (Kromm and White 1986). This plurality shifts to a lopsided majority in Texas, where Shelley found that irrigators would favor mandatory regulations on water use subject only to a majority vote of local farmers. Only in New Mexico, the sole state with strongly centralized water management, has research shown a significant preference for state rather than local management (Kromm and White 1986). This anomaly could represent satisfaction with the current water management system, including informal but important accommodations between interest groups and officials. Smith (1984), for example, reported that farm opinion leaders in New Mexico favored state management in contrast to local only as long as the existing state engineer remained in office.

Irrigators and to a lesser extent the general High Plains population do not favor regulatory management tools (Taylor et al. 1985; Shelley 1983; Kromm and White 1986). Support is strong only for programs that emphasize voluntary, technical conservation practices that can be adopted by individual farmers. Such measures include tailwater recovery systems, minimum tillage, monitoring of soil moisture, and high-efficiency irrigation equipment. The sole regulatory tool consistently favored is the regulation to control well spacing or well density (Shelley 1983; Baird 1976; Keller et al. 1981). Constraints on capacity or pumping, along with any form of financial incentive such as pump taxes, are uniformly and strongly rejected.

Residents in the High Plains have supported local control, regulation of well spacing, and voluntary conservation education and demonstration programs, a pattern of attitudes remarkably matched in practice. People have tended to support existing management institutions consistently, and they resist any more stringent regulation of water use, mirroring the political difficulties such proposals have encountered.

A MODEL OF GROUNDWATER MANAGEMENT

Any evaluation of groundwater management programs depends crucially on a conceptual model of management. What is the problem? Whose behavior contributes? What needs to happen to solve the problem? The "Tragedy of the Commons" is "the dominant framework within which social scientists portray environmental and resource issues" (Godwin and Shepard 1979). Whether in the form of Garret Hardin's (1968) colorful analogy to the common grazing land of an English country village or in more sober neoclassical formulations (Friedman 1971), the problem is the existence of common-property institutions that yield free and unregulated access to a finite resource. Groundwater is a fugitive resource that cannot be possessed until it is pumped to the surface; while it is still in the ground, it is common property. This holds whether the legal doctrine defining groundwater rights is that of absolute ownership, as in Texas, reasonable use, as in Nebraska, or prior appropriation, as in New Mexico. The theory of common property maintains that users will not limit pumping to a socially desirable level, a level usually taken to be "economic efficiency," which is the criterion of maximum economic well-being identified by neoclassical economic theory (Randall 1981). People are "unlikely to restrain their own behavior when the immediate benefits of their actions are their own but the costs are passed on to society as a whole (or other specific groups), and any longer-term or external benefits that might accrue from an individual's self-instigated" moral restraint are indiscernible in effect (McCay and Acheson 1987). A "free-for-all" ensues, "with users competing with one another for a greater share of the resource to the detriment of themselves, the resource, and society as a whole" (Ciriacy-Wantrup and Bishop 1975).

This model generates a number of outcomes, including resource depletion, dissipation of economic surplus, and overcapitalization, the last effect having special significance because it locks users into rapid resource depletion (McCay and Acheson 1987). Highly capitalized users are able to succeed in the race to grab the resource, but the cost of that capital then renders them dependent on high-input/high-output production. Furthermore, the model predicts that users will resist change in the system, even though change would be to their collective benefit. Each is afraid that the individual user will pay the cost for any larger social benefit under management.

Both conservative and liberal solutions to the tragedy of the commons exist, perhaps helping to account for the popularity of the model, as McCay and Acheson suggest (1987). Common property can be made private, or the use of common property can be regulated by the larger public; either approach can generate an optimal, or efficient, rate of aquifer depletion. The "new resource economics" school has developed schemes to define "transferable property rights" in groundwater (Anderson, Burt, and Fractor 1983). This school favors privatization over regulation not only because of the incentives to protect and conserve resources provided by private ownership but also because of mistrust of the politics and bureaucracy that accompany regulation (Cuzan 1983). Advocates of regulation are far more numerous (Friedman 1971; Aiken 1984; Johnson 1982, 1986; Kelly 1983). They recognize the solution of privatization theoretically but question whether transferable groundwater rights can be defined completely enough in practice to eliminate the need for regulation. If property rights to groundwater do not allow users to maintain all rights to the future use of water they "save" in the ground, then privatization will provide incentives to deplete rather than to conserve. Property schemes that provide complete protection to those who save water do not exist.

AN APPRAISAL

Pragmatic appraisals of the adequacy of groundwater management institutions in the High Plains have taken a generally pessimistic tone. Johnson (1982, 1986) and Templer (1983) identified serious deficiencies in Texas groundwater law, including no judicial protection against water-level declines, only minimal sanction against waste, and no deliberate policy on the proper rate of depletion for nonrecharging aquifers. Templer (1983) noted that deeply entrenched political resistance virtually precluded rapid reform. In particular, the prevailing support for local versus state management reflects an assessment of those likely to favor little control. Keller et al. (1981) concluded that the unwillingness of northern-plains district officials to go beyond voluntary policies to regulatory policies ensured that management will have little impact. Emel and Maddock (1986) and Wescoat (1985) emphasized that the traditional aim of groundwater management programs in many western states has been to protect property rights rather than to ensure maximum beneficial use. Such protection puts a high priority on security of rights in order to encourage resource development, but it also can limit the incentives for conservation and flexibility of use necessary to encourage efficient resource development.

Aiken (1984) focused on the failure of most states in the High Plains to force existing users to share groundwater deficits with potential users, thereby creating an unfair burden on those denied access. Indeed, analysis has suggested that the significant changes in law and practice over the past twenty years in these states represent changes in the form of management rather than in substance (Emel and Brooks 1988; Roberts and Gros 1987). Rules replaced discretionary standards, and administrative organizations replaced judges for defining rights and settling disputes (Emel and Brooks 1988). Irrigators supported water-rights reform because it translated their traditional common-law water rights into more clearly defined and protected statutory rights at a time when state or federal governments threatened regulatory intervention.

The Tragedy of the Commons as a conceptual model underlies many of these appraisals of groundwater management programs in the High Plains. The model identifies "efficiency," or maximum befical use, as the goal of management and presumes inefficiency in the absence of regulation because of the fugitive character of the groundwater resource. The model also predicts that water users will resist beneficial regulation, resulting in weak, locally controlled, and voluntary management programs in the absence of external compulsion. The most commonly implemented management tools have been well spacing and conservation education rather than more strenuous withdrawal limitations; only New Mexico has a long history of managing withdrawals. Local control is predominant in Texas, Kansas, and Nebraska, and local interests figure in state-level policymaking in the other states. Questions arise about the willingness of individualistic irrigators to subject themselves to collectively beneficial regulations. The legal literature has come closest to recognizing goals other than maximum beneficial use, such as protection of property rights (Emel and Maddock 1986; Wescoat 1985). Yet the theoretical justification for protecting property rights within the law relies heavily on the same utilitarian formulations underlying the neoclassical theory of externalities from which the Tragedy of the Commons is derived.

QUESTIONS

Despite the widespread acceptance of the tragedy of the commons as the appropriate model for understanding groundwater management, recent research questions its importance to groundwater depletion in the High Plains by pursuing two lines of analysis. The first questions the magnitude of the tragedy or the inefficiency to be remedied. The second challenges the conclusion that states and localities have been unable to resolve the problems of the commons (Roberts and Emel 1991).

The model of the Tragedy of the Commons assumes that common property is freely available to all, a condition known as "open access." When the number of "firms" with access to a common-property fishery is limited in a neoclassical model, too many boats still catch too many fish, but the inefficiency is smaller than in the open-access case (Dasgupta and Heal 1979). The inefficiency decreases as the number of firms declines. The analogy to development of an aquifer is clear. Rights to use groundwater, however, are not open-access rights but are restricted to overlying landowners, and the number of such landowners is limited by complex historical and economic forces, with the number decreasing over time. Therefore, one would expect the restricted access inherent in surface-property rights to reduce the inefficiency substantially.

Models combining economic and hydrologic components can assess the significance of the inefficiency remaining under limited access to an aquifer. Gisser and Sanchez (1980), and Allen and Gisser (1984) concluded that "under hydrologic conditions that are likely to prevail in many irrigation basins . . . , welfare loss . . . under the regime of no control would be nearly zero." The necessary hydrologic conditions require that both the recharge and the annual water use be small compared to water stored in the aquifer; such conditions are approximated over significant portions of the Ogallala, especially where saturated thickness is greatest. They also found that welfare loss under management is sensitive to misspecification of the demand curve for water, which implies that restrictions on withdrawals, without careful prior economic analysis, may introduce greater welfare loss than no management. Feinerman and Knapp (1983) reviewed a number of hydrologic/economic models and came to similar conclusions. They found that optimal management may bring negligible benefits and that allocation schemes may easily generate an economic loss as a result of reducing water use too much. They also found that benefits are sensitive to the demand curve. Thus, research concludes that efficiency benefits to management of groundwater may be small, and management may be more likely to do harm than good.

Research also indicates that the conclusions usually drawn from the Tragedy of the Commons model are far too pessimistic about the capacity of states and especially of localities to manage groundwater problems. The survey of groundwater management programs reveals considerable recent activity. New Mexico is no longer the sole state with management capability; Northwest Kansas GMD No. 4 and the Nebraska Upper Republican NRD are cases in point. Both have introduced metering in the past few years, a step irrigators are usually reluctant to consider, and both have initiated allocation schemes that place real constraints on water use by individual farmers. The safe-yield goal in Northwest Kansas GMD No. 4 is especially striking. Significantly, these steps have taken place in districts with strong local control, raising the possibility that local control supports management instead of detracting from it as the Tragedy of the Commons model predicts. In fact, the director of Northwest Kansas GMD No. 4 reports that local control will be essential to implementing the safe-yield goal effectively. "Bureaucratic mistrust associated with regulation can be substantially reduced or possibly even eliminated if the bureaucracy is local enough to be considered 'ourselves,' such as in the case of a well-organized and tight-knit local government" (Bossert 1990).

Anthropological evidence confirms the capacity of local communities to manage the commons. McCay and Acheson (1987) emphasized that the "thesis of the tragedy of the commons fails to distinguish between common property as a theoretical condition in which there are no relevant institutions (open access) and common property as a social institution (the commons)." A variety of case studies indicates that groups of local users do in fact develop formal and informal institutions to solve common-property problems, although this need not necessarily be the case (McCay and Acheson 1987; Maass and Anderson 1978). The adequacy of institutions needs to be evaluated on a case-by-case basis rather than on the blanket assumption that local people are too individualistic to resolve their problems; case studies of the U.S. fisheries demonstrate this capacity. Despite the limits of antitrust laws on organization by fishers, local fishing communities have developed a variety of means to limit access, including individual fishing territories in the Maine lobster fishery, gear restrictions, area closures, and controls on entry in the Gulf fishery (Johnson and Libecap 1982; Acheson 1987).

The implications for groundwater management in the High Plains are clear; management programs must be evaluated from a new perspective that recognizes the capacity of local communities. In this light, groundwater management efforts in the High Plains can compare with commons management institutions in the fisheries. Surveys show that irrigators are aware and concerned about the problem of groundwater depletion and that management programs enjoy fair-to-active support from farmers. Management tools designed to limit access are widely employed, from well spacing and conservation education to metering, allocation, and basin closure. In the political processes underlying management, districts do deal with commons issues. Managers in Texas speak of developing procedures to prevent the "stealing" of water (Bowers 1990; Hoelscher 1990). In implementing its safe-yield goal, Northwest Kansas GMD No. 4 wrestled with questions of the commons: "Will we be placing ourselves at an economic disadvantage by achieving zero depletion if others do not? How can we provide a property scheme to protect the water rights of those who sacrifice to achieve the greater public good? How is the best way to overcome the overcapitalization problem?" (Bossert 1990).

These conclusions are supported by recent empirical analyses of the effects of groundwater management institutions in the southern High Plains of Texas and New Mexico (Emel and Roberts 1991). Examination of the statutory and regulatory wording would seem to indicate that New Mexico has provided the greatest active protection to water levels over the past thirty-five years and that Texas has provided the least of any state in the High Plains. Statistical analysis, however, indicates that most variation across the region in 1930–1980 water-level declines and in current irrigated land-use patterns can be explained by the variation in biophysical parameters such as soils, hydraulic conductivity, saturated thickness, and depth to water. In neither study is the difference between New Mexico and Texas in approaches to management important. The analysis of water-level declines identifies a difference between management and no management; the analysis of irrigated land use does not even mark this distinction. Thus, even management approaches as apparently polarized as those of Texas and New Mexico may be equally capable of eliminating inefficiencies in groundwater use. Tools that initially appear to be inadequate—well spacing, prohibitions against excessive waste, and voluntary conservation programs—may be more effective than one thinks.

A REAPPRAISAL

Legislation in all the High Plains states grants broad powers to state agencies and local districts to manage groundwater depletion from the Ogallala Aquifer. Until recently, resulting groundwater management programs were characterized by voluntarism and a hesitancy to employ regulatory tools. Groundwater management in Texas, Nebraska, and Kansas was exercised by voluntarily formed, locally controlled districts; groundwater policy in other states was strongly influenced by irrigators' interests. Only well spacing and voluntary adoption of technical conservation measures were widely adopted tools. New Mexico, with strong centralized state control, was the only state to exert substantial control over pumpage allocations. Surveys indicated both residents and irrigators strongly supported the local, voluntary approach to management already established. Many analysts concluded that strong local control or influence was related to a weak management stance and that prospects for improvement were poor, conclusions that harmonized with the

Tragedy of the Commons model. In the rush to appropriate a common, fugitive resource, users would neither restrain themselves nor submit voluntarily to a cooperative solution.

Evidence accumulating during the 1980s reveals that these judgments no longer hold. Perhaps most impressive is the emergence of innovative, aggressive groundwater management programs in the High Plains. The programs undertaken in Kansas and Nebraska are cases in point: Northwest Kansas GMD No. 4 is implementing an ambitious safe-yield goal requiring planned reduction of withdrawals, and Nebraska's Upper Republican NRD has limited allocations for all farmers in its GCA to 15 acre-inches per year. Actions by other states and districts indicate similar trends. Active conservation education and technical-assistance programs are increasingly common. Surprisingly, these initiatives are concentrated in states where local control is pronounced and where management officials view local control as essential to their effectiveness. These developments question profoundly the logic underlying earlier, more pessimistic, analyses that assumed the inevitability of a tragic ending to the commmons problem; instead, they support a more optimistic assessment. Communities have the potential, although not all will choose to exercise it, to resolve the difficulties of the commons.

REFERENCES

Acheson, James M. 1987. "The Lobster Fiefs Revisited: Economic and Ecological Effects of Territorialty in Maine Lobster Fishing." In Bonnie J. McCay and James M. Acheson, eds., *The Question of the Commons* 37–65. Tucson: University of Arizona Press.

Aiken, J. David. 1984. "Depleting the Ogallala: High Plains Ground Water Management Policies." In George A. Whetstone, ed., *Proceedings of the Ogallala Aquifer Symposium III*, 451–64. June. Lubbock, Tex.

Allen, Richard C., and Micha Gisser. 1984. "Competition versus Optimal Control in Groundwater Pumping When Demand Is Nonlinear." *Water Resources Research* 20, 7:752–56.

Anderson, Terry L., Oscar R. Burt, and David T. Fractor. 1983. "Privatizing Groundwater Basins: A Model and Its Applications." In Terry L. Anderson, ed., *Water Rights: Scarce Resource Allocation, Bureaucracy, and the Environment*, 223–48. San Francisco: Ballinger.

Baird, Frank L. 1976. "District Groundwater Planning and Management Policies on the Texas High Plains: The Views of the People." Lubbock, Tex.: High Plains Underground Water Conservation District.

Bossert, Wayne. 1990. Manager, Northwest Kansas Groundwater Management District No. 4. Personal communication. September 12.

Bowers, Richard. 1990. Manager, Texas North Plains Underground Water Conservation District. Personal communication.

Ciriacy-Wantrup, S. V., and Richard C. Bishop. 1975. " 'Common Property' as a Concept in Natural Resource Policy." *Natural Resources Journal* 15, 4:713–26.

Cuzan, Alfred G. 1983. "Appropriators versus Expropriators: The Political Economy of Water in the West." In T. L. Anderson, ed., *Water Rights: Scarce Resource Allocation, Bureaucracy, and the Environment*, 13–43. San Francisco: Ballinger.

Dasgupta, P. S., and G. M. Heal. 1979. *Economic Theory and Exhaustible Resources.* Digswell Place, Welwyn, Eng.: James Nisbet.

Emel, Jacque L., and Elizabeth Brooks. 1988. "Changes in Form and Function of Property Rights Institutions under Threatened Resource Scarcity." *Annals of the Association of American Geographers* 78, 2:241–52.

Emel, J. L., and T. Maddock. 1986. "Effectiveness and Equity of Groundwater Management Methods in the Western United States." *Environmental Professional* 8:225–36.

Emel, Jacque L., and Rebecca S. Roberts. 1991. "It Works: An Empirical Study of Groundwater Management on the Southern High Plains." Unpublished paper. Graduate School of Geography, Clark University, Worcester, Mass.

Feinerman, Eli, and Keith C. Knapp. 1983. "Benefits from Groundwater Management: Magnitude, Sensitivity, and Distribution." *American Journal of Agricultural Economics* 65, 4:703–10.

Friedman, Alan E. 1971. "The Economics of the Common Pool: Property Rights in Exhaustible Resources." *UCLA Law Review* 18:855–87.

Gisser, Micha, and David A. Sanchez. 1980. "Competition versus Optimal Control in Groundwater Pumping." *Water Resources Research* 16, 4:638–42.

Godwin, R. K., and W. B. Shepard. 1979. "Forcing Squares, Triangles and Ellipses into a Circular Paradigm: The Use of the Commons Dilemma in Examining the Allocation of Common Resources." *Western Political Quarterly* 32, 3:265–77.

Hardin, Garrett. 1968. "The Tragedy of the Commons." *Science* 162:1243–48.

Hoelscher, Mark. 1990. Martin County, Texas, Underground Water Conservation District. Personal communication.

Johnson, Corwin W. 1982. "Texas Groundwater Law: A Survey and Some Proposals." *Natural Resources Journal* 22, 4:1017–30.

———. 1986. "The Continuing Voids in Texas Groundwater Law: Are Concepts and Terminology to Blame?" *St. Mary's Law Journal* 17, 4:1281–95.

Johnson, Ronald N., and Gary D. Libecap. 1982. "Contracting Problems and Regulation: The Case of the Fishery." *America Economic Review* 72, 5:1005–22.

Keller, Lawrence F., Craig G. Heatwole, and James W. Weber. 1981. "Managing Crisis: The Effectiveness of Local Districts for Control of Groundwater Mining." *Water Resources Bulletin* 17, 4:647–54.

Kelly, Michael J. 1983. "Management of Groundwater through Mandatory Conservation." *Denver Law Journal* 61, 1:1–24.

Kromm, David E., and Stephen E. White. 1985. "Conserving the Ogallala: What Next?" Manhattan: Kansas State University.

———. 1986. "Variability in Adjustment Preferences to Groundwater Depletion in the American High Plains." *Water Resources Bulletin* 22, 5:791–801.

———. 1987. "Interstate Groundwater Management Preference Differences: The Ogallala Region." *Journal of Geography* 86:5–11.

———. 1990. "Conserving Water in the High Plains." Manhattan: Kansas State University.

Lacewell, Ronald D., and John G. Lee. 1988. "Land and Water Management Issues: Texas High Plains." In Mohamed T. El-Ashry and Diana C. Gibbons, eds., *Water and Arid Lands of the Western United States*, 127–67. Cambridge: Cambridge University Press.

Luckey, Richard R., Edwin D. Gutentag, and John B. Weeks. 1981. "Water-Level and Saturated-Thickness Changes, Predevelopment to 1980, in the High Plains

Aquifer in Parts of Colorado, Kansas, Nebraska, New Mexico, Oklahoma, South Dakota, Texas, and Wyoming." Atlas, HA–652. U.S. Geological Survey.

Maass, Arthur, and Raymond L. Anderson. 1978 . . . *and the Desert Shall Rejoice.* Cambridge, Mass.: MIT Press.

McCay, Bonnie J., and James M. Acheson, eds. 1987. *The Question of the Commons: The Culture and Ecology of Communal Resources.* Tucson: University of Arizona Press.

Randall, Alan, 1981. *Resource Economics.* Columbus, Ohio: Grid Publishing.

Roberts, Rebecca S., and Jacque L. Emel. 1991. "Uneven Development and the Tragedy of the Commons: Competing Images for Nature–Society Interaction." Unpublished paper. Department of Geography, University of Iowa, Iowa City, Iowa.

Roberts, Rebecca S., and Sally L. Gros. 1987. "The Politics of Ground-Water Management Reform in Oklahoma." *Ground Water* 25, 5:535–44.

Shelley, Fred M. 1983. "Groundwater Supply Depletion in West Texas: The Farmer's Perspective." *Texas Business Review* (Nov.–Dec.):279–83.

Smith, Zachary A. 1984. "Centralized Decisionmaking in the Administration of Groundwater Rights: The Experience of Arizona, California and New Mexico and Suggestions for the Future." *Natural Resources Journal* 24:641–48.

Tarlock, A. Dan. 1985. "An Overview of the Law of Groundwater Management." *Water Resources Research* 21, 11:1751–66.

Taylor, Jonathan G., Mary W. Downton, and Thomas R. Stewart. 1985. "Adapting to Environmental Change: Perceptions and Farming Practices on the Ogallala Aquifer." In *Proceedings: Arid Lands, Today and Tomorrow.* International Arid Lands Research and Development Conference. Oct. 20–25. Tucson, Ariz.

Templer, Otis W. 1983. "Groundwater Management Institutions in Texas." In Randall J. Charbeneau, ed., *Proceedings.* American Water Resources Association Symposium, 43–52. October. Washington, D.C.

———. 1985. "Water Conservation in a Semi-Arid Agricultural Region." In Otis W. Templer, ed., *Proceedings.* Forum of the Association for Arid Lands Studies, 31–38. April 24–27. Lubbock, Tex.

Weeks, John B., and Edwin D. Gutentag. 1981. "Bedrock Geology, Altitude of Base, and 1980 Saturated Thickness of the High Plains Aquifer in Parts of Colorado, Kansas, Nebraska, New Mexico, Oklahoma, South Dakota, Texas, and Wyoming." Atlas, HA–648. U.S. Geological Survey.

Wescoat, James L. 1985. "On Water Conservation and Reform of the Prior Appropriation Doctrine in Colorado." *Economic Geography* 61, 1:3–24.

CHAPTER SIX

Irrigation Technologies

J. T. Musick and B. A. Stewart

Major advances in irrigation in the groundwater region of the High Plains began in Texas in the late 1930s. Its evolution followed the technological development of rotary well-drilling, deep well turbine pumps, right-angle gear drives, improved internal combustion engines and electric motors, and widespread availability of natural gas and electricity for pumping energy. Major drought and the availability of development capital through the Reconstruction Finance Corporation stimulated the initial expansion of irrigation; favorable crop prices and a widespread drought in the 1950s accelerated it after World War II. Initially, expansion of groundwater-based irrigation centered on graded furrow systems on extensive areas of favorable soils having relatively flat slopes. Most of the changes that followed have been associated with the introduction of new technologies.

Furrow irrigation developed using unlined ditches for on-farm distribution and siphon tubes for furrow application. Underground concrete pipelines came into use in the 1950s and plastic underground pipe in the late 1960s. The replacement of unlined ditches with underground pipe coincided with the adoption of aluminum gated pipe application to furrows. As plastics were improved to resist degradation by sunlight, plastic gated pipe was introduced in the late 1970s. Graded furrow application resulted in substantial end-of-furrow tailwater runoff, and reuse systems came into general service in the early 1960s. Tailwater runoff was collected in temporary field ditches, drained by gravity to a holding pond, and then was pumped through a pipeline, supplementing the supply from wells. Pipeline distribution from wells to the point of application and reuse systems for irrigation runoff resulted in relatively high-field application efficiencies.

The availability of affordable equipment such as aluminum pipe and impact sprinkler heads stimulated the expansion of sprinkler irrigation

Contribution from USDA, Agricultural Research Service, Conservation and Production Research Laboratory, P.O. Drawer 10, Bushland, Tex. 79012. This chapter was prepared by U.S. government employees as part of their official duties and legally cannot be copyrighted.

after World War II. Later, development of center pivot sprinkler systems allowed irrigation of soils having rough terrain and sandy textures unsuited for surface irrigation. The major introduction of sprinkler irrigation occurred during the 1950s and 1960s; its expansion on the Texas High Plains illustrates the trend in center pivot sprinkler irrigation (Figure 6.1.).

We shall examine the technologies of furrow and sprinkler irrigation, the two systems widely used in the groundwater-irrigated areas of the High Plains. With furrow irrigation, we emphasize technologies for limiting excessive water intake as well as management and efficient use of limited water supplies. These technologies include wide-spaced and alternate-furrow irrigation, tractor-wheel compaction of furrows, surge flow, reducing or eliminating runoff, and skip-row systems. With sprinkler irrigation, technologies have been introduced over the past three decades for improvement in center pivot systems and in management, and we compare the application-efficiency advantage of center pivot over furrow irrigation. Management practices include irrigation scheduling, limited irrigation, preplant irrigation, crop response to irriga-

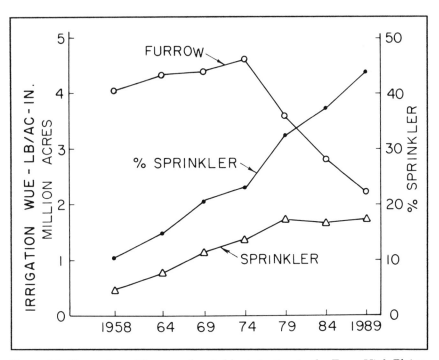

Figure 6.1. Expansion of the use of sprinkler irrigation in the Texas High Plains, 1958–1989

tion, precipitation as a water resource, cultural practices, and actions to limit pumping energy costs.

Geographically, the High Plains represents the Ogallala Aquifer regions of central and western Nebraska, eastern Colorado, western Kansas, eastern New Mexico, the Oklahoma Panhandle, and the Texas High Plains; the central High Plains includes areas in Nebraska, Colorado, and Kansas; the southern High Plains, New Mexico, Oklahoma, and Texas.

FURROW IRRIGATION

Furrow irrigation, especially on moderately permeable soils (primarily 0.2 to 0.6 inch/hour basic-intake rate), is characterized by relatively large water applications and substantial losses to profile drainage and field runoff. Because of low-salinity groundwater in the High Plains, non-saline soils, and periodic leaching by precipitation, the need for irrigation-leaching requirements is very low. Irrigation management practices have been developed to reduce excessive water application in graded furrow systems and to limit losses to profile drainage.

Furrow-application efficiencies commonly range from 50 to 80 percent without tailwater reuse, with the higher values occurring on slowly permeable clays that lose little to profile drainage. Furrow-irrigated clay soils with tailwater-reuse systems have application efficiencies that compare favorably with sprinkler irrigation. In managing furrow irrigation for efficient water application and use, application depths need to be limited to the root-zone soil-profile storage capacity. Reducing application depths reduces losses to profile drainage and tailwater runoff, tends to lower the amount of soil water stored in the soil profile at harvest (which can significantly reduce precipitation storage between harvest and planting), and provides some additional storage capacity for precipitation following irrigation. Several practices have been used successfully to reduce water intake in graded furrows.

Wide-Spaced and Alternate-Furrow Irrigation

Conventional furrow spacing as practiced in the High Plains is usually 30 to 40 inches; alternate and wide-spaced furrow spacing is usually 60 to 80 inches. Wide-spaced furrow irrigation tests have been conducted in Nebraska, Oklahoma, and Texas in which application was reduced from about one-fourth to one-half compared with conventional furrow irrigation with only modest or no-yield reduction, thus increasing irrigation water-use efficiencies for crop yields (Crabtree et al. 1985; Fischbach and Mulliner 1974; Longenecker et al. 1969 and 1970; Musick and Dusek 1974;

Gravity-fed furrow irrigation in Lamb County, Texas.

Stone et al. 1979 and 1982). Many of the tests did not report tailwater runoff and net-water intake, but reduction in intake was probably substantially less than reduction in application.

In irrigating summer row crops (almost all irrigated crops except forages and winter small grains grown in narrow rows), a crop row should have one side adjacent to an irrigated furrow to prevent excessive water deficits. Many irrigated crops have higher yield potential when planted in narrow row spacings, and planting summer row crops in 30-inch rows and irrigating 60-inch furrow spacings have proven to be good practices for many crops. The use of wide-spaced furrows becomes less successful on steeper sloping and with coarse-textured soils, for crops such as corn sensitive to yield reduction from plant-water stress, and in very dry seasons.

The favorable yield response to wide-spaced and alternate-furrow irrigation is believed to be associated with reduced losses to profile drainage, to reduced tailwater runoff, and from reduced evaporation from partial wetting of the surface soil between the wide-spaced furrows. Precipitation is rather uniform in occurrence over a field and can limit water-deficit effects from nonuniform-irrigation water storage, especially in seasons of above-average precipitation.

Some irrigators use wide-spaced furrows in wide bed-furrow systems in which wheel traffic is maintained on the wide beds, not in the irrigation furrows (Longenecker et al. 1969; Allen and Musick 1972; Allen 1985). Tractor wheels in furrows reduce water intake, accelerate water advance, increase nonuniformity among wheel-track and nonwheel-track furrows, and increase surface runoff. Using a wide-spaced bed-furrow system with wheel traffic on the beds improves uniformity of advance down the field and eliminates the normally high runoff from wheel-track furrows or the labor required for readjusting the nonuniform flow-rate advance. Wide-spaced and alternate furrow irrigation systems that partially wet the soil profile provide some additional storage capacity for precipitation. In alternate furrow systems where the same furrow is irrigated each time, furrow dams or dikes can be used in the nonirrigated furrows to minimize storm runoff (Stewart et al. 1983).

Tractor-Wheel Compaction of Furrows
for Water-Intake Control

Furrow compaction by tractor wheels can effectively reduce excessive irrigation water intake in graded furrows. In tests on a clay loam in the Texas High Plains, a tractor-wheel pass was used in 60-inch spaced furrows to increase bulk density to a 3-inch depth in the furrow bottom from a loose-soil condition to about 1.6 grams per cubic centimeter. The increased soil density in furrows reduced water intake during six irrigations for corn on a one-fourth-mile furrow length by 33 percent (Musick et al. 1985; Musick and Pringle 1986). The practice greatly reduced percolation losses below a caliche layer that limited rooting depth (Figure 6.2). Irrigations were applied at about 50 percent of the profile soil-water depletion and the reduction in intake by furrow compaction more closely balanced water-intake quantity with profile-storage capacity at the time of irrigation. The tractor-wheel furrow compaction was removed by primary tillage after harvest.

Surge-Flow Irrigation

Surge flow is a surface-irrigation technique developed at Utah State University in the late 1970s and extensively tested in the Great Plains and in the western states in the 1980s (Stringham 1988). A controller-valve assembly is used for intermittent water application of constant or variable duration. The most common application for surge flow is furrow irrigation using gated pipe. An available water supply (primarily from wells in the High Plains) irrigates more soil than is irrigated in conventional continuous flow by alternating the surges to a set of furrows on each side of a controller-valve assembly. A larger area can be irrigated proportionate to the reduction in water intake by surge application. Surge flow can be

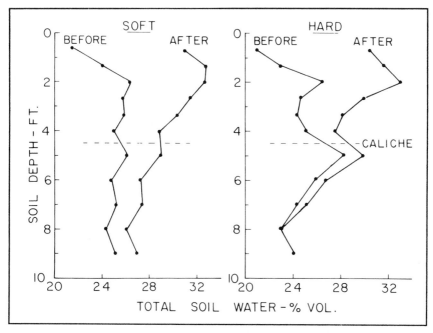

Figure 6.2. Average seasonal soil water before and after irrigation on Olton clay loam treatment plots having nonwheel-track furrows (SOFT) and wheel-track furrows (HARD)

managed for nearly continuous tailwater runoff by using a short-cycle time (less than 15 minutes) during the runoff phase, during which surge advances tend to catch up with recession flow to provide nearly continuous furrow flow on lower field sections. This permits lower-field wetting with reduced tailwater runoff.

A time-controlled valve alternates water-inflow surges to a set of furrows on each side of the valve. The on-and-off flow cycles are effective in reducing water-intake rates for many soils and soil conditions. The primary reason for the reduced-intake rate associated with the off cycle is believed to be the effect of surface-tension forces developed during the desaturation off cycle, causing soil surface-layer consolidation (Kemper et al. 1988; Saleh and Hanks 1989). Soil loosened by tillage benefits most. The surge effect is reduced when the surface soil is consolidated by wheel traffic, tillage, or previous irrigations.

In seasoned irrigation tests for corn on a nonswelling clay loam, surge flow reduced intake by 32 percent when the soil was in a loosened condition from tillage compared with continuous flow. The reduction averaged 17 percent for seasonal irrigations when the surface soil was

Surge-flow system with solar-powered controls on top. Chase County, Nebraska.

consolidated from previous irrigation (Musick et al. 1987). Also, surge flow resulted in similar profile storage from irrigation, similar corn yields, and improved down-the-field uniformity of profile wetting.

Reducing or Eliminating Field Runoff

Many farmers manage irrigation in graded furrow systems to reduce or eliminate tailwater runoff for crops having drought tolerance. As pumping yields of wells have declined and energy costs have increased, farmers in the Texas High Plains have reduced tailwater runoff from about 30 to 40 percent of water applied when pumping costs were lower to about 15 to 20 percent in recent years (Musick and Walker 1987). About 60 percent of the furrow-irrigated area is on slowly permeable swelling clays (Musick et al. 1988). About one-third of the total water intake on these soils results from initial filling of shrinkage cracks. After approximately three to five hours of flow time, when lateral wetting from furrows greatly slows, the slowly permeable B2t horizon below the tillage depth controls the intake rates, which drop to a basic rate of about 0.1 inch per hour. The low basic rate limits the additional intake volume and the additional lower field yield response from extending the duration of tailwater flow.

Stewart et al. (1983) developed and successfully tested a limited irrigation dryland (LID) system on a clay loam designed to prevent irrigation tailwater and storm runoff from leaving a field. Water was applied for grain sorghum to fully irrigate the upper one-half of a 1,900-foot length of run. Tailwater from the fully irrigated section was used on the next one-fourth field section. The lower one-fourth field section was dryland sorghum with furrow dams to retain and use precipitation and thus prevent storm runoff. Irrigation was applied to alternate 30-inch furrow spacing, and furrow dams were maintained for the complete field length of the alternating nonirrigated furrows. The average results from a three-year test on three LID treatments have been compared with full irrigation and dryland cropping (Table 6.1).

Skip-Row Systems

Graded furrow-irrigated skip-row systems involve planting alternating strips of two or four rows of summer row crops and leaving one, two, or four rows unplanted. In the most common system, farmers plant two 30- or 40-inch rows, leaving one row unplanted, and irrigate the one furrow between the paired crop rows. This practice greatly reduces average field-irrigation water-intake depth in graded furrow systems. Skip-row planting and irrigation of fewer furrows than crop rows have been tested for sorghum and corn (Musick and Dusek 1982) and for cotton (Newman 1967; Longenecker et al. 1963, 1969, and 1970).

Farmers widely practice skip-row planting and irrigation of fewer furrows in the irrigated-cotton area of the south Texas High Plains, a region of limited groundwater storage and many small wells. Newman (1967) conducted tests at Lubbock, Texas, by planting two 40-inch cotton rows and leaving out either one or two skip rows and then evaluated limited irrigation of the one furrow between the paired rows. In the plant-two, skip-one system, average irrigation water-use efficiencies for lint production were increased by 52 percent and in the plant-two, skip-two system by 21 percent, compared with the conventional every-row-

Table 6.1. Comparison of LID Treatments, Full Irrigation, and Dryland Cropping, Three-year Average, Bushland, Texas

Treatment	Applied Irrigation (Inches)	Grain Yield (Lb/acre)	Seasonal[1] ET[2] (Inches)	Water-use Efficiency	
				ET	Irrigation
				(Lb/acre-inch)	
Dryland	—	2,260	11.5	190	—
Full irrigation	20.3	6,460	24.2	265	208
LID–10.0 inches	9.2	5,080	20.5	245	308
LID–7.5 inches	6.8	4,580	18.3	247	340
LID–5.0 inches	4.7	3,990	16.2	245	385

[1]Seasonal rainfall averaged 9.8 inches.
[2]ET = evapotranspiration.
Source: Stewart et al. (1983), "Yield and Water-use Efficiency," *Agronomy* 75:629–34.

planted and every-furrow-irrigated system. Although irrigation water is used efficiently in skip-row planted and irrigated systems, seasonal precipitation is used less efficiently because of increased loss to evaporation from the bare soil separating the paired crop rows.

SPRINKLER IRRIGATION

Sprinkler irrigation generally conserves water. Application efficiencies of sprinkler and furrow irrigation of moderately and slowly permeable soils indicate a 20 to 25 percent application-efficiency advantage with sprinkler irrigation on moderately permeable soils but little advantage on slowly permeable soils with tailwater reuse (Musick et al. 1988). In inventories conducted in the Texas High Plains by the Soil Conservation Service (SCS), furrow-application efficiency estimates averaged 59 percent for moderately permeable soils and 72 percent for slowly permeable soils without considering tailwater reuse; when the SCS conducted 223 center pivot sprinkler evaluation tests on the Texas High Plains in the early 1980s, application efficiencies averaged 83 percent.

There is an advantage of sprinkler over furrow irrigation for reducing groundwater pumped to irrigate corn on moderately permeable soils (Figure 6.3). The figure's probability distribution curves of groundwater pumped represent the irrigation of sixty-five corn fields in Parmer and Castro counties of the Texas High Plains during 1983 and 1984 (Rettman and McAdoo 1986). The curves indicate a high degree of similarity in groundwater amounts pumped for all sprinkler-irrigated fields and for furrow-irrigated fields having slowly permeable soils. The median application (50 percent probability occurrence) indicated that an additional 12 inches of water was pumped for furrow-irrigated fields on moderately

Tailwater pit in Gray County, Kansas.

permeable soils. For the 20 percent of the fields that received the highest water application, an additional 19 inches of water was pumped. These results obtained in a groundwater area with high-yielding wells suggest that conversion from furrow to sprinkler irrigation on moderately permeable soils can permit substantial reduction in groundwater pumping and probably substantial reduction in losses to profile drainage below the root zone.

The use of electric operating controls in the late 1960s and the associated ease of movement increased the attractiveness of center pivot systems to irrigators. The improved controls enabled irrigators to move the systems without applying water and provided variable speed of application. The center pivot's higher application efficiency and its automation led to an extensive replacement of furrow systems with sprinkler systems. Based on irrigation surveys by state Agricultural Extension Services and the Texas SCS, the 1989 sprinkler-irrigated area on the High Plains was estimated to average 48 percent of the total acreage irrigated for a six-state area.

Sprinkler irrigation in the High Plains is primarily accomplished with center pivot systems, which accounted for 96 percent of the total in the Texas High Plains in 1984 (Musick et al. 1988). Most machines are one-fourth mile long and irrigate about 130 acres of a 160-acre quarter-section of land. In the relatively flat terrain of the High Plains a recent

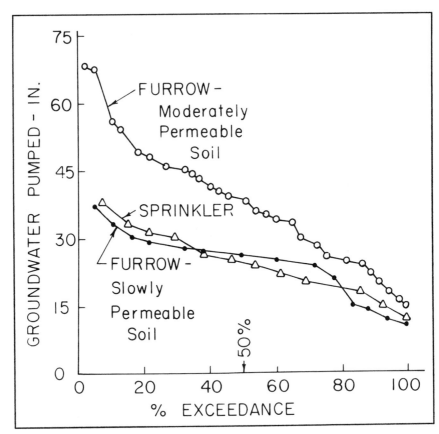

Figure 6.3. Percentage distribution of groundwater pumped for irrigation of sixty-five cornfields with sprinkler- or furrow-irrigation systems

trend has been the installation of new systems of one-half-mile machines that irrigate an area similar to four one-fourth-mile systems at about the initial cost of three one-fourth-mile machines (L. L. New, personal communication, 1990). Turnkey installation costs in 1990 for one-fourth-mile systems were about $35,000 (without the end gun) compared with about $100,000 for one-half-mile systems (W. L. Harman, personal communication, 1990).

Reduction in labor is a major attraction of center pivot systems. Duke (1989) wrote, "While a single irrigator may be able to handle irrigation of 1,000 to 2,000 acres under center pivot machines, he can seldom keep up with more than 300 to 500 acres of surface irrigated land, depending on the type of delivery system used. Where minimal tillage is needed and labor intensive operations such as planting and harvest can be handled by seasonal labor or custom operations, the savings in labor costs can go far toward paying the extra capital and operating expense of sprinkler irrigation systems."

Many improvements have been made over the years in the design, management, and use of center pivot systems. Improved technologies include (1) tires having higher flotation for improved traction and reduced rutting, (2) electric drive systems, (3) reduced-pressure application with computer-designed sprinkler-nozzle packages for more uniform application, (4) management techniques for use with reduced-pressure systems to reduce or eliminate surface runoff, (5) multifunctional systems for applying water and chemicals (chemigation, the application of fertilizers and pesticides through an irrigation system), (6) improved sprinkler heads for jet breakup into desired droplet size and distribution patterns, (7) positioning of spray and low-energy precision application (LEPA) heads on drop tubes much closer to the crop or soil surface for reducing wind drift and evaporation losses (Lyle and Bordovsky 1983), (8) remote monitoring through radio telemetry and computer on-off control capability, (9) use of LEPA on new systems and as retrofit packages, and (10) management techniques such as reduced tillage and circular planting of row crops (using pivot-tower tire tracks as guides) with positioning of the drops between the circular crop rows.

Following the escalation of pumping energy costs after the OPEC price increases of 1973, system conversion from high pressure to medium and low pressure was widely adopted along with selection of low-pressure sprinkler packages by those investing in new systems. Heermann (1990) gave the ranges of high, medium, and low pressure as having pivot-input pressures of 50 to 70 pounds per square inch (psi), 35 to 50 psi, and less than 35 psi, respectively. In 1989 an SCS inventory of counties in the Texas High Plains showed that the percentage of low-pressure center pivot systems in use was primarily associated with the age of the systems and averaged 74 percent for the 1.75 million acres of sprinkler-irrigated crops. New indicated that about four hundred LEPA systems were in use in the Texas High Plains in spring 1990 (L. L. New, personal communication, 1990).

Reduced-pressure technology involves reducing high-discharge jet angles of 23 to 27 degrees for conventional impact heads to 5 to 7 degrees for low-angle, reduced-pressure heads, increasing use of spray-nozzle systems, using drop tubes to position spray nozzles near the top or into the crop canopy, and positioning LEPA heads on drops about 8 to 16 inches above the soil surface. LEPA heads can be operated in a spray mode for crop germination, a bubble mode that applies water in an umbrella pattern with a 16- to 18-inch diameter at the soil surface, or in a chemigation mode that uses a splash plate to direct a spray pattern up into the canopy for insecticide application to taller crops such as corn. One person can change the application mode on a one-fourth-mile system in about 45 minutes.

Efficient application and uniform distribution of sprinkler-irrigation water involve reducing droplet wind-drift and associated evaporation losses and reducing or eliminating field runoff. Application losses were estimated by New et al. (1990) as 2 to 4 percent for LEPA heads in the bubble mode, 12 percent for spray nozzles, and 15 to 25 percent for impact sprinklers. Wind-drift losses have been reduced by lowering the jet trajectory angle on impact heads and by placing spray and LEPA heads on drop tubes. Wind speed and direction affect spray distribution and drift losses. In areas having a continental climate such as the High Plains, nighttime wind speeds normally decrease sufficiently to enhance application efficiency and distribution uniformity. Successive center pivot irrigations can be scheduled to alternate day and night at a given site.

Runoff losses have been reduced by using faster travel speeds that result in smaller applications, basin tillage (furrow dams or dikes), in-row ripping for increased intake rates, surface crop residue management, circular planting, and by keeping tractor-tire traffic out of the drop-applicator furrows with drops positioned in alternate furrows. Improved sprinkler-package designs also limit the kinetic energy of water droplets and lessen the effects of surface-layer dispersion and consolidation (surface crust) on reducing intake rates.

Sprinkler irrigation enhances management of reduced tillage and maintenance of crop residues on the soil surface; in addition, crop emergence has been improved substantially by the ability to apply a small irrigation (0.7 to 1.0 inch) rapidly through a center pivot after planting. Rainfall after planting can cause a surface crust on some soils that prevents crop emergence. A small sprinkler application can be used to soften the surface crust and thus ensure the crop stand.

IRRIGATION SCHEDULING

Irrigation scheduling, the forecasting of water-application timing and amount for optimal crop production, is essential for efficient management and use of irrigation water. Rational scheduling requires knowledge of plant available soil water storage capacity, rooting depth, soil water content, and the expected changes in soil water over a subsequent five- to ten-day period. Water-use rates are affected by weather conditions that influence evaporative demand and by precipitation.

Farmers use water budgets for irrigation scheduling based on soil-water contents, irrigation applied, losses to deep percolation and surface

Operating center pivot system with drop tubes and low pressure emitters. Lamb County, Texas.

runoff, precipitation, and estimates of evapotranspiration (ET). Computer-based irrigation-scheduling programs use meteorological data, crop coefficients (a function of crop development), and reference crop ET for predicting actual crop ET. The early scheduling programs used mainframe computers and access terminals; more recently, researchers have developed and validated scheduling software programs for personal computers.

Center pivot sprinkler systems are usually scheduled to apply predetermined application depths, and timing of application is allowed to vary. In graded furrow systems, however, both the timing and the amount can vary widely. Center pivot systems can be operated to refill the soil profile partially and to maintain some storage capacity for precipitation that may occur following irrigation. On low-water storage-capacity soils, however, maintaining profile-storage capacity for precipitation following irrigation is generally not advisable. On these soils, it is more important to maintain a fully wet profile, thus providing a margin of safety should the system malfunction or the crop encounter an unusually high water-use period.

Computer scheduling is most widely practiced in the Great Plains for center pivot irrigation of corn. On the low-water storage soils, scheduling can be managed for both high yields and efficient water use by avoiding rapidly developing water deficits and excess application that results in water losses to profile drainage and leaching of nitrates (Heermann et al. 1976). Computer scheduling can also be accomplished by using crop-growth simulation models such as Ceres Maize for sprinkler-irrigation management for corn grown in the southern Great Plains (Howell et al. 1989). The growth models also forecast crop yields.

Scheduling can be based on root-zone soil-water contents determined from core samples or neutron probes or from root-zone soil-water potentials determined from tensiometers or gypsum blocks. Approaches involving measurement of plant water stress such as leaf-diffusive resistance and water potentials are usually limited to research projects.

The hand-held infrared thermometer is a recent scheduling tool that allows rapid, quantitative field measurements of plant-water stress. The instrument is small, portable, and is operated as a "gun" that measures thermal radiation (i.e., plant temperature) emitted from all parts of the canopy within view of the instrument. Crop stress increases canopy temperature from reduced transpirational cooling and can be assessed by comparing canopy temperature elevation for a desired field site with the temperature of a nearby site that is known to be adequately irrigated and nonstressed.

Drop tubes on a linear sprinkler system in Moore County, Texas. The pipe in the foreground carries the water flow from the well and moves with the system.

A more precise stress assessment involves the calculation of a crop-water stress index from an energy-balance equation involving canopy air temperature difference and current meteorological data (Jackson 1982). The preferred diurnal time of measurement is during the period of maximum stress, normally within a plateau of high evaporative demand following solar noon for approximately the next three hours. The method performs best on clear days with relatively high solar radiation and when it is used to target plant leaves to exclude low-transpiring plant parts such as sorghum heads and corn tassels and to minimize soil background in the target area. Clouds affect canopy temperatures from variable incoming solar radiation, which can be a problem in using infrared thermometers in the High Plains environment.

Visual observations of stress are widely used in irrigation scheduling for drought-resistant crops in the High Plains. Symptoms of stress that can be observed visually include leaf roll, droop, or movement to reduce incoming radiation interception, stress-related chlorophyll degradation as indicated by changes in shades of green leaf color, slowed leaf expansion and accelerated senescence of older leaves, and evening or morning stress recovery or both. Although afternoon stress may be allowed under deficit irrigation of crops possessing drought resistance, the stress should be alleviated by irrigation before it becomes severe enough to prevent overnight recovery. Stress that develops to this point slows growth greatly, indicates that depletion of available soil water is near the lower limit, and can cause rapid loss of yield potential.

LIMITED IRRIGATION

Limited irrigation is a management strategy that uses limited water supplies to irrigate larger field areas by allowing crops to experience periods of slight to moderate plant-water stress; its main purpose is to increase total farm production or net returns by reducing the area of dryland crops. Adequate and limited irrigation are both widely practiced in the High Plains. Farmers practice limited irrigation primarily with drought-resistant crops that are also grown without irrigation. Occurrence of normal to above-normal precipitation is important for the success of limited irrigation in the High Plains; limited irrigation becomes less successful during major dry seasons.

A common practice is to about double the area that is fully irrigated for maximum yields. System designs by SCS in the Texas High Plains have allowed flexibility within the range of 3 to 10 gallons per minute (gpm)/acre compared with 7 to 10 gpm/acre for adequate irrigation to meet peak water requirements. Center pivot systems having LEPA drops in alternate furrows (circle-planted) have been designed and operated for irrigation of cotton in the Texas High Plains with water supplies of 3 gpm/acre (L. L. New, personal communication, 1990).

While modest yield reductions are allowable in order to use available limited water supplies for irrigating larger areas, limited-irrigation management should be weighed carefully before being adopted. Musick (1989) summarized seven rules to apply in making the decision. (1) Consider only soils that are relatively deep and that have moderate to high water-storage capacity; (2) consider only crops possessing drought resistance (avoidance or tolerance or both); (3) consider increasing the contribution of precipitation to crop water needs; (4) consider crop growth stage and cutoff date in managing water; (5) consider the need for preplant irrigation; (6) in furrow systems, consider methods for reducing water intake and field runoff; and (7) consider modifying some cultural practices for limited irrigation.

PREPLANT IRRIGATION

Preplant irrigation is the system of irrigating to wet the soil profile partially or fully before planting a crop and has been widely practiced in the semiarid High Plains since the early expansion of pump irrigation from the Ogallala Aquifer in the late 1930s. Under some conditions, preplant irrigation is essential for the establishment of timely stands and for high yields. In many situations, however, the large application depths required for surface irrigation result in inefficient soil water storage and low-yield response. Smaller and more precise preplant irrigation-application amounts are possible with center pivot sprinkler systems to wet the soil partially, in preparation for planting. Also, early-season irrigations can be applied when water use rates are low, which provides flexibility in rewetting the soil profile, thus eliminating the need for large preplant-irrigation depths that increase soil profile drainage losses and leaching of nitrates.

Preplant irrigation accomplishes different objectives, including wetting the soil profile, germinating crop volunteer plants and weeds that can be killed by tillage before planting, and providing an adequate seed-zone soil physical condition and water content to facilitate planting and stand establishment (Musick 1987). The benefits are likely to be greatest in four situations: (1) when the soil profile is dry as planting approaches, (2) when seasonal irrigations are not applied to drought-tolerant crops or are reduced in amount, (3) when early planting is desirable and soil wetting by precipitation is not likely by the desired planting time, and (4) when preplant irrigation plus seasonal precipitation on deep, high water-

Metering water use is an effective and relatively inexpensive management tool. Texas A & M Research Station near Etter, Texas.

storage soils can result in moderately high yields without seasonal irrigation. The benefits are likely to be low when soil profiles are moderately wet at the time of irrigation, when planting dates are flexible and can follow precipitation for stand establishment, and when seasonal irrigation provides adequate water to meet plant requirements.

Yields of preplant-only irrigated grain sorghum as a percentage of adequately irrigated yields were analyzed (Table 6.2). Multiyear tests were conducted at five locations in the central and southern High Plains. The locations have similar average seasonal precipitation of 8 to 10 inches, and each produced similar adequately irrigated yields. The comparisons indicate that preplant-only irrigated yields, expressed as a percentage of adequately irrigated yields, were higher in the central than in the southern High Plains. Seasonal water use is lower in the central High Plains, and the test sites had relatively deep soils.

Results from the five test sites indicate that when yields from preplant irrigation were low compared with adequate seasonal irrigation, the yield response to seasonal irrigation was relatively high. Also, when yields from preplant irrigation on the high-water-storage soils were relatively high compared with adequately irrigated yields, the yield response to seasonal irrigation was relatively low (Figure 6.4). The data are from a

Table 6.2. Yields of Preplant-Only Irrigated Grain Sorghum as a
Percentage of Adequately Irrigated Yields, Various Soils, Central and
Southern High Plains

Location	Soil	No. of Test Years	Yield as Percentage of Adequate Irrigation (Preplant Only)	Data Source
Southern High Plains				
Bushland, Tex.	Pullman clay loam	7	40	Musick 1987
Clovis, N. Mex.	Pullman silty clay loam	3	54	Finkner and Malm 1971
Central High Plains				
Garden City, Kans.	Ulysses clay loam	8	57	Erhart 1970
Garden City, Kans.	Richfield clay loam	6	66	Musick and Grimes 1961
Garden City, Kans.	Richfield silty clay loam	6	79	Hooker 1985
Tribune, Kans.	Ulysses silty clay loam	3	81	Stone et al. 1987
Colby, Kans.	Keith silt loam	3	95	Bordovsky and Hay 1975

three-year study with grain sorghum for treatments of preplant only and preplant plus three levels of seasonal irrigation on Keith silt loam at Colby, Kansas.

Water intake during preplant irrigation frequently exceeds profile-storage capacity and losses occur as rapid drainage below the root zone. In addition, in the absence of root extraction for an extended period of time following the preplant irrigation, slow profile drainage occurs as unsaturated flow on the deep-silt (loess) profiles in western Kansas. Profile drainage losses from preplant irrigation to planting were measured in the 2- to 3-inch range on Ulysses clay loam at Tribune, Kansas (Stone et al. 1987). The most efficient use of irrigation water on this soil was made when the water was applied as closely as possible to the time of plant need (Stone et al. 1980).

CROP RESPONSE

Corn is one of the most economically important irrigated crops grown in the High Plains. As a stress-sensitive crop, especially during pollination, it is most often grown with adequate water and other production inputs

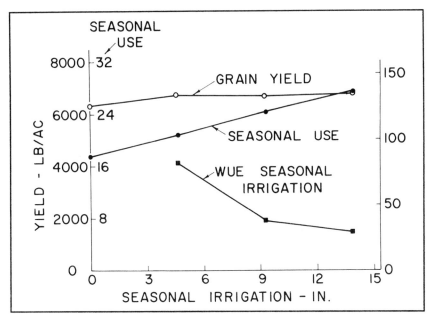

Figure 6.4. Yield, seasonal water use, and irrigation water-use efficiency (WUE) of grain sorghum response to seasonal irrigation, Keith silt loam, Colby, Kansas

for high yields (Musick and Dusek 1980). Adequate irrigation of corn for high yields has contributed to the dramatic trend in yield increase, (Figure 6.5). Other crops that are generally grown under adequate irrigation are alfalfa, soybeans, sugar beets, and vegetables. The major crops grown extensively under limited irrigation are winter wheat and grain sorghum in the central High Plains and wheat, grain sorghum, and cotton in the southern High Plains. Minor crops include barley, millet, forage sorghum, cool-season grasses, alfalfa for seed, sunflowers, and grapes (Musick and Walker 1987). Late-season water deficits can enhance yield quality such as improved cotton-fiber properties, grain protein, and grapes for wine. Some crops are grown under both adequate and limited irrigation and as dryland crops on different fields of the same farm.

Most crops grown with limited-irrigation tend to resist drought through the capability of plants to tolerate plant water deficits as growth continues, normally at a reduced rate, or through the ability to avoid and thus delay stress by deep-rooting, with a greater use of water from deeper in the profile, and/or by the use of shorter growing-season cultivars. Sunflowers provide an excellent example of drought avoidance by combining a very deep root system for water extraction with the relative short growing season of commercial hybrids.

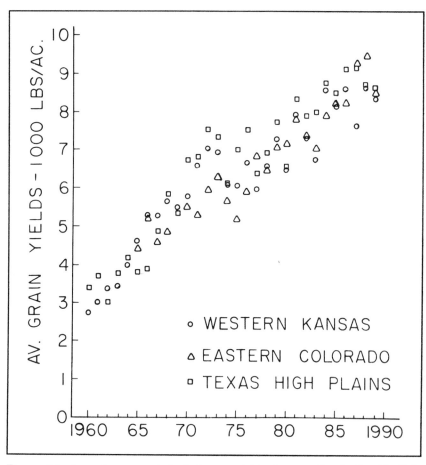

Figure 6.5. Annual average irrigated corn yields for counties in the Ogallala Aquifer boundaries, 1960–1989 (western Kansas, 31 counties; eastern Colorado, 11; Texas High Plains, 41)

In the absence of root-restricting zones in the soil profile, deep-rooted crops such as sunflowers, sugar beets, and alfalfa extract soil water approximately to the 7- to 8-foot depth and wheat, sorghum, and cotton approximately to the 4- to 6-foot depth. Winter wheat has a longer vegetative growing period and thus a deeper root system than spring wheat. Extraction of available soil water in the lower one-quarter of the profile is normally limited by sparse rooting densities.

When deficits are allowed and irrigation water is applied stages of crop growth can have substantial effects on yield response. Yield sensitivity of grain sorghum is low during its early-season vegetative growth, increases substantially during the boot stage through flowering, and de-

Table 6.3. Average Grain Sorghum Yield Increases and
Irrigation Water-use Efficiency, Etter, Tex., 1969 and 1972

	6–8 Leaf	Mid- to Late-boot	Heading to Flowering	Milk to Soft Dough
Grain-yield increase per irrigation (lb/acre)				
1969	342	2,388	2,550	254
1972	499	1,096	1,708	696
Irrigation water-use efficiency (lb/acre-inch)				
1969	86	597	637	64
1972	125	274	427	174

Source: Shipley and Regier (1975), "Water Response," Tex. Agri. Exp. Station, MP 1202.

clines during grain filling (Musick and Dusek 1971) (Table 6.3). Timing of water deficits involving development stages can result in a substantial range of sorghum yields from a given level of seasonal water use (Musick and Dusek 1971).

For some perennial crops such as cotton and alfalfa for seed, late-season irrigation may stimulate continued vegetative growth at the expense of economic yield. Cotton grown in the Texas High Plains needs a stress period near the end of August and the beginning of September for new fruiting cutout since late-season initiated bolls do not mature in this climatic environment (Krieg 1986). A late-season deficit that limits the continued vegetative growth of cotton hastens maturity and improves lint quality.

The timing of irrigation in relation to critical-development stages increases in importance as the number of seasonal irrigations are reduced and plants experience increasing levels of water stress (Table 6.4). A single seasonal irrigation for sorghum in the Texas High Plains should not be applied as the only irrigation either during early vegetative growth or during mid-to-late grain filling. However, at higher water levels involv-

Table 6.4. Average Irrigation-use Efficiency (1969 and 1972)
from One 4-inch Seasonal Irrigation (lbs/acre-inch)

Number of Seasonal Irrigations	6–8 Leaf	Mid- to Late-boot	Heading to Flowering	Milk to Soft Dough
1	0	505	481	23
2	90	460	545	122
3	156	386	536	137
4	208	404	537	150

Source: Shipley and Regier (1975), "Water Response," Tex. Agri. Exp. Station, MP 1202.

ing additional applications for high yields, the yield contribution of early and late irrigations increases.

When growth-stage responses to limited irrigation of winter wheat and grain sorghum are compared in the High Plains, irrigation of wheat during early-spring vegetative growth can be more critical. This comparative growth period occurs about six months after planting winter wheat, compared with about one month after planting sorghum. Soil-water depletion at this growth stage is normally greater for wheat because of the much longer period for water use. Although wheat is more responsive than sorghum to irrigation during early vegetative growth, it is normally less responsive to irrigation during grain filling because of increasing spring precipitation that peaks during this period.

PRECIPITATION AND IRRIGATION

Precipitation increases in its importance for meeting crop-water needs in areas where farmers practice limited irrigation (Stewart and Musick 1987). In the irrigated semiarid central and southern High Plains, precipitation normally provides about 30 to 60 percent of seasonal crop-water requirements for high yields. In the major wet seasons, irrigation can be reduced substantially; in the major dry seasons, increased irrigation is needed to compensate for both reduced precipitation and increased evaporative demand from the prevailing warm, dry air.

The contribution of precipitation in meeting crop-water needs and thus in reducing irrigation requirements can be enhanced by (1) using precipitation for stand establishment without preplant irrigation, (2) irrigating to wet the profile partially, which allows some storage capacity for precipitation (by limiting application depths using sprinkler irrigation, wide-spaced furrows, wheel-track compaction of irrigated furrows, or surge flow to reduce water intake), (3) reducing or eliminating precipitation runoff (by using conservation tillage, furrow dams, and land leveling), (4) reducing applications during above-normal precipitation periods, and (5) managing irrigation to use more fully the available profile water storage by the end of the season, thus enhancing precipitation storage between crops.

The average long-term January-through-December precipitation patterns have been analyzed for sites in the central and southern High Plains (Figure 6.6). These graphs, presented as fifteen-day totals for three-day periods, moving from north to south—Colby, Kansas, to Amarillo and Lubbock, Texas—illustrate the normally dry winter months of the continental climate, the increasing spring precipitation patterns, and some north-to-south differences in summer distribution patterns.

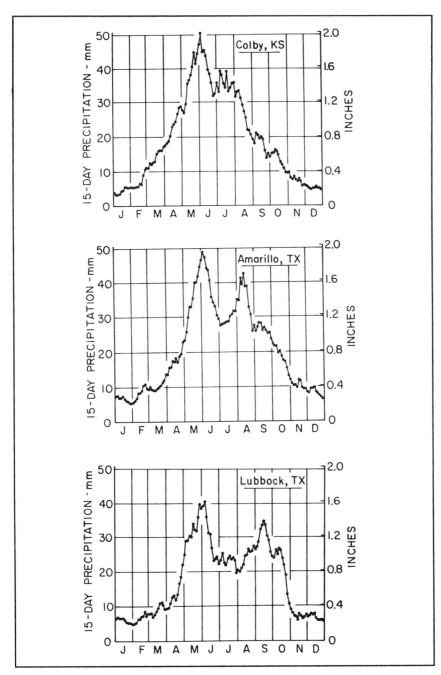

Figure 6.6. Average fifteen-day precipitation, January through December, for central and southern High Plains

Early irrigation cutoff increases storage capacity for nongrowing-season precipitation between harvest and planting the next crop and thus increases the efficiency of precipitation storage. In a three-year test involving grain sorghum irrigation treatments on clay loams at Bushland, precipitation storage efficiency after the harvest declined from the 40- to 50-percent range when the soil profile was dry after harvest (from early irrigation cutoff at boot stage) to about 10 percent or less when the profile was wet after harvest (from late cutoff at dough stage of grain) (Figure 6.7). During major drought periods, paucity of precipitation may necessitate shifting limited water supplies to more stress-sensitive crops such as corn or soybeans, and crop areas under limited irrigation may need to be reduced.

CULTURAL PRACTICES

Cultural practices influence the successful management of irrigated-crop production, and those that are useful in facilitating management of limited irrigation are conservation tillage, plant densities, planting dates,

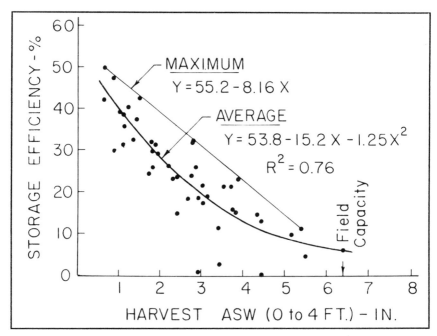

Figure 6.7. Effect of plant-available soil water after harvest of grain sorghum on preseason precipitation-storage efficiency, Pullman clay loam, Bushland, Texas

maturity-length cultivars, and cropping systems, including the use of fallow between crops to increase precipitation storage and to eliminate preplant irrigation. Some practices used for limited irrigation are also common to dryland agriculture in the High Plains.

Conservation tillage (including no-tillage) involves management of crop residues on the soil surface for increased precipitation storage. The dryland-cropping system of wheat-sorghum-fallow, two crops in a three-year sequence having about eleven months fallow between harvest and planting of each crop, has been successfully tested under limited irrigation at Bushland (Musick et al. 1977). The system has been employed as no-tillage, using herbicides for weed control, and as a combination of very limited tillage, combined with the use of herbicides. One-sweep tillage operation has been successfully practiced to loosen the surface soil, improving seed-zone physical conditions for planting, to control weeds before planting, and to inject anhydrous ammonia fertilizer under the sweep blades.

Three other cropping systems have been tested successfully for efficient use of limited irrigation: alternating equipment-width field strips of wheat and sorghum combined with wide-spaced furrow irrigation, with the outside crop rows benefiting from a border effect during the non-growing period of the adjacent crop strip (Musick and Dusek 1972 and 1975); double cropping of sorghum and wheat combined with no-till seeding (Allen et al. 1975; Musick et al. 1977); and combination systems of irrigated and dryland crops (Stewart et al. 1983; Unger and Wiese 1979; Unger 1984).

The use of moderate plant densities may be desirable for crops that do not tiller extensively in order to limit interplant competition for water and to allow more gradual development of water deficits. Under adequate irrigation, narrow row spacing for grain sorghum increases yields (Grimes and Musick 1960; Porter et al. 1960). With limited irrigation, the increased yield response from narrow row spacing may not occur. However, narrow row culture is not likely to reduce yield under limited irrigation when high plant densities are avoided (Musick and Dusek 1969). Use of moderate plant densities is of lesser importance for wheat because of tiller compensation when plant density is reduced.

In the water-limited areas of the south Texas High Plains where irrigated grain sorghum is a secondary crop to cotton, farmers plant sorghum early, using medium-maturity hybrids, and limit irrigation to early-season application before the cotton-irrigation season begins. However, north of the cotton production boundary (about 35° north latitude), grain sorghum is the primary irrigated crop in many counties and is planted early, using medium-late-maturity hybrids, and mostly irrigated for high yields.

Cablegation sequentially opens gates in order to flood furrows. Chase County, Nebraska.

LIMITING PUMPING ENERGY COSTS

National energy costs after 1973 varied significantly, peaking in 1984 for natural gas and in 1985 for electricity, two of the three major fuels used for pumping irrigation water. Prices climbed again in 1990 following disturbances in the Persian Gulf. Energy costs can be lowered for irrigation by reducing the pumping head and volume and by increasing pumping-plant efficiencies. Energy costs may be restricted also by management that reduces peak-load demand, high costs that electric utility suppliers subsequently pass on to users. Three significant trends have developed to contain pumping energy costs: (1) reduced water application for the drought-resistant crops that are widely grown under limited irrigation, (2) adoption of low-pressure application for center pivot systems, and (3) conversion from graded furrow to center pivot systems.

Comparing groundwater pumped from irrigation inventories in the Texas High Plains illustrates the reduction in water application. When three years of low pumping energy costs (1964, 1969, and 1974) were compared with three inventory years of much higher costs (1979, 1984, 1989), average water application for grain sorghum declined by 18 percent, for winter wheat by 19 percent, and for cotton by 35 percent (Musick et al. in press). Average water application for all other crops except corn declined by 15 percent. Groundwater pumped for corn increased by 17 percent in association with a trend in increasing yield (see Figure 6.5). The reduction in groundwater applied for most crops over time has partially offset the increased pumping energy costs.

The control of peak-load demands is an important factor in billing for utility power suppliers (Heermann et al. 1990). Stetson et al. (1975) reported that many power suppliers offer reduced rates for interruptible power to reduce peak loads, which can significantly decrease the cost of energy for irrigation. Scheduling/load-control programs can successfully decrease the peak energy demands by limiting the use of irrigation pumping to nonpeak periods.

Heermann et al. (1984) developed an integrated system for irrigation scheduling and power control during peak electrical-use periods. It monitors the irrigation system's operation, provides on-off control, schedules irrigation, and controls electric-power demand. The power supplier monitors the electrical demand and sends radio signals to a computer-based controller at the farm headquarters when it is necessary to interrupt the load. The computer-based system then stops irrigation on individual units based on a priority for all irrigation systems under control. The irrigator monitors all systems to see that they are operational when power is available, exercising personal priorities, and changes the priority using the computer-based controls when desired.

Minimizing pumping energy costs requires high-efficiency pumping equipment. The acceptable energy-efficiency standard for deep-well turbine pumps is 75 percent. Energy-efficiency tests of 360 irrigation pumping plants in the southern High Plains by New and Schneider (1988) averaged 59 percent. The study indicated that efficiencies were lower in areas having smaller pumping units and older equipment. Installation of new wells greatly declined during the 1980s. The low rate of replacement wells and the aging of equipment will probably result in the continued decline in pump efficiencies, thus further increasing pumping energy costs.

In the northern Plains in 1980, electricity was used as the pumping energy for 30 percent of the irrigated area, diesel for 25 percent, and natural gas for 32 percent (Sloggett 1983). Comparative values for the southern Plains were 22 percent electricity, 2 percent diesel, and 66 percent natural gas. Use of gasoline and liquid-petroleum gas accounted for the balance. The Department of Energy has projected increases in national rates for electricity and natural gas through 2010, based on 1989 dollars (adjusted for inflation; see Figure 6.8). The reported national prices for different user groups that were the closest to those of irrigators in the High Plains were average commercial-user rates for electricity and industrial-user rates for natural gas. Natural-gas prices closely parallel diesel prices on an energy-equivalent basis.

The much more stable prices projected would cause electricity increasingly to become the energy of choice for pumping irrigation water in the High Plains. Yet the lack of utility service at many well sites, the high costs of extending electric lines, and the peak-demand problems caused by irrigation pumping to electric-utility suppliers may limit future conversions from natural gas and diesel fuel to electricity. Thus further increases in pumping energy costs undoubtedly contribute to future decline in groundwater use for irrigation in the High Plains.

Skold and Young (1987), in an economic analysis of intermediate and long-range water costs for favorable and less favorable commodity prices, concluded that groundwater irrigation in the Ogallala Aquifer region remains profitable only because producers are living off previous investments in wells, pumps, and irrigation distribution systems and because government payments are sufficient to augment operating losses. The High Plains has experienced some decline in the production of crops dependent on groundwater irrigation in recent years and further declines are anticipated.

Irrigation technologies developed and adopted during the rapid expansion of groundwater-based irrigation in the High Plains following

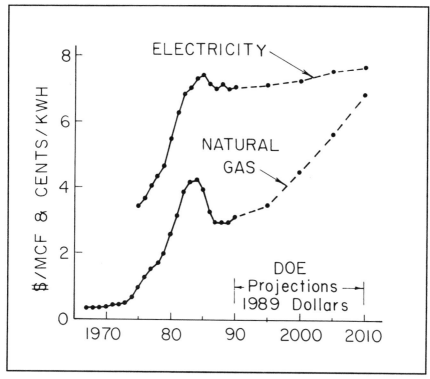

Figure 6.8. Average national electricity rates (commercial users) since 1974, natural gas rates (industrial users) since 1967, and projections by Department of Energy to 2010

World War II have had a major impact on conservation and on efficient water use. The major technologies include (1) on-farm underground-pipeline distribution that replaced open ditches, (2) gated pipe replacement of furrow siphon tubes that allowed much greater flexibility in adjusting furrow flow-rates, (3) tailwater-reuse systems for field runoff, and (4) center pivot sprinkler irrigation that replaced hand-move and side-roll systems. More recent developments have been the major extension of center pivot sprinkler irrigation to sandy soils and to rolling topography not suited to surface irrigation and the replacement of less efficient furrow systems with center pivot systems. The substitution of graded-furrow with center pivot sprinkler systems has greatly reduced labor requirements for irrigation.

A major limitation to attaining high field-application efficiencies with furrow irrigation has been excessive water application and field intake on the relatively long furrow-length fields (mostly one-fourth to one-half mile) and excessive losses to profile drainage below the crop root zone. Technologies that substantially reduce water intake are irrigation of alternate and wide-spaced furrows, including skip-row planting systems, tractor-wheel compaction of furrows, and surge-flow application. Other technologies for water-intake management include deep tillage for increased water intake on the slowly permeable soils and controlled traffic systems that exclude wheel traffic from irrigated furrows, for example, wide bed-furrow systems in which all wheel traffic is maintained on the wide beds. Many useful technologies for irrigation scheduling and timing of application have been developed, including computer irrigation scheduling, which is most widely used for center pivot application to adequately irrigated crops such as corn.

Because of the limited and declining groundwater supplies in important areas of the High Plains regional aquifer and the relatively high pumping energy costs, we have emphasized limited-irrigation management for efficient use of available water supplies. These technologies apply primarily to irrigation of drought-resistant crops on farms having inadequate water supplies for full irrigation. Useful methods include (1) timing irrigation in relation to critical crop-development states for water-deficit effects on yields, (2) reducing or eliminating the preplant irrigation, (3) reducing or eliminating field runoff, and (4) employing practices that effectively use precipitation for partially meeting crop-water requirements on irrigated land. Limited irrigation management probably should not be practiced on low water storage soils, for production of stress-sensitive crops, and during periods of major drought.

High pumping energy costs have contributed to a decline in irrigation in the High Plains. The U.S. Department of Energy projections suggest that in the future, electricity will become the dominant and preferred energy source for pumping irrigation water. The projected doubling of natural gas prices (adjusted for inflation) by 2010 will have the most adverse effect in the southern plains, where it is the predominant energy used for pumping water.

Future trends in technology will emphasize a continuation of present trends for more efficient application systems and for management that reduces losses to profile drainage below the root zone as well as losses associated with field runoff and soil evaporation. Over the next two decades, increased efficiencies in water application and use are projected to lead to a reduction in irrigation water requirements by 15 to 25 percent. A major challenge for research is to develop further the technologies needed for increasing water use efficiencies for irrigated crop production, both from irrigation and from precipitation on irrigated land. A major need is to increase the crop-yield levels and net returns attained by irrigators and to maintain competitive production from irrigated land.

The financial viability of irrigated agriculture in the High Plains is essential to the development and adoption of the new technologies.

REFERENCES

Allen, R. R. 1985. "Reduced Tillage—Energy Systems for Furrow Irrigated Sorghum on Wide Beds." *Transactions ASAE* 28, 6:1736–40.
Allen, R. R., and J. T. Musick. 1972. "Wheat and Grain Sorghum Irrigation in a Wide Bed-Furrow System." *Transactions ASAE* 15, 1:62–63.
———. (In press.) "Effect of Tillage and Preplant Irrigation on Sorghum Production." *ASAE Applied Engineering in Agriculture*.
Allen, R. R., J. T. Musick, F. O. Wood, and D. A. Dusek. 1975. "No-till Seeding of Irrigated Sorghum Double Cropped after Wheat." *Transactions ASAE* 18, 6:1109–13.
Bordovsky, R., and D. Hay. 1975. "Irrigating Grain Sorghum." *Kansas Agricultural Experiment Station Bulletin* 592.
Crabtree, R. J., A. A. Yassin, I. Kargougou, and R. W. McNew. 1985. "Effects of Alternate-Furrow Irrigation: Water Conservation on the Yields of Two Soybean Cultivars." *Agricultural Water Management* 10:253–64.
Duke, H. R. 1989. "Irrigation System Conversions." *Proceedings of the Central Great Plains Irrigation Short Course*. Colby, Kans. Feb. 13–14, 57–64.
Erhart, A. B. 1970. "Winter Irrigation of Sorghums." Kansas Agricultural Experiment Station Report of Progress, 154. Garden City, Kans.
Finkner, R. E., and N. R. Malm. 1971. "Grain Sorghum Row Spacing, Plant Population, and Irrigation Studies on the High Plains of Eastern New Mexico." *New Mexico Agricultural Station Bulletin* 578.
Fischbach, P. E., and H. R. Mulliner. 1974. "Every-other Furrow Irrigation of Corn." *Transactions ASAE* 17, 3:426–28.
Grimes, D. W., and J. T. Musick. 1960. "Effect of Plant Spacing, Fertility, and Irrigation Management on Grain Sorghum Production." *Agronomy Journal* 52:647–50.
Heermann, D. F. 1990. "Overview of New Developments in Sprinkler Irrigation." *Proceedings of the Central Plains Irrigation Short Course*, Wray County. Feb. 5–6, 5–12.
Heermann, D. F., G. W. Buchleiter, and H. R. Duke. 1984. "An Integrated Water-Energy Management-System—Implementation." *Transactions ASAE* 27, 5:1424–29.
Heermann, D. F., H. R. Haise, and R. H. Mickelson. 1976. "Scheduling Center Pivot Sprinkler Irrigation Systems for Corn Production in Eastern Colorado." *Transactions ASAE* 19, 2:284–87.
Heermann, D. F., D. L. Martin, R. D. Jackson, and E. C. Stegman. 1990. "Irrigation Scheduling Controls and Technologies." In B. A. Stewart and D. R. Nielsen, eds., *Irrigation of Agricultural Crops*. Ch. 17. *Agronomy Monograph* 30:510–36.
High Plains Underground Water Conservation District No. 1. Lubbock, Tex. 1990. "Water Well Permits Issued in District." *Cross-Section* 36, 3:4.
Hooker, M. L. 1985. "Grain Sorghum Yield and Yield Component Response to Timing and Number of Irrigations." *Agronomy Journal* 77, 5:810–12.
Howell, T. A., K. S. Copeland, A. D. Schneider, and D. A. Dusek. 1989. "Sprin-

kler Irrigation Management for Corn—Southern Great Plains." *Transactions ASAE* 32, 1:147–54, 160.

Jackson, R. D. 1982. "Canopy Temperatures and Crop Water Stress." In D. Hillel, ed., *Advances in Irrigation*. Vol. 1. New York: Academic Press, 43–85.

Kemper, W. D., T. J. Trout, A. S. Humpherys, and M. S. Bullock. 1988. "Mechanisms by Which Surge Irrigation Reduces Furrow Infiltration Rates in a Silty Loam Soil." *Transactions ASAE* 31, 3:821–29.

Krieg, D. R. 1986. "Cotton Growth and Development." *Proceedings of the DRIP Irrigation Cotton Symposium*. Texas Agri. Ext. Serv. Midland. Feb. 18–19.

Longenecker, D. E., E. L. Thaxton, Jr., J. J. Hefner, and P. J. Lyerly. 1970. "Variable Row Spacing of Irrigated Cotton." *Texas Agricultural Experiment Station Bulletin 1102*.

Longenecker, D. E., E. L. Thaxton, Jr., and P. J. Lyerly. 1963. "Cotton Production in Far West Texas with Emphasis on Irrigation and Fertilization." *Texas Agricultural Experiment Station Bulletin 1001*.

———. 1969. "Variable Row Spacing of Irrigated Cotton as a Means for Reducing Production Costs and Conserving Water." *Agronomy Journal* 61, 1:101–4.

Lyle, W. M., and J. P. Bordovsky. 1983. "LEPA Irrigation System Evaluation." *Transactions ASAE* 26, 3:776–81.

Musick, J. T. 1970. "Effect of Antecedent Soil Water on Preseason Rainfall Storage in a Slowly Permeable Irrigated Soil." *Journal Soil and Water Conservation* 25, 3:99–101.

———. 1987. "Preplant Irrigation in the Southern High Plains—a Review." ASAE Paper No. 87–2558. St. Joseph, Mo.

———. 1989. "Managing Deficit Water Supplies." Proceedings of the Central Great Plains Short Course. Colby, Kans. Feb. 13–14, 1–23.

Musick, J. T., and D. A. Dusek. 1969. "Grain Sorghum Row Spacing and Planting Rates under Limited Irrigation in the Texas High Plains." Texas Agricultural Experiment Station MP 932.

———. 1971. "Grain Sorghum Response to Number, Timing, and Size of Irrigations in the Southern High Plains." *Transactions ASAE* 14, 3:401–4, 410.

———. 1972. "Irrigation of Grain Sorghum and Winter Wheat in Alternating Double-Bed Strips." *Journal Soil and Water Conservation* 27, 1:17–20.

———. 1974. "Alternate-Furrow Irrigation of Fine-Textured Soils." *Transactions ASAE* 17, 2:289–94.

———. 1975. "Limited Irrigation of Grain Sorghum in Alternating Strips with Wheat." 1975. *Transactions ASAE* 18, 3:544–48.

———. 1980. "Irrigated Corn Yield Response to Water." *Transactions ASAE* 23, 1:92–98.

———. 1982. "Skip-Row Planting and Irrigation of Graded Furrows. *Transactions ASAE* 25, 1:82–87.

Musick, J. T., and D. W. Grimes. 1961. "Water Management and Consumptive Use by Irrigated Grain Sorghum in Western Kansas." Kansas Agricultural Experiment Station Technical Bulletin 113.

Musick, J. T., and F. B. Pringle. 1986. "Tractor Wheel Compaction of Wide-Spaced Irrigated Furrows for Reducing Water Application." *Applied Engineering in Agriculture* 2, 2:123–28.

Musick, J. T., F. B. Pringle, W. L. Harman, and B. A. Stewart. (In Press.) "Long-term Irrigation Trends—Texas High Plains." *ASAE Applied Engineering in Agriculture*.

Musick, J. T., F. B. Pringle, and P. N. Johnson. 1985. "Furrow Compaction for Controlling Excessive Irrigation Water Intake." *Transactions ASAE* 28, 2:502–6.

Musick, J. T., F. B. Pringle, and J. D. Walker. 1988. "Sprinkler and Furrow Irrigation Trends—Texas High Plains." *Applied Engineering in Agriculture* 4, 1:46–52.

Musick, J. T., and J. D. Walker. 1987. "Irrigation Practices for Reduced Water Application—Texas High Plains." *Applied Engineering in Agriculture* 3, 2:190–95.

Musick, J. T., J. D. Walker, A. D. Schneider, and F. B. Pringle. 1987. "Seasonal Evaluation of Surge Flow Irrigation for Corn." *Applied Engineering in Agriculture* 3, 2:247–51.

Musick, J. T., A. F. Wiese, and R. R. Allen. 1977. "Management of Bed-Furrow Irrigated Soil with Limited- and No-Tillage Systems." *Transactions ASAE* 20, 4:666–72.

New, L., G. Buchleiter, W. Spurgeon, and B. Unruh. 1990. "Low Energy Precision Application (LEPA) for Center Pivot Machines." Proceedings of the Central Great Plains Irrigation Short Course. Wray County. Feb. 5–6, 13–18.

New, L., and A. D. Schneider. 1988. "Irrigation Pumping Plant Efficiencies—High Plains and Trans-Pecos Areas of Texas." Texas Agricultural Experiment Station MP 1643.

Newman, J. S. 1967. "Yields and Fiber Properties of Cotton Planted in Solid and Skip-Row Systems under Minimal Soil Moisture Levels, Texas High Plains, 1963–65." Texas Agricultural Experiment Station MP 843.

Porter, K. B., M. E. Jensen and W. H. Sletten. 1960. "The Effect of Row Spacing, Fertilizer, and Planting Rate on the Yield and Water Use of Irrigated Grain Sorghum." Agronomy Journal 52:431–34.

Rettman, P. L., and G. D. McAdoo. 1986. "Irrigation Data from Castro and Parmer Counties, Texas, 1983–84." USGS Open-File Report 85–699.

Saleh, A., and R. J. Hanks. 1989. "Field Evaluation of Soil Hydraulic Property Changes Caused by Surge Water Application." *Soil Science Society America Journal* 53:1526–30.

Shipley, J., and C. Regier. 1975. "Water Response in the Production of Irrigated Grain Sorghum, High Plains of Texas." Texas Agricultural Experiment Station MP 1202.

Skold, M. D., and R. A. Young. 1987. "The Role of Natural Resources in the Changing Great Plains Economy." Symposium. Proceedings of the Rural Great Plains of the Future, Great Plains Agricultural Council. Denver, Nov. 3–5.

Sloggett, G. 1983. "Energy and U.S. Agriculture: Irrigation Pumping, 1974–80." USDA Agricultural Economics Report No. 495. Washington, D.C.

Stetson, L. E., D. G. Watts, F. C. Corey, and I. D. Nelson. 1975. "Irrigation System Management for Reducing Peak Electrical Demands." *Transactions ASAE* 18, 2:303–6, 311.

Stewart, B. A., and J. T. Musick. 1987. "Conjunctive Use of Rainfall and Irrigation in Semiarid Regions." *Advances in Irrigation*. Vol. 1. New York: Academic Press, 1–24.

Stewart, B. A., J. T. Musick, and D. A. Dusek. 1983. "Yield and Water Use Efficiency of Grain Sorghum in a Limited Irrigation-Dryland Farming System." *Agronomy Journal* 75:629–34.

Stone, J. F., J. E. Garton, B. B. Webb, H. E. Reeves, and J. Keflemariam. 1979. "Irrigation Water Conservation Using Wide-Spaced Furrows." *Soil Science Society America Journal* 43:407–11.

Stone, J. F., H. E. Reeves, and J. E. Garton. 1982. "Irrigation Water Conservation by Using Wide-Spaced Furrows." *Agricultural Water Management* 5:309–17.

Stone, L. R., C. G. Carlton, T. L. Hanson, R. E. Gwin, Jr., P. Gallagher, and M. L. Horton. 1983. "Amount of Profile Water in Early Spring Resulting from Increased Profile Water in the Fall." *Soil Science Society America Journal* 47, 2:305–9.

Stone, L. R., R. E. Gwin, Jr., and M. A. Dillon. 1978. "Corn and Grain Sorghum Yield Response to Limited Irrigation." *Journal Soil and Water Conservation* 33:235–38.

Stone, L. R., R. E. Gwin, Jr., and P. Gallagher. 1980. "Overwinter Soil Water Loss." Proceedings of the Irrigation Workshop, Kansas State University. Manhattan. Feb. 19–20, 7–20.

Stone, L. R., R. E. Gwin, Jr., P. J. Gallagher, and M. J. Hattendorf. 1987. "Dormant-Season Irrigation: Grain Yield, Water Use and Water Loss." *Agronomy Journal* 70, 4:632–36.

Stringham, G. E., ed. 1988. "Surge Flow Irrigation." Final Report of the Western Regional Research Project, W–103. Res. Bull. 515. Utah Agri. Exp. Stn. Logan.

Unger, P. W. 1984. "Tillage and Residue Effects on Wheat, Sorghum, and Sunflower Grown in Rotation." *Soil Science Society America Journal* 48, 4:885–91.

Unger, P. W., and A. F. Wiese. 1979. "Managing Irrigated Winter Wheat Residues for Water Storage and Subsequent Dryland Grain Sorghum Production." *Soil Science Society America Journal* 43, 3:582–88.

CHAPTER SEVEN

Groundwater Use
Monitoring Techniques

M. Duane Nellis

Assessments of groundwater management programs in the High Plains region are often limited by inadequate information on water demand and water quality. Although an extensive network of metered wells and sampling of water quality would provide the spatial and temporal information necessary for better management of groundwater, economic and political factors preclude such approaches. Meter installation and associated retrofitting, for example, would cost several million dollars in each of the High Plains states (Nellis 1987). Additional costs of regular meter maintenance and collection of data on water use and quality make these labor-intensive approaches impractical, and irrigators frequently resist attempts by policy makers to require such data collection as an invasion of their right to manage water as they choose. But because comprehensive information about water demand and water quality is critical to water resource planners, we need to explore alternative monitoring methods. Successful techniques include the use of remote sensing and geographic information systems.

AN INTRODUCTION TO REMOTE SENSING

Several researchers (Heines and Luckey 1980; Loveland and Johnson 1983; and Nellis 1987) have focused on integrating remotely sensed, land-cover data and water-response rates by cover type to estimate water use. Past studies (e.g., Astroth et al. 1990) illustrated the general advantage of remote sensing in providing land-cover data—crop type (e.g., wheat) and irrigation method (e.g., center pivot)—for water resource investigations because the information can supply water estimates for individual fields within geographically large areas in a cost-effective manner when the proper system is used. Thus, remote sensing can provide synoptic information about water use to assist the water manager in making decisions.

Generally, most of the remote sensing research associated with groundwater monitoring in the High Plains has followed one of three approaches. Initial investigations provided direct measurements of irrigation acreage for water resources planning programs (Poracsky 1979). Later research focused on either a two- or a three-step procedure for predicting groundwater use (e.g., acre-feet of water used for a specific area) (Nellis 1987). In the two-step sequence, the remote sensing data were first classified into categories of land cover or land use; land cover was differentiated by irrigated or nonirrigated and by specific, irrigated crops. Then, a representative value of the hydrologic or water-related parameter for that land-use category was estimated through a mathematical model. Some studies have since added to this two-sequence approach by developing a direct relationship between the land-cover/water parameters and other landscape characteristics to predict a third characteristic of the water management system such as the energy requirements for irrigation (Loveland and Johnson 1983). For example, land-cover/water parameters have been linked with the characteristics of slope and of distance from the water source to assess requirements for energy pumpage.

MEASURING IRRIGATED ACREAGE
WITH REMOTE SENSING

Several investigators have been successful in determining irrigated and nonirrigated crop areas using aerial photography and Landsat imagery. Such inventories are useful to the regional, state, and federal water-resource managers who need accurate information on the dynamics of irrigated acreage. Nellis (1987), for example, employed color infrared photography with a spectral sensitivity from 0.5 to 0.9 micrometers (sensitivities to green, red, and near-infrared earth radiation with high hue values representing irrigated wheat) in northwest Kansas to map irrigated and nonirrigated crops successfully as part of an initial investigation into predicting water demand (see illustration, p. 147). Color infrared photography (sensitive to the near-infrared) has also been used to monitor crop conditions and uniformity of water distribution in irrigated areas of the High Plains (Bye 1987). This type of photography is more widely available than thermal infrared imagery and its costs per unit area are lower.

Hoffman (1983), Kolm and Case (1984), and others used Landsat imagery to identify and locate land irrigated by center pivot systems in the High Plains of Nebraska and South Dakota. The current Landsat satellite has two sensors on board: a multispectral scanner and a thematic mapper. These provide spatial and spectral resolutions relative to monitoring water resource/irrigation agriculture (Table 7.1). The Landsat

High-altitude infrared photograph of irrigated wheat in the High Plains of northwest Kansas.

thematic mapper has greater utility than the multispectral scanner for more detailed mapping of irrigated crops because of its increased spatial and spectral resolution.

In Texas, integrating both aerial photography and satellite remote sensing has proven useful for mapping irrigated areas. The Texas Natural Resources Information System, which combines remote sensing and geographic information systems, provides water managers in Texas with additional information on irrigated cropland and the dynamics of cropland changes (McCulloch 1983).

Studies by Poracsky (1979) and others indicate that the Landsat multispectral scanner band 2 (Landsat thematic mapper band 3) is useful for mapping irrigated land in Kansas because actively growing vegetation reflects a high level of red light. Poracsky employed the Landsat imagery

Table 7.1. Landsat Sensor Spatial, Spectral Resolutions,
and Utility for Water Resource Monitoring

Spatial Band Resolution		Spectral Resolution	Utility
Multispectral sensor			
1	79 meters	0.5–0.6um(green)	water pollution
2	79 meters	0.6–0.7um(red)	irrigated-land mapping
3	79 meters	0.7–0.8um(near IR)	water stress in vegetation
4	79 meters	0.8–1.1um(near IR)	drainage-system mapping
Thematic mapper			
1	30 meters	0.45–0.52um(bl-green)	bathmetric mapping
2	30 meters	0.52–0.60um(green)	water stress in plants; water pollution
3	30 meters	0.63–0.69um(red)	water stress in plants
4	30 meters	0.76–0.90um(near IR)	irrigation water distribution and plant biomass
5	30 meters	1.55–1.75um(near IR)	moisture content
6	120 meters	10.4–12.5um(far IR)	soil moisture
7	30 meters	2.08–2.35um(mid IR)	mineral characteristics of soil

to produce maps of six Kansas High Plains counties. A statistical analysis of accuracy derived from a detailed study of Finney County indicated a mapping accuracy of 85 to 99 percent (depending on the particular crop) and an aggregated areal statistical accuracy of 99 percent for the three major crops: wheat, corn, and sorghum.

Although techniques of visual interpretation are useful for many studies that identify irrigated lands in the High Plains, Kolm and Case (1984) discovered that ratioed classifications of logarithmically stretched images based on the Landsat multispectral band 4/band 2 ratio and on an unsupervised-supervised (decision-maker assisted) smoothing technique of multiple-band images produced the best interpretation in the High Plains of South Dakota. Using this approach, they found that irrigated alfalfa was more effectively identified and mapped using May Landsat imagery, but irrigated corn and soybeans were most easily mapped using an August Landsat image.

In his research in western Kansas, Nellis (1987) used a combination of ratioing and supervised classification to delineate irrigated cropland. Supervised classification incorporates ground-reservation information in the classification procedures to enhance accuracy. A two-band scattergram of band 4 relative to band 2 of Landsat multispectral scanner data illustrates the utility of this combination for classifying irrigated cropland in western Kansas (Figure 7.1). Band 4 values are based on the intensity of reflectance by the crop in infrared light; band 2 shows the level of reflective response by the crop in the red-light region of energy. To further

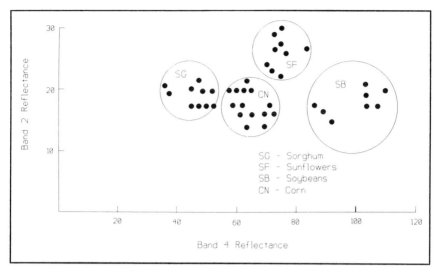

Figure 7.1. A two-band scattergram of Landsat data for northwest Kansas

refine the ratioing technique Nellis applied a supervised-maximum-likelihood classifier to all four Landsat multispectral bands. This procedure allowed for an analysis of variance and a correlation of the irrigated cropland category's spectral-response patterns when classifying an unknown pixel (grid location in the raster-based Landsat data file). The resulting classification proved to be 80 to 90 percent accurate depending on the crop. Baumgardner (1983) achieved similar results in his research in the Texas High Plains.

ASSESSING CROP-WATER NEEDS
WITH REMOTE SENSING

Measurement of crop canopy temperatures, using an aerial thermal scanner, has also proven useful to irrigators and to regional water managers for acquiring information about soil water status in the High Plains, which can be useful for determining the water needs of irrigated and nonirrigated crops. In Nebraska, Blad et al. (1981) employed thermal infrared remote sensing to study sorghum and corn. The study defined the relationship between crop canopy temperatures and moisture stress in plants and evaluated factors affecting canopy temperatures. The thermal scanner detected radiation in the 8.7 to 11.5 micrometer range of electromagnetic energy (far-infrared region). Blad found that nonirrigated sorghum was a few degrees warmer than irrigated sorghum from mid-afternoon to late evening. In addition, corn under stress was as much as 12.8° C (55° F) warmer than nonstressed corn in the afternoon. Such findings offer significant potential for assessing the conditions of irrigated and nonirrigated crops; they also provide information that could lead to more effective management of irrigation water by determining the water needs of irrigated crops through the variations in irrigated crop-canopy temperatures.

A similar approach using thermal infrared remote sensing was developed by the Earth Resources Data Corporation (1985) to estimate water requirements of crops, water-distribution uniformity, mechanical failures, soil moisture, and water-use scheduling. The research was based on the functions of plant physiology. High temperatures indicate stress because plants conduct water and nutrients through their vessels and exchange carbon dioxide through their leaf surfaces. If the plant is stressed from too little water or from disease, insects, or salts in the soil, the movement of water and nutrients and the exchange of gasses is reduced. Stressed plants usually transpire less than unstressed plants. The leaf temperatures in crops not receiving adequate irrigation water, for example, remain high because they lack the cooling effect of full transpiration.

A model developed by Van Bavel (1984) for use in the Texas High Plains combines the information obtained from microwave remote sensing (the moisture in the top 2 inches of the soil) with moisture-distribution patterns for particular types of soil. The model also considers moisture loss by evaporation and moisture gained from precipitation. Such information would be of significant value to farmers and to irrigation-management specialists who are required to make decisions regarding crop water needs and for increasing the efficiency of ground-water use.

From a broader regional perspective, the National Oceanic and Atmospheric Administration (NOAA) satellite has been used in Nebraska to assess vegetative conditions (Peters and Greegor 1987) as they relate to crop water needs. Although designed as a meteorological data collector, two of the five bands on board the satellite are useful for land-resource investigations: Channel 1 records visible red light, and channel 2 records near-infrared energy from the earth's surface. Since red light is absorbed and near-infrared energy is highly reflected by living vegetation, a calculation of channel 2 minus channel 1 divided by channel 2 plus channel 1 has proven useful for indicating the condition of living vegetation. This calculation highlights the degree of live biomass that can then be correlated with irrigated cropland. The resulting data have proven useful for anticipating groundwater demands associated with irrigation based on the condition of the vegetation as determined by the NOAA satellite. As with other satellite data, NOAA data is readily available to the general public and would be of value to regional water resource managers.

ESTIMATING WATER DEMAND USING REMOTE SENSING AND GEOGRAPHIC INFORMATION SYSTEMS

Data derived from remote sensing of irrigated cropland can be integrated with other data to estimate water demand. Such information is critical to water resource managers in their assessment of the effectiveness of their decisions. Heines and Luckey (1980) evaluated the use of Landsat multi-spectral data in combination with water use according to crop to estimate groundwater demand in parts of Colorado, Kansas, Nebraska, New Mexico, Oklahoma, South Dakota, Texas, and Wyoming. The results provide general information on water use by the region, but the scale of application of this particular project made it difficult for scientists to assess the accuracy of the estimation.

Similar types of data on irrigated crop acreages have been combined with water-use rates in areas outside the High Plains region to estimate evapotranspiration (Raymond and Owen-Joyce 1986). Within the High Plains region Walsh (1986) investigated the relationship between the crop-moisture index, a meteorologically based drought index, and the characteristics of vegetation assessed through remotely sensed data sampled during a growing season in Oklahoma. He derived remotely sensed data using a one-kilometer resolution Advanced Very High Resolution Radiometer of the NOAA satellite. The method provided insight for water planners relative to demands on the groundwater resources during periods of high drought.

Still other research offers a three-step approach for understanding more aspects of the groundwater management system in the High Plains. With such an approach, remote sensing data is classified into categories of irrigated and nonirrigated land cover. The data are then integrated with a water-use rate according to the land cover. The third step combines this information with topographical data to predict another aspect of the water management system. A study by Astroth, Trujillo, and Johnson (1990) provided a procedure for combining remote sensing with geographic information systems to determine energy-related factors of the groundwater management system in Oregon. In the High Plains, where pumping costs for irrigation continue to increase, such an approach promises insights into methods for the prediction of energy requirements for particular areas of irrigation and their potential for development.

WESTERN KANSAS CASE STUDY

The need for accurate statistics on water demand in the limited groundwater resource areas of the Kansas High Plains has led to increased interest by the state of Kansas in exploring methods other than flow meters for estimating this demand. The political and economic constraints associated with meters necessitate alternatives. The cost of a meter (excluding labor) on a new well in northwest Kansas is approximately $400. Retrofitting existing irrigation wells with meters would cost $500 to $3,000, depending on the pipe configuration at the well. Since a large majority of the wells would require retrofitting, the cost of installing meters on wells throughout northwest Kansas alone would be approximately $1.8 million, excluding maintenance and monitoring costs. The meters generally have a life expectancy of seven to ten years (Bossert 1987).

To provide accurate information on water demand at a low cost in the Kansas High Plains, the U.S. Department of Interior and the Kansas Water Resources Research Institute funded a project, completed in 1987, to determine the potential for using remote sensing in combination with other information for estimating water demand in Northwest Kansas Groundwater Management District No. 4. The district has required meters on all new irrigation wells since May 1981 and thus can serve as a case study, providing critical data on irrigation pumping rates and water demand that can be used in developing a model.

The spatial model required input on the crop area derived from remote sensing and field transects, including method of irrigation, crop water requirements, metered water-use rates, and precipitation (Figure 7.2). The irrigated crop area was determined using Landsat multispectral scanner data acquired for different dates during the growing season. Dates in late April, early May, late July, early to mid-August, and early September were required to provide crop response for the range of cropping calendars associated with crop types in the district and to avoid cloud cover during some stages of the satellite overpass. Landsat digital data were converted into major categories of irrigated crop type, using multiband ratioing of bands 4 and 2 and a maximum likelihood classification procedure (Table 7.2). Data also included a classified irrigated crop area, using the maximum likelihood classification procedure.

The maximum likelihood approach applies two weighted factors to a probability estimate. First, the analyst determines the anticipated likelihood of an occurrence for each class in the scene. For example, when classifying a pixel or a digital value for the image, the probability of irrigated corn may be weighted more heavily than a less likely crop.

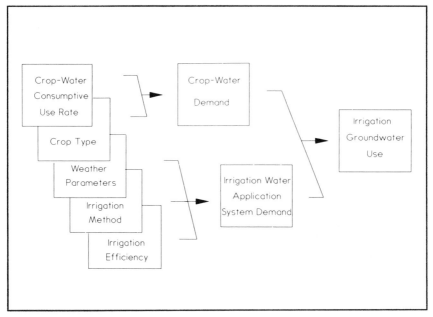

Figure 7.2. The key indicators in the water-demand model used in northwest Kansas to predict water demand

Second, the weight or "cost" of misclassification is applied to each class. These two factors act to minimize misclassifications (Lillesand and Kiefer 1987).

Because of the annual variation in growing-season precipitation (April–October), the amount of water required for irrigated crop production varies. Therefore, the irrigation coefficients by crop type and the irrigation method as determined by the U.S. Department of Agriculture were modified by a precipitation coefficient, which reflects the deviation of precipitation from a normal distribution. Baker demonstrated the approach (1983) by correlating precipitation amounts during the crop-growing season with crop water requirements and by using the resulting data to estimate rates of groundwater withdrawal in southwest Kansas. The precipitation in 1986 was less than 1 percent (0.9) above the norm and is reflected in the irrigation requirements by crop (see Table 7.2).

When one compares the predicted value using the remote sensing model with metered well data, the accuracy for the model is approximately 96 percent. The annual costs associated with such an approach are less than $20,000 for an area the size of northwest Kansas, a significant savings over retrofitting for metered wells.

Table 7.2. Remote Sensing Derived Irrigated Land Cover Data and Irrigation Requirements, 1986 Irrigation Season, Northwest Kansas (in acre-feet/acre)

Crop Type	Acres	Irrigation Requirement	Water Demand
Alfalfa	53,400.6	2.01	107,335.21
Corn	163,946.2	1.27	208,211.67
Sorghum	69,839.0	1.08	75,426.12
Soybeans	28,323.9	1.04	29,456.86
Sunflowers	46,575.1	1.05	48,903.86
Wheat	69,946.8	0.93	65,050.52
Total			534,384.24

Source: M.D. Nellis (1987), *Estimating Water Demand,* Manhattan: USGS and Kansas Water Resources Research Institute.

USING REMOTE AND GEOGRAPHIC INFORMATION SYSTEMS FOR MONITORING GROUNDWATER QUALITY

Scientists have used the techniques of remote sensing and geographic-information systems for monitoring groundwater quality in the High Plains region (Ripple and Miller 1982; Pritchard 1987–1988). In spring 1979, the South Dakota Department of Water and Natural Resources initiated a project with the aid of the state Planning Bureau for water-quality planning. Using color infrared aerial photography and Landsat imagery, planners developed maps of potential groundwater pollution based on information concerning land cover, soil permeability, location of the water table, and slope gradient. This approach alleviates the problems of obtaining current, comprehensive land-use/land-cover data and combines information effectively. By using a storage and retrieval system of georeferenced computer-data information, the planners gained many options. This particular case study demonstrates the potential savings in applying this approach to more extensive areas of the High Plains region.

In a more recent effort, the Center for Advanced Land Management Information Technologies (CALMIT) has utilized a remote sensing/ geographic information system for mapping areas of an aquifer's vulnerability as part of the Nebraska Department of Environmental Control's effort to designate special groundwater protection areas (Pritchard 1987–1988). The system, called "DRASTIC," combines information on hydrogeology and soils into one map that shows the vulnerability of the aquifer to pollution in a specific region (Figure 7.3). DRASTIC is the acronym for the seven mappable factors:

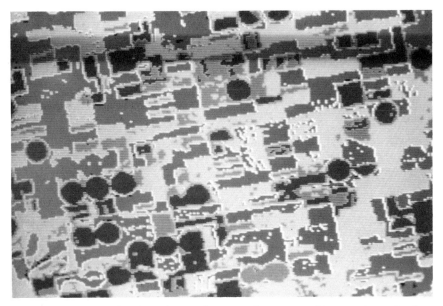

Landsat maximum likelihood classification of an area of irrigated cropland in northwest Kansas.

D = Depth to water
R = Recharge
A = Aquifer media
S = Soil media
T = Topography
I = Impact of the unsaturated zone
C = Hydraulic conductivity

Developed in 1985 by the National Water Well Association and the U.S. Environmental Protection Agency, DRASTIC was first used as a joint project by CALMIT and the Nebraska Department of Health to evaluate the potential for groundwater pollution at Cozad, Nebraska. The Nebraska Department of Environmental Control became interested in the technology as a means of determining special protection areas after the passage in 1986 of the Nebraska Groundwater Management and Protection Act. The act was the legislative response to increasing groundwater contamination by nitrates and other nonpoint source pollutants. Before a special protection area can be designated, however, a detailed study of the area must be conducted. DRASTIC allows a standardized approach for determining the vulnerability of groundwater.

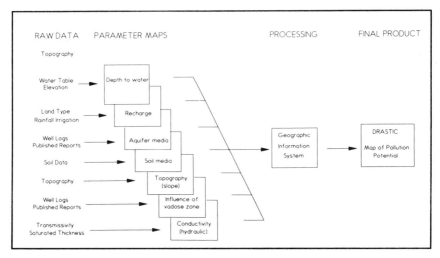

Figure 7.3. DRASTIC: remote sensing and geographic information system network

Each factor of DRASTIC is given a rating of 1 to 10, with 10 as most
vulnerable and 1 as least vulnerable. The rating scale is weighted relative
to the seven factors present in a specific area. Depth to water, for example, is one of the more important factors in determining pollution potential. A range of 0 to 5 feet in depth to water is rated at 10; 100 feet or more is
rated at 1. Topography or the slope of the land surface affects how quickly
a contaminant penetrates the soil; a flatter surface allows a contaminant to
infiltrate the soil more rapidly. A 0 to 2 percent slope, for example, is rated
at 10; an 18-plus percent slope is rated at 1. The computer combines the
data onto a single map that shows the aquifer's vulnerability.

As decisions about water resources grow more critical in the High Plains
region, the need for more data and for improved methods of storage and
retrieval increases correspondingly. Thus remote sensing technology
and geographic information systems are serving as valuable tools for the
High Plains water resource manager. With the improvement in resolution of sensors and in analysis, remote sensing will play an ever more
important role in providing information about irrigated areas, cropland
changes and conditions, water needs, uniformity of water distribution in
irrigated fields, and variations in water demand and in pollution of
groundwater resources.

Software and hardware for remote sensing and geographic information systems continue to decrease in cost. Computer-compatible

data bases (e.g., soils, topography, and land) are increasingly available from state and regional organizations at low cost; microcomputer technology has moved to the county and to the offices of regional water management. Water managers are limited only if they are uncomfortable with user-friendly software packages.

Remote sensing and geographic information systems can provide water-resource data on a variety of levels. On a small scale, data focusing on irrigated acreage and water demand are important to the regional, state, and federal decision makers; on a large scale, data centering on crop stress associated with irrigation and water quality are more useful to the individual operators. Remote sensing and geographic information systems have grown ever more sophisticated since the late 1980s, particularly the two- and three-dimensional models, and can be processed on microbased computer systems at all levels of the water management system. As these technologies continue to improve, so too will the potential for groundwater monitoring.

REFERENCES

Astroth, J., J. Trujillo, and G. Johnson. 1990. "A Retrospective Analysis of GIS Performance: The Umatilla Basin Revisted." *Photogrammetric Engineering and Remote Sensing* 56: 359–64.
Baker, C. 1983. *Estimates of Groundwater Withdrawals for Irrigation in Western Kansas.* Topeka: Kansas Water Office.
Baumgardner, R. 1983. "Mapping Irrigated Agriculture in the Texas High Plains." In C. Palmer and L. Childs, eds., *Texas Natural Resources Inventory and Monitoring System.* Austin: TNRIS and NASA, 67–84.
Blad, B., B. Gardner, D. Watts, and N. Rosenberg. 1981. "Remote Sensing of Crop Moisture Stress." *Remote Sensing Quarterly* 3, 2: 4–20.
Bossert, W. 1987. Manager, Northwest Kansas Groundwater Management District No. 4. Personal interview.
Bye, S. 1987. "Monitoring Crops with the Infrared Eye in the Sky." *Sunflower* 13: 18–19.
Earth Resources Data Corporation. 1985. *Integrated Crop Monitoring.* Overland Park, Kans.: Earth Resources Data Corporation.
Heines, F., and R. Luckey. 1980. *Evaluating Methods in the High Plains in Parts of Colorado, Kansas, Nebraska, New Mexico, Oklahoma, South Dakota, Texas, and Wyoming.* Denver: U.S. Geological Survey.
Hoffman, R. 1983. *Center-Pivot Irrigation Systems in Nebraska.* Lincoln, Nebr.: Remote Sensing Center, Conservation and Survey Division.
Kolm, K., and H. Case. 1984. "The Identification of Irrigated Crop Types and Estimation of Acreages from Landsat Imagery." *Photogrammetric Engineering and Remote Sensing* 50: 1479–90.
Lillesand, T., and R. Kiefer. 1987. *Remote Sensing and Image Interpretation.* 2d ed. New York: John Wiley & Sons.
Loveland, T., and G. Johnson. 1983. "The Role of Remotely Sensed and Other

Spatial Data for Predictive Modeling: The Umatilla, Oregon, Example." *Photogrammetric Engineering and Remote Sensing.* 49: 1183–92.

McCulloch, S. 1983. "Development of the Texas Natural Resources Inventory and Monitoring System (TNRIS)." In *Texas Natural Resources Inventory and Monitoring System.* Austin: INRIS and NASA, 21–32.

Nellis, M. D. 1987. *Estimating Water Demand in Northwest Kansas.* Manhattan: U.S. Geological Survey and Kansas Water Resources Research Institute.

———. 1990. "Interfacing Remote Sensing and Geographic Information Systems for Rural Land Use Analysis." *Photogrammetric Engineering and Remote Sensing* 56: 329–32.

Peters, A., and D. Greegor. 1987. *Vegetative Growing Conditions in Nebraska as Viewed by Satellite: 1987 Growing Season.* Lincoln, Nebr.: Center for Land Management Information Technologies (CALMIT).

Poracsky, J. 1979. "Irrigation Mapping in Western Kansas Using Landsat." *Symposium Proceedings on Remote Sensing of Irrigated Lands.* Omaha, Nebr.: Missouri River Basin Commission, 48–54.

Pritchard, K. 1987–1988. "Mapping Aquifer Vulnerability: A Cooperative Effort for CSD, DEC." *Resource Notes: Quarterly of the Nebraska Conservation and Survey Division* 2, 2: 2–3.

Raymond, L., and S. Owen-Joyce. 1986. "Estimates of Consumptive Use and Evapotranspiration in Palo Verde Valley, California, 1981 and 1983." In A. Johnson and A. Rango, eds., *Remote Sensing Applications for Consumptive Use (Evapotranspiration).* Bethesda, Md.: American Water Resources Association.

Ripple, B., and S. Miller. 1982. "Remote Sensing and Computer Modeling for Water Quality Planning in South Dakota." In C. Johannsen and J. Sander, eds. *Remote Sensing for Resource Management.* Ankeny, Iowa: Soil Conservation Society of America, 309–16.

Van Bavel, C. 1984. "Studying from a Distance." *Texas Water Resources* 10, 5:1–2.

Walsh, S. 1986. "Drought Assessment through Advanced Very High Resolution Radiometer Satellite Data." *Papers and Proceedings of Applied Geography Conferences.* Vol. 9. West Point, N.Y.: U.S. Military Academy, 45–55.

CHAPTER EIGHT

The Nebraska Sandhills

Steve Gaul

The Sandhills region of Nebraska presents a striking contrast to the remainder of the High Plains, not only in terms of its more generous groundwater reserves but also in the unique nature of its soils and topography. The area covers over 19,000 square miles, primarily in north-central Nebraska, and is the largest sand dune area in the Western Hemisphere (Figure 8.1). Beneath a land surface stabilized by a grass cover lies about half of Nebraska's groundwater in storage. It is thus not surprising that the issues surrounding the use of groundwater in the Sandhills vary significantly from those in other areas of the High Plains. Groundwater quantity remains a concern, but more in terms of local water-table levels and potential export than in terms of total reserves. Soil erosion and water-quality problems related to groundwater development receive a higher level of attention. Although we shall be examining issues of land and water development in the Sandhills, it should be kept firmly in mind that the region remains overwhelmingly ranching country. Only about 5 percent of its total area is under cultivation, and it remains sparsely populated. The Sandhills account for about one quarter of Nebraska's area but contain a mere 1.4 percent of the state's population.

PHYSICAL GEOGRAPHY

Although groundwater provides the key to understanding the use and the potential of the Sandhills, the topography is the feature more likely to catch the eye. The grass-covered dunes are up to 400 feet in height, as much as 20 miles in length, and have slopes as steep as 25 percent (Bleed and Flowerday 1989). The dunes were probably formed during episodes of eolian activity over the last ten thousand years; the more extensive activity probably ceased about fifteen hundred years ago (Swinehart 1989). The stabilizing grass cover is fragile, however, and human activities can cause blowouts that modify the topography. Topsoils on the Sandhills dunes are thin and contain very little organic matter (Lewis 1989). Sandhills soils are also highly permeable, which contributes to the unique

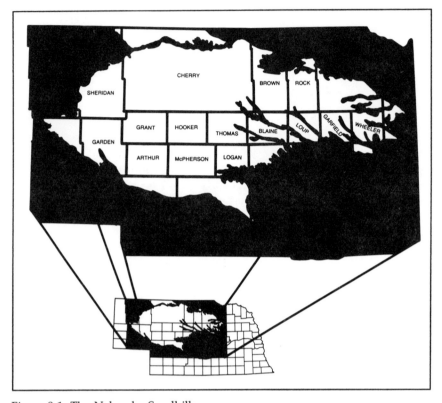

Figure 8.1. The Nebraska Sandhills

characteristics of the hydrology of the area. In addition, soils are often used to indicate the boundaries of the Sandhills.

Most precipitation falling in the region infiltrates the sand, resulting in very low levels of overland runoff and accounting in part for the relatively small ratio of tributaries to streams in the area. Streamflow is supplied almost entirely by groundwater seepage. The regulating effect of the groundwater reservoir and the low level of water consumption result in an unusually steady flow rate in Sandhills streams. Groundwater also helps support lakes, wetlands, subirrigated meadows, human settlement, and ranching and contributes to pressures to develop land. Its quality, abundance, and proximity to the surface combine to make groundwater one of the most remarkable resources in the Sandhills region.

Although the Sandhills compose only a quarter of Nebraska's area, they probably contain about half its groundwater. Geologic data continues to be gathered, and the total amount of water in storage has not yet been measured accurately. In the 1960s Reed estimated that between 700 and 800 million acre-feet of groundwater are in storage beneath the Sandhills (Keech and Bentall 1971). This compares with an estimate of about 3 billion acre-feet in the Ogallala formation in a six-state region (High Plains Study Council 1982). Recent information indicates that the groundwater system in the Sandhills may be more complex than previously thought; therefore, any estimates of the amount of water in storage are subject to debate.

A thick set of permeable rocks and sands and occasional impermeable layers, known as the Ogallala group, underlies the entire Sandhills and much of the rest of Nebraska. Together with older groups, younger alluvial deposits, and sand beneath the dunes, they form an excellent groundwater reservoir. The aquifer contains over 900 feet of saturated thickness in parts of Grant and Hooker counties and large portions of the Sandhills have over 500 feet of saturated thickness. That water is generally of high quality and is very low in dissolved solids. Shallow lakes and wetlands are common in many of the northern and western portions of the Sandhills, with estimates of the number of lakes ranging from 2,490 (Steen 1961) to 1,500 (McCarraher 1977). Lake sizes appear to vary in response to precipitation cycles, and thus it can be difficult to distinguish between lake and wetland. Although lakes and wetlands are considered to generally be groundwater discharge areas, their intricate relationship with groundwater is not fully understood.

Depth to the water table varies considerably in much of the Sandhills; in the valleys it may be near the surface or may intersect it, resulting in subirrigated meadows, wetlands, lakes, and streams. Artesian springs and flowing wells are found in some areas. Because of human dependence on these resources, development that causes water-table fluctuations can result in problems even though it may have a minimal effect on the amount of groundwater in storage.

HISTORY OF LAND USE

Evidence that mass bison kills occurred between eight to ten thousand years ago appears in several areas surrounding the Sandhills (Holen 1989), and Folsom arrow points that are 10,500 years old have been found in a blowout site in Blaine County. Since the dunes were formed during the last ten thousand years, people were probably present in the region while dune formation was still occurring. More substantial human impact on the land has occurred since Euro-American settlement. The first account of a European viewing the Sandhills dates from 1795; but the Nebraska-Kansas Act in 1854 opened the Nebraska Territory to settlement, and cattle ranching actually began in the Sandhills in the late 1870s.

Cultivation began under the provisions of the Homestead Act, which allowed settlers to acquire title to 160 acres by farming and improving the land. During the late 1890s a severe drought contributed to a loss of population in much of western Nebraska. The Homestead Act and other federal laws designed to encourage settlement based on farming or forestry were not useful to ranchers, who needed large tracts of land to sustain an operation in the region. Consequently, landowners attempted to stretch the laws in a variety of ways. In many cases unclaimed land was ranched, and fences were often built without regard for ownership. Legislative attempts to change laws also occurred so that larger tracts could be acquired, in the belief that more acreage would facilitate a viable operation. In 1904, Congress passed the Kinkaid Act, which permitted homestead claims of 640 acres in thirty-seven western Nebraska counties and allowed more practicable farm and ranch operations. Interestingly, as of 1982 the average farm or ranch size in the Sandhills was around 3,700 acres (Soil Conservation Service [SCS] 1989). Nonetheless, the Kinkaid Act helped populate western Nebraska and converted government grazing land in the Sandhills into private parcels. Between 1900 and 1920 the total population of thirteen interior counties in the Sandhills nearly doubled.

Long-term economic conditions did not sustain this level of settlement. The area's population began a long decline, and population numbers in the interior region are now only marginally above the levels reached before passage of the Kinkaid Act. Miller (1989) reported that in most of the thirteen counties that lie predominantly within the Sandhills "the acres under cultivation declined after the 1930s drought and did not return to the levels recorded for 1930." The expansion of center pivot irrigation in the 1970s reversed this trend in some areas. For instance, in Rock County some 3.5 percent of the land was in corn in 1921; that figure dropped to about 0.4 percent in 1960 but rose to about 6.7 percent by 1980. In Wheeler County approximately 6.3 percent of land was in corn in 1921, 3.1 percent in 1960, and 12.7 percent in 1980. Garfield County had 8.8 percent of its acreage in corn in 1921, 3.2 percent in 1960, and 5.8 percent in 1980 (Nebraska Agricultural Statistics, various years).

Throughout this time hay production remained dominant in terms of acreage harvested, with wild hay accounting for the vast majority of the total acres in hay. In 1980 all wild and tame hays combined accounted for 67.8 percent of all acres harvested in Rock County and 55.8 percent of all acres harvested in Wheeler County. Some small grains are also grown

Windmill-powered pump and tank to provide water for livestock in the Sandhills.

in the region, although they are much less common today than they were in the first half of the century.

The abundant groundwater in the Sandhills provided for multiple stock wells and watering places, facilitating ranching in the region and also allowing some irrigation in level areas. The potential of the groundwater was unlocked, however, when Frank Zybach patented the center pivot irrigation system in 1952. In the mid-1950s Zybach began a demonstration project in Holt County near the edge of the Sandhills. The pivot was labor saving and economical, it could irrigate sandy soils, and it was useful even on somewhat variable topography. In the Sandhills the groundwater's potential was especially evident on sandsheets found in the eastern margins that constitute about 16 percent of the region (SCS 1989). Their gentler slopes resulted in better prospects for converting rangeland to irrigated cropland. The pivots in these areas are used primarily for corn production; however, ranchers throughout the Sandhills use pivots to produce hay or alfalfa as supplemental feed for their cattle. Generally these crops require fewer chemicals and involve less exposure and erosion of the soil than corn.

The impact of the center pivot on the Sandhills was quite different from its effect in most other areas of the High Plains. Groundwater was abundant and easily reached, but soils and topography presented severe limitations to development even with the pivot. Thus, in the Sandhills, groundwater depletion was a relatively minor concern, but problems with erosion were significant. Although the ensuing irrigation development would primarily involve only small amounts of land on the perimeter of the Sandhills, the continued productivity of some of the best land in the Sandhills was affected by potential erosion. Also, unlike most other areas of the High Plains, the change in land use was not from predominantly dryland agriculture to irrigated agriculture but from ranching and hayland to irrigation. After development, even the more developed eastern fringes of the Sandhills would remain overwhelmingly an area of ranches.

A combination of technological innovation, high crop prices, and possibly drought may have helped to fuel the center pivot boom of the early and mid-1970s. By 1970 most of the mechanical problems had been removed from pivot technology, and it had gained a measure of acceptance among farmers. Between 1972 and 1974 crop prices exploded, more than doubling in constant dollars (Wellman and Lutgen 1988). This rise in crop prices can be correlated with the increases in acres of irrigated corn harvested and in well registrations in Wheeler, Rock, and Garfield counties (Figures 8.2 and 8.3). From 1974 to 1976 the area was dry (1974 in particular was a drought year), reinforcing the belief in the benefits of irrigation. Some of the fluctuations in irrigated-corn acreage were no doubt influenced by federal farm programs (see Figure 8.2). Irrigated acreage decreased considerably in 1983 because the federal payment-in-kind program offered incentives to remove land from production. The number of acres of corn harvested in 1987 was 31,000 less than in 1985 for the three counties. In 1987 Rock and Wheeler counties had almost 17,500 acres in the Conservation Reserve Program (U.S. Bureau of Census 1987), which provides annual payments for highly erodible cropland taken out of production for a ten-year period.

In a few counties on the eastern margin of the Sandhills the changes during the period of 1970–1984 were dramatic (Table 8.1). The most pronounced development was in Wheeler County; in 1970 about 1.5 percent of the land there was irrigated, but by 1984 that figure had expanded to about 15.2 percent. The figures for Arthur and Grant counties indicate a lesser impact from irrigation in some of the western Sandhills counties. Notably, irrigation development was increasing on a statewide basis during the same period. Although some of the development in the eastern counties was in the Sandhills, a great deal also took place on land just outside the Sandhills boundaries (Figure 8.4). In a number of cases, series of pivots were developed on adjacent tracts of land. Although pivots can operate on moderate slopes, land leveling was sometimes used to remove

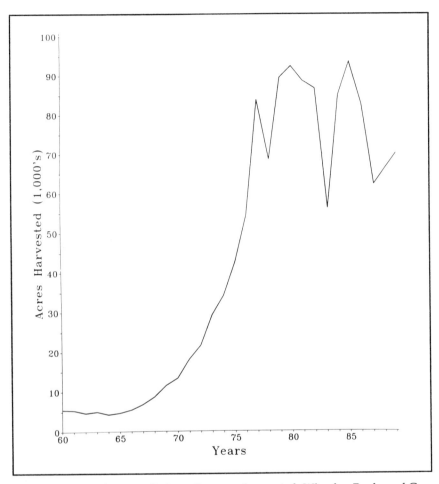

Figure 8.2. Corn for grain (irrigated)—acres harvested, Wheeler, Rock, and Garfield counties (totals), 1960–1987. *Source:* Nebraska Agricultural Statistics (1989 data are preliminary)

the steeper areas from the hills so that pivots could be used. The rate of development was rapid between 1972 and 1981, but the number of wells drilled per year has declined since then (see Figure 8.3).

Along with the transition from ranching to irrigation came another change: feeding cattle. The Nebraska Natural Resources Commission reported that "in Wheeler and Garfield counties . . . calf production and cows two years old and older declined 13 percent and 12 percent respectively, from 1967 to 1980. Cattle on feed increased 78 percent and the number of hogs on farms increased 14 percent in that period" (Nebraska

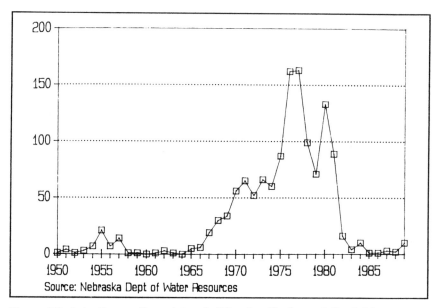

Figure 8.3. Irrigation wells registered, Wheeler, Rock, and Garfield counties, 1950–1989. *Source:* Nebraska Department of Water Resources

Natural Resources Commission 1981). One result of the change was arguably economic progress, but an examination of annual county personal income as a percentage of state personal income between 1969 and 1986 for Rock and Garfield counties revealed no readily apparent trends (U.S. Dept. of Commerce, Local Area Personal Income). Wheeler County experienced dramatic increases in its share of personal income between 1980 and 1987, however.

Population levels also help measure the change. Total population increased between 1970 and 1980 in Rock and Wheeler counties and declined minimally in Garfield County (Table 8.2). The figures illustrate an interesting trend in ranking during the period of center pivot development. Between 1970 and 1980, years of major center pivot development, Rock, Wheeler, and Garfield counties experienced a higher rank in percentage of population change than in either the preceding or the following decade. Any conclusions about income or population changes in the three counties must be tempered by the knowledge that the total population of the area remains quite small and thus does not provide a large enough sample for adequate evaluation.

By the 1980s some of the conditions that had helped cause the high rate of center pivot development were changing. The farm economy had weakened; difficulties experienced by those who had developed unsuit-

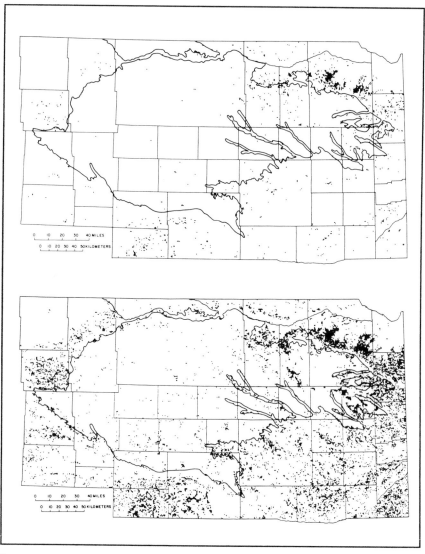

Figure 8.4. Center pivots as determined from Landsat imagery, 1972 (top) and 1984 (bottom)

Table 8.1. Acres Irrigated and Percentage of Total Land Area
Irrigated in Selected Counties, 1970 and 1984

County	Acres Irrigated		Percentage of Land Area Irrigated	
	1970	1984	1970	1984
Wheeler	5,700	56,000	1.55	15.19
Rock	10,500	62,000	1.63	9.60
Brown	37,600	74,000	4.83	9.51
Garfield	8,900	33,000	2.44	9.06
Arthur	2,500	12,000	0.55	2.66
Grant	600	4,000	0.12	0.82
Nebraska	3,998,000	7,800,000	8.17	15.93

Sources: Nebraska Agricultural Statistics, 1971 and 1987, Nebraska Dept. of Agriculture

Table 8.2. Population Change, Rank in Percentage Population
Change, 1960–1990, Wheeler, Rock, and Garfield Counties

Year	Population	Percentage Change		Rank in Percentage Change
Wheeler County				
1960	1,297	—		—
1970	1,051	−19.0	(60-70)	86
1980	1,060	+0.9	(70-80)	39
1990	948	−10.6	(80-90)	58
Rock County				
1960	2,554	—		—
1970	2,231	−12.6	(60–70)	65
1980	2,383	+6.8	(70–80)	19
1990	2,019	−15.3	(80–90)	84
Garfield County				
1960	2,699	—		—
1970	2,411	−10.7	(60–70)	55
1980	2,363	−2.0	(70–80)	52
1990	2,141	−9.3	(80–90)	44

Source: U.S. Bureau of the Census, Census of Population, 1960, 1970, 1980, 1990.

able land were more apparent and investors were increasingly cautious.
Problems in managing irrigated land may have contributed to financial
troubles and bankruptcy for some landowners and a general slowing of
land development although that is hard to measure accurately. Moreover,
federal tax reforms in the mid-1980s removed some of the incentives that
might have brought investors to the Sandhills.

As economic conditions changed, a few center pivots were taken out
of use. In 1985 the Soil Conservation Service (SCS) surveyed idle irriga-

tion systems in Nebraska and found sixty-seven in Garfield, Wheeler, and Rock counties, accounting for 8,769 acres. Seven thousand six hundred fifty-one acres of that land normally would have severe erosion hazards. A total of 2,116 acres could potentially erode at a rate of at least twice the established soil-loss tolerance. Interestingly, although these three counties made up only 2.4 percent of Nebraska's acreage with active irrigation systems, they accounted for 26.7 percent of idle-system acreage, 35 percent of idle acreage with severe erosion hazards, and 29.4 percent of idle acreage with severe erosion hazards and erosion at a rate of at least twice the soil-loss tolerance. The condition of center pivot lands no longer irrigated in Wheeler, Garfield, Rock, Brown, and Cherry counties was investigated by the Natural Resources Commission in 1985 and 1986. Most of the land had been removed from production two to three years earlier, and erosion did not appear to be a serious problem because most of the fields had adequate weed cover (Nebraska Natural Resources Commission 1989).

CURRENT LAND USE AND LAND-USE PROBLEMS

The dominant land use in the Sandhills has long been and is likely to remain cattle ranching. Rangeland accounts for 80 percent of land use in the region, wild hay for 10 percent, and cultivated crops (many of which are types of hay) for only 5 percent. Woody vegetation (including planted pine forest in Thomas, Blaine, and Cherry counties) takes up 2 percent and water another 1 percent. All other uses combined account for the remaining 2 percent of the land. The SCS (1989) estimated that about 3 percent of the Sandhills is irrigated although Miller estimated 4 percent (1989). The SCS also has estimated total annual groundwater use in the Sandhills to be about 410,000 acre-feet, with 384,000 acre-feet used to irrigate crops (1989). The only urban center actually within the physiographic Sandhills is Valentine (population 2,826, 1990). The lack of towns and the predominant use of land as range helps explain why only about 22,300 people live in the Sandhills region; the area has an average of slightly more than one person per square mile.

With such a large proportion of rangeland one would expect range management to be the major issue in the Sandhills. However, Stubbendieck (1989) characterized the region as "one of the few rangeland areas of the world in which the grazing resource has improved since it was first used by domestic animals," citing the control of wildfires and the easy detection of problems as the two reasons. He noted "If the rancher starts to make a grazing management mistake, the moving sand is an indicator."

Moving cattle along the highway in Garfield County, Nebraska.

Issues have been raised more often about the 5 percent of land that is cropped and have addressed primarily land productivity, water quality, and water-table declines. Although these concerns are important, the small proportion of land involved should also be considered. On first examination, land productivity would not seem to be a problem associated with center pivot installation when the pivot is properly sited and good management is used. Converting rangeland to irrigated cropland substantially increases the land's value. Nonetheless, proper management of Sandhills cropland can be difficult, and in the past some land developers were unaware of the form needed. Moisture must be applied to the crop more often than in other areas because of the soil's low moisture retention. If sand does begin to blow in any area of the field, it can damage crops through blasting and sometimes by spreading and covering areas of adjacent fields. Blowing sand can also cause problems with maintenance of machinery.

If a pivot is poorly sited, if land is badly managed, or if the pivot owner, sometimes from bankruptcy, stops irrigating the land without reestablishing a good grass cover, wind erosion can result. Sometimes "blowouts" or conical-shapes from wind erosion develop and if not treated expand. In areas where cropping is discontinued, range productivity may not return to former levels unless the area is properly seeded. Establishing a good native-grass cover on Sandhills lands that were formerly cropped can be expensive. Reversion of land may occur because owners are in financial difficulty or have filed for bankruptcy. If the pivot is removed without establishing a cover of native grass, the costs of reestablishing it can amount to more than the land's market value. Government programs and funds may ultimately be used to help accomplish revegetation. Soil Conservation Service data show that in 1982, the major area that constitutes the Sandhills had 180,800 acres or 49.1 percent of its irrigated cropland adequately treated compared with about 52.6 percent of irrigated cropland in the state itself (SCS 1984). Sandhills irrigated cropland does not appear to suffer from a significantly higher incidence of inadequate treatment than irrigated land in other areas.

Sandhills soils require substantial management for successful cropping. The SCS classifies soil capability into eight groups that indicate progressively greater limitations and narrower choices for practical use. As of 1982, almost 79 percent of irrigated cropland in Nebraska was classed in groups 1 through 3, the least limited for use. But almost 82 percent of irrigated cropland in the Sandhills was classed in groups 4 through 8, as land with the most severe restrictions. The limitations on Sandhills soils in general are even more severe. The SCS has noted that 97 percent of the Sandhills would be considered either as highly erodible or as wetland (1989). The limitations on Sandhills soils indicate that extensive management is needed to ensure that a cover is maintained on the land at all times.

Issues over water quality and Sandhills development relate to the area's sandy soils, the abundant groundwater, and a water table that is often near the surface. Attaining high yields on irrigated lands usually requires the use of fertilizers and pesticides, but the coarse-textured soils of the Sandhills allow those chemicals to be leached through the root zone relatively quickly. The degree to which this poses a threat to the water supply in areas near intensive developments is not extensively documented, but work on potential nitrate leaching in the Sandhills has been completed by the University of Nebraska.

Problems related to the water table vary; declines can cause problems for stock wells, domestic wells, and wet-meadow productivity. The Nebraska Natural Resources Commission surveyed twenty landowners thought to have potential well problems in highly developed northern Wheeler and Greeley counties; seventeen of them identified 114 of 302 stock wells as having problems. Most of the landowners surveyed also identified adverse changes in the productivity of their wet meadows over the years (Nebraska Natural Resources Commission 1983). Since portions of the Sandhills are dotted with lakes, and many of those lakes are water-table exposures, groundwater pumping has the potential to lower lake levels; other wetlands could experience similar effects. Many Sandhills operations include subirrigated wet meadows that supply hay and other forage plants, which could be seriously affected by a drop in the water table. Since streams in the Sandhills are almost entirely derived from groundwater seepage, streamflow would also be reduced. Although its findings were disputed, the Bureau of Reclamation reported that a planned surface water irrigation system in the Cedar River Basin in the south of Wheeler County was no longer feasible because streamflow was expected to decrease, the result of intensive irrigation development.

Another controversy has been over the potential use of the Sandhills groundwater reservoir as a source for large-scale water transfers to other states. When the state conducted a study of possible changes in water-transfer statutes, residents and local governments in the Sandhills region voiced concern (Water Management Board 1988). Although the region does possess much larger groundwater reserves than surrounding areas, the high cost of moving water makes lengthy transfers seem unlikely in the immediate future. Large- or medium-scale energy consumption or industrial use within or near the Sandhills may occur. Pumping water from near Argo Hill in Sheridan County to a power plant to be built near Hemingford in Box Butte County was one possibility; building a water-cooled power plant near Dunning in Blaine County was another but neither of those ideas was implemented.

GOVERNMENTAL POLICY AND IRRIGATION DEVELOPMENT

Governmental policy has played a significant role in Sandhills land and water management, but that role should not be overemphasized. Ninety-five percent of the area is not cropped, and agricultural programs have had comparatively little impact on privately owned ranch land. In the portion that is cropped, the erratic nature of prices for agricultural commodities is significant: The incentive to develop land is greater when prices are high; when they are low it may be more advantageous to let the land go back to grass.

The first governmental policy that brought about plowing the land was the Kinkaid Act, which resulted in the cultivation of some unsuitable land that was then abandoned. Between the exit of the Kinkaid settlers and the spread of the center pivot in the early 1970s, governmental programs played a comparatively marginal role in Sandhills land development and the region retained its character as a ranching area. In 1936 the Department of Agriculture's Agriculture Conservation Program established the federal government as a source of financial assistance for re-seeding efforts, a program that has continued. Over time governmental policy, landowner decisions, and commodity-price fluctuations have combined to produce "go back" lands, as they are sometimes called in the region. These areas that once were cropped and then left to return to grass naturally are sometimes less productive as rangeland although in many cases they have been reseeded successfully. If seed of improved varieties is used, the quality, production, and disease resistance can be better than the native grasses; however, it is not unusual for seed from native harvest to be used. In other cases cropped lands may have been removed from production and then brought back at a later date. Both irrigated and dryland cropping occurred between the 1920s and 1970, primarily on a small scale. In the 1970s federal, state, and local governments began to consider policies to address the somewhat larger-scale changes that were occurring.

STATE AND LOCAL POLICY

When rapid irrigation development began in the 1970s no state-level strategy existed for dealing with the resulting problems. The right to use groundwater in Nebraska was and is generally based upon ownership of the land overlying a water supply. Beginning in the 1970s, Nebraska passed legislation that would be important to land and water development throughout the state, including the Sandhills. Some of those efforts included groundwater control areas, groundwater management areas, the Chemigation Act, special water-quality protection areas, the Sediment and Erosion Control Act, Soil Conservation funding, and a constitutional amendment banning nonfamily corporate farms. Although many of these laws could affect the use of Sandhills land for irrigated agriculture, their current impact is limited.

Nebraska's role is often perceived as giving local governments sufficient powers to deal with the problems. In that regard the unicameral legislature took a significant step even before substantial irrigation development occurred in the Sandhills. In 1972 Nebraska consolidated eighty-six soil and water conservation districts and various watershed districts into twenty-four natural resources districts (two were subsequently combined, resulting in twenty-three districts currently) and gave them powers to plan and execute a number of works and programs, including those related to soil conservation, flood prevention, water development and management, water conservation, pollution, drainage, wildlife habitat, and recreation facilities. Since the districts have the authority to tax local property, they have significant financial resources and realistic prospects of addressing problems in their areas. The district funds have been used for soil-conservation cost sharing and for the other programs.

As issues related to natural resources have arisen, the unicameral has significantly increased the power of the districts. Yet this increase in authority must be balanced against the observation that funding increases to accomplish the new duties have been limited. This is exacerbated in that districts in the Sandhills have few cities and thus have a much lower tax base than many of Nebraska's other natural resources districts. The districts do have powers to limit groundwater development for reasons of both quantity and quality as well as having regulatory powers relating to areas with excessive soil erosion. Should large-scale center pivot development occur in the Sandhills again, natural resources districts may well play a more significant regulatory role.

FEDERAL POLICY

Federal tax policies and commodity programs have influenced decisions over irrigation development throughout the High Plains. In the Sandhills the role of capital-gains tax policy possibly may have been accentuated by the difference between the value of the undeveloped grazing land and the developed irrigated cropland. The marginal nature of the land also means that recent soil conservation requirements for participation in federal farm programs may affect development decisions more heavily in the Sandhills than in the other areas of the High Plains.

The reasons for a continued federal role are largely economic. Until very recently federal monies for soil conservation practices were considerably above the combined Nebraska state and local totals. Federal tax policy helps determine the economics of farming. Federal price-support programs help control the price of agricultural commodities and thus the pressures to use the land; under current conditions access to federal farm programs is almost a necessity for many farmers. Perhaps most significantly, access to those programs depends upon implementation of conservation plans. Whether this power of the purse will halt environmentally unsuitable development on Sandhills lands is uncertain, but it has that potential.

A number of aspects of the farm program have affected land use in the Sandhills, including the Agriculture Conservation Program, the Great Plains Conservation Program, the Conservation Reserve Program, federal tax policy, price-support programs, and the 1985 Food Security Act, with its sodbuster and swampbuster provisions. The Agriculture Conservation Program of the Agricultural Stabilization and Conservation Service has provided funds for constructive land practices in Nebraska: land leveling, terraces, sod waterways, livestock water dams and pits, erosion and storage dams, and grass seeding.

The Great Plains Conservation Program of the SCS has played an important role in the Sandhills, providing funds to solve erosion problems regardless of their source. Thus when physically unsuitable land is developed for irrigation in the Sandhills, program funds can be used to reseed the area to grass if the cropping venture fails. Although the decision on expenditure of the funds is federal, local natural resources districts approve plans involving disbursement of the program's funds.

Natural resources districts approve the Conservation Reserve Program's plans for reseeding highly erodible cropland to grass or trees. In the past, a few natural resources districts in the Sandhills area have refused to approve the program's plans for reseeding some of the land that had been developed for irrigated cropping and was reverting to grassland. The districts argued that the land was unsuitable for crop development and that government should not be asked to bear the expense of bad business decisions. No statistics have been published on total governmental costs involved in reseeding previously cropped Sandhills land to grass, so the magnitude of this problem is difficult to determine. If the plans are not signed by the natural resources district, they can still be approved after a short waiting period.

Federal tax policy has played a somewhat controversial role in Sandhills irrigation development. Tax features influencing Sandhills investment decisions at various times since 1972 include the capital-gains exemption, accelerated depreciation, the investment tax credit, and deductibility of conservation expenses. Evidence indicates that investors in high-income brackets were able to reduce their tax rates through land development. Although these tax features have provided incentives for development, the federal tax reforms of 1986 have reduced their influence by eliminating the capital-gains exemption and the investment tax credit and by reducing allowable levels of accelerated depreciation. In early 1992 partial restoration of the capital-gains exemption was still under consideration.

A significant work on the role of tax incentives is Baker, Lundeen, and Gessaman's "Analysis of Tax Incentives for Intensive Irrigation Development in the Nebraska Sandhills" (1983), which examined budgets for investments, crop production costs and returns, and the resulting tax liabilities for irrigation developers who were either ranchers, farmers, or long-term or short-term investors. They reported that:

> while the cost of production before tax is greater than the before tax gross income, after-tax cash flows were positive for all of the cases studied.
>
> The after-tax cash flows increase with increases in leverage and marginal tax rates. Thus the developers who are in the highest mar-

ginal tax bracket and who have the capability of obtaining a highly leveraged position are receiving the greatest total returns."

A tax incentive seems apparent, especially for the high-tax-bracket investor who chose to develop in the Sandhills before 1986. Documentation on the amount of influence tax breaks actually had on development and the degree to which investors from outside the Sandhills were involved is lacking, nor has there been a study of the role of taxes from 1972 to 1981, when much of the development took place. Capital-gains taxes may have played a role in development elsewhere in the High Plains where land was often converted from dryland to irrigated cropland. Still, because grazing land has a higher value than land used for hay and irrigated crops, the advantages of the capital-gains tax policy were probably greater in the Sandhills.

Federal price-support programs are another incentive to develop land in the Sandhills for irrigation purposes. Corn is the crop of choice on much of the developed marginal land and has been receiving price supports in most years. Without those supports incentives for development would be reduced, but if applied nationwide the programs could have a negative financial impact on all corn producers. The passage of the Food Security Act in 1985 may have provided a method to uncouple those subsidies from inadequately treated marginal land without affecting other producers. In any case, some landowners may not be in the farm program; a rancher who installs a center pivot and grows a hay crop or grains and then feeds the product to his own cattle may not require a subsidy.

By any standards, the 1985 Food Security Act is a major change in federal policy for marginal lands and will probably reduce pressures for irrigation development in the Sandhills. The act requires that by 1990 anyone farming highly erodible cropland must have a conservation plan to reduce soil losses to required levels. Failure to comply will cause landowners to be ineligible for U.S. Department of Agriculture programs on all their lands. By 1995 landowners must have an approved conservation system. Although the act does not prohibit breaking out highly erodible grassland for crop production, the sodbuster provisions require that in order for landowners to stay eligible for USDA programs their lands must be farmed under a conservation system approved by the local natural-resources district. The act's swampbuster provisions make landowners ineligible for most U.S. Department of Agriculture programs if they convert wetlands to crop production. The law also initiated a Conservation Reserve Program that issues ten-year federal contracts to return land to grass or trees and to prohibit their harvest.

The act's impact on Sandhills irrigation development may prove significant because of the high percentage of uncropped and highly erodible land in the region. For instance, the sodbuster provisions and the expense of conservation measures are likely to help prevent breakout of new grassland. The SCS currently permits alternative conservation systems that allow for erosion to be higher than the soil's tolerable limit where highly erodible lands were previously in production. However, sodbuster lands must meet more rigid conservation standards that bring average erosion losses down to the soil's tolerable level. The act's swampbuster provisions will provide some degree of protection to the lakes, wetlands, and wet meadows found in parts of the Sandhills. The Conservation Reserve Program also should protect marginal areas.

POTENTIAL FOR CHANGE

Changes in agricultural markets, governmental policy, and the perceptions of land managers seem to weigh against an immediate repeat of the rapid center pivot development the Sandhills experienced in the early and mid-1970s. Yet current laws do not necessarily meet with everyone's approval, and a change in markets or modifications in governmental policy could encourage at least some degree of development on unsuitable lands.

Market conditions could conceivably influence irrigation development on unsuitable lands, even under current governmental policies. Marginal lands become valuable in times of high crop prices, and those prices can become high enough to justify breaking the land out for crops. Controversy over government subsidies for such action will no doubt continue. Because of the cyclic nature of agricultural markets, relatively high crop prices are likely to return temporarily. Two changes in governmental policy could affect the future price of agricultural commodities. First, the level of government price supports for corn and other grains could change. Currently, budget constraints indicate those support levels are unlikely to increase much, but supports do provide a floor price that generally helps encourage decisions to cultivate the subsidized crops. Second, governmental policy on tax subsidies for ethanol could be changed to affect future crop prices significantly, especially corn prices.

Changes in the Federal Food Security Act are also possible. The act does not require complete implementation of conservation plans until 1995. Because some owners of marginal lands are likely to experience difficulties or expenses in meeting those requirements, political pressure either to change the law or to soften the regulations or their enforcement seems likely. Notably, the Food Security Act was passed in times of relatively modest crop prices; pressure to soften the law and to allow more intensive use of the land comes in periods of high crop prices. When crop prices are favorable there is also less need to stay in the program. Long-term government funding of agricultural programs may decrease; if that does occur, farmers may find it less worthwhile to stay in those programs. Thus the long-term effect of the Food Security Act on development of marginal land remains uncertain.

The tax-code changes of 1985 are also subject to the winds of political change. Congressional debate on partial restoration of the capital-gains exemption continues and decisions on capital gains, the investment tax credit, and accelerated depreciation will probably be made more in reference to their impact on the nation than to their effect on marginal lands.

Policy changes are also possible at the state level. In 1987 and 1988 the Nebraska Unicameral considered a legislative bill that would have addressed breakout of all highly erodible grassland in the state, not just that in the federal farm programs. Although that legislation was not passed, the bill also contained provisions to ensure reseeding of abandoned cropland in such areas. Powers that state and local governments possess but have not yet exercised could prove important if conditions in the Sandhills change in the future.

Finally, an important condition that has changed through time and may change again is the perception of the capability of the land. The governmental perception that it made economic sense to encourage dryland cropping throughout western Nebraska helped establish the Kinkaid Act. Although the program did encourage settlement, dryland cropping in the Sandhills was not generally successful. The center pivot expansion of the 1970s again tested the land's limits. The difficulties of some land developers may encourage caution in future investors; still, memories do not last forever, and land management technologies are subject to change. At some point in the future there may once again be strong pressure for cropland development, but for now, crop prices, the Food Security Act, tax changes, and concerns about the capability of the land seem likely to curb large-scale land development efforts in the Sandhills.

REFERENCES

Baker, Maurice, Michael Lundeen, and Paul Gessaman. 1983. "Analysis of Tax Incentives Intensive Irrigation Development in the Sandhills." Lincoln, Nebr.: Department of Agricultural Economics.
Bentall, Ray. 1989. "Streams." In *An Atlas of the Sandhills*. Resource Atlas No. 5. Lincoln: Conservation and Survey Division, University of Nebraska.
Bleed, Ann. 1989. "Groundwater." In *An Atlas of the Sandhills*. Resource Atlas No. 5. Lincoln: Conservation and Survey Division, University of Nebraska.

Bleed, Ann, and Charles Flowerday. 1989. "Introduction." In *An Atlas of the Sandhills*. Resource Atlas No. 5. Lincoln: Conservation and Survey Division, University of Nebraska.

Bleed, Ann, and Charles Flowerday, eds. 1989. *An Atlas of the Sandhills*. Resource Atlas No. 5. Lincoln: Conservation and Survey Division, University of Nebraska.

High Plains Study Council. 1982. "A Summary of Results of the Ogallala Aquifer Regional Study with Recommendations to the Secretary of Commerce and Congress." Washington, D.C. Dec. 13.

Holen, Steven R. 1989. "Anthropology: The Native American Occupation of the Sandhills." In *An Atlas of the Sandhills*. Resource Atlas No. 5. Lincoln: Conservation and Survey Division, University of Nebraska.

Keech, C. F., and Ray Bentall. 1971. "Dunes on the Plains: The Sandhills Region of Nebraska." Conservation and Survey Division, Resource Report No. 10: University of Nebraska-Lincoln.

Lewis, David T. 1989. "Origin of Properties of Sandhills Soils." In *An Atlas of the Sandhills*. Resource Atlas No. 5. Lincoln: Conservation and Survey Division, University of Nebraska.

McCarraher, D. B. 1977. "Nebraska Sandhills Lakes." Lincoln: Nebraska Game and Parks Commission.

Miller, Susan. 1987. "Evaluation of the Kinkaid Act." Lincoln: University of Nebraska, Department of Political Science. December.

————. 1989. "Land Development and Use." In *An Atlas of the Sandhills*. Resource Atlas No. 5. Lincoln: Conservation and Survey Division, University of Nebraska.

Nebraska Department of Agriculture. Nebraska Agricultural Statistics Service. Nebraska Agricultural Statistics, various years.

Nebraska Department of Water Resources. 1981. Well Registration Data. Nebraska Natural Resources Commission. Sandhills Area Study Decision Document, March 19.

Nebraska Natural Resources Commission. 1981. Sandhills Area Study Decision Document, March 19.

————. 1983. "An Economic Survey of Ranchers and Farmers Impacted by Externalities of Irrigation in the Eastern Section of the Sandhills." Draft, March.

————. 1989. Sandhills Area Study, Eastern Section. Status Report, draft, July.

Steen, M. O. 1961. "Sandhills Lake Survey, Report for the Period July 1 to December 1960." Lincoln: Nebraska Forestry and Parks Commission.

Stubbendieck, James. 1989. "Range Management." In *An Atlas of the Sandhills*. Resource Atlas No. 5. Lincoln: Conservation and Survey Division, University of Nebraska.

Swinehart, James B. "Geology-Wind Blown Deposits." In *An Atlas of the Sandhills*. Resource Atlas No. 5. Lincoln: Conservation and Survey Division, University of Nebraska.

U.S. Department of Agriculture. 1984. Soil Conservation Service. Nebraska Final NRI Tables. October 15.

————. 1989. Soil Conservation Service. Forest Service in Cooperation with the Nebraska Natural Resources Commission. Nebraska Sandhills Cooperative River Basin Study.

U.S. Department of Commerce, Bureau of the Census. 1987. *Census of Agriculture*, various years.

————. *Census of Population*, decennial years.

————. 1989. *Population Estimates,* July 27.

————. Bureau of Economic Analysis. *Local Area Personal Income,* various years.

Water Management Board. 1988. State of Nebraska. Report on the Water and Water Rights Transfer Study. November.

Wellman, Allen C., and Lynn H. Lutgen. 1988. "Crop and Livestock Prices for Nebraska Producers." April.

CHAPTER NINE

Groundwater Management in Northwest Kansas

Wayne A. Bossert

In 1974 the Kansas Legislature passed the Groundwater Management District Act, which established a new approach for the state with respect to groundwater. The act provided a process whereby residents in an area could organize and assume responsibilities for groundwater resource management based upon their own local needs. Within four years five established districts were beginning to develop local programs designed to address their specific problems. These districts continue to work on a wide range of concerns involving issues of both water quality and quantity and to implement programs designed to address all locally perceived concerns. The districts began their existence as virtual clones of one another, but each district evolved independently and now clearly exists as a unique unit. One of these groundwater management districts (GMDs) is located in the northwest corner of the state, and since 1977 it has designed, developed, and implemented efforts in that area to manage the groundwater resources.

THE GROUNDWATER MANAGEMENT DISTRICT ACT

The Kansas Groundwater Management District Act sets state policy regarding groundwater management as follows:

> It is hereby recognized that a need exists for the creation of special districts for the proper management of the groundwater resources of the state; for the conservation of groundwater resources; for the prevention of economic deterioration; for associated endeavors within the state of Kansas through the stabilization of agriculture; and to secure for Kansas the benefit of its fertile soils and favorable location with respect to national and world markets. It is the policy of this act to preserve basic water use doctrine and to establish the right of local water users to determine their destiny with respect to the use of the groundwater insofar as it does not conflict with the basic laws

and policies of the state of Kansas. It is, therefore, declared that in the public interest it is necessary and advisable to permit the establishment of groundwater management districts.

The act spells out the authorities and responsibilities to be given an organized district, including the methodology and monetary limits of their assessment authority, and other operational procedures.

In practice, the act stipulates that any area may file a declaration of intent to form a district with the chief engineer, Division of Water Resources, State Board of Agriculture. The declaration must be signed by at least fifteen eligible voters, the first seven of whom become the official steering committee. This committee then prepares a map of the proposed boundaries and, in concert with the chief engineer, determines these boundaries and circulates a petition calling for the formation of the district. Once the petition has been signed by at least fifty voters, the steering committee files it with the secretary of state, who reviews the document for sufficiency. If it is approved, the secretary transmits the petition to the chief engineer, who must also act upon it and subsequently notify the steering committee and the secretary of state of his or her findings within ninety days. The chief engineer's approval is conditioned upon finding that

1. the lands proposed to be included in the district substantially constitute a hydrologic community of interest,
2. the proposed district would not include any of the lands of an existing groundwater management district,
3. the statement of purposes contained in the petition conforms with the intent and purposes of the act,
4. the lands within the proposed district or part thereof overlie an aquifer or aquifers subject to management,
5. the map attached to the petition is substantially correct,
6. the area of the district and existing and prospective uses of groundwater within the district are sufficient to support a groundwater management program,
7. the public interest will be served by the creation of the proposed district.

Following the chief engineer's approval, the steering committee holds an election; if a majority votes in favor of it, the district is declared formed and is ready to conduct its first annual meeting and elect its initial board of directors. No action attacking the legality of the incorporation of the district can be maintained unless it is begun within ninety days after the secretary of state issues the certificate of incorporation.

The district's first responsibility is to develop a management program. This document must first be approved by the chief engineer and then locally adopted by the district board, following a public hearing. The chief engineer's review is solely to determine if the proposed plan conforms to the Kansas Water Appropriation Act and cannot be used to change the plan except for those items that are in conflict with the act. This process is designed to retain as much local direction as possible.

District financing is an important section of the act. The boards are authorized to fund their operations by levying a land assessment not to exceed $.05 per acre of land, a water user charge not to exceed $.60 per acre-foot of established water right, or both. In some cases landowners are authorized to petition the board to exclude their land from the assessment, thus abandoning their voter eligibility. The act states that "any . . . landowner who is the owner . . . of land comprising not less than 640 acres in area . . . on which no water is being used or from which no water is being withdrawn, may have such tracts of land on or from which no water is being withdrawn, excluded from district assessment." Water-rights holders may also verify annually to the district a lesser amount of water pumped than is registered on their rights and then be assessed only for that lesser amount. The other funding authority of the GMDs is a unique provision allowing for a special assessment against lands benefited by a specific project, following a board resolution to that effect. In these cases, a team of appraisers is hired to assess the relative benefits accruing to each tract of land affected by the project and to certify their findings to the board, which then imposes a special land assessment in addition to the customary land assessment.

Every political body has authorities. Basic powers of the GMDs, among others, are to

1. sue and be sued;
2. maintain, equip, and staff an office;
3. hold and sell property and water rights;
4. acquire land up to 1,000 acres by gift or exchange;
5. construct and operate works for drainage, recharge, storage, distribution, or importation of water;
6. levy water user charges and land assessments, issue bonds, and incur indebtedness;
7. contract with persons, firms, associations, or agencies of state or federal government;
8. extend or reduce district boundaries;
9. conduct research and demonstration projects;
10. require installation and reading of meters or gauges;

11. provide assistance in the management of drainage, storage, recharge, surface water, and other problems;
12. adopt, amend, and enforce by suitable action policies relating to the conservation and management of groundwater;
13. recommend to the chief engineer rules and regulations necessary to implement and enforce board policies;
14. enter upon private property for inspection purposes to determine conformance with policies;
15. seek and accept grants or other financial assistance from federal, public, or private sources; and
16. recommend to the chief engineer the initiation of proceedings to establish an intensive groundwater use control area.

Final sections of the Kansas Groundwater Management District Act cover the extension or reduction of boundaries, the dissolution of districts, and the designation of intensive groundwater use control areas.

In 1975 and 1976 the Northwest Kansas Groundwater Management District No. 4 followed all the necessary organizational procedures. In the election on February 24, 1976, 1,058 persons cast votes and by a two-to-one margin supported district formation. Immediately prior to staffing, the steering committee held the district's first annual meeting and passed three resolutions affecting the board's composition. First, they decided that eleven board positions would be created. Counties wholly within the district would seat two positions each; others would seat one member each or together seat one member, depending on the area of inclusion. The one county with only twenty-one sections of land within the district would be represented by members from an adjacent county. The steering committee also agreed to a two-term limitation for all board positions except for the position that may represent the three western districts on the Kansas Water Authority. The district's first manager was hired and began work March 1, 1977; as of this writing, there are four full-time employees on the staff.

In December 1991, GMD No. 4 contained just over 3.11 million acres of land, of which approximately 2.46 million were being assessed. The remaining acreage had been excluded from district assessment by landowners. Approximately 899,000 acre-feet of water rights were appropriated within the district. The 1991-1992 annual budget was approved at $212,416.00 and necessitated a land and water fee of $.05 and $.09, respectively. This schedule means that a typical irrigated tract of land is assessed at three times more than a nonirrigated tract of the same size. This three-to-one ratio has been maintained by the board since a water user charge was implemented in 1980.

REGIONAL SURVEY OF NORTHWEST KANSAS

Northwest Kansas Groundwater Management District No. 4 includes Sherman, Thomas, and Sheridan counties and portions of Cheyenne, Rawlins, Decatur, Graham, Gove, Logan, and Wallace counties (Figure 9.1). The district covers approximately 3 million acres and is located in the High Plains section of the Great Plains physiographic province. Elevations range from approximately 3,900 feet above sea level at the district's western boundary to approximately 2,200 feet above sea level at its eastern edge.

The major cities within the district include St. Francis, Goodland, Colby, Hoxie, Oakley, and Quinter, with a combined population of 16,120 people in 1990. These communities collectively lost 1,423 inhabitants between 1980 and 1990. These towns and people are served by a highway network including Interstate 70 and Kansas Highways 23, 24, 25, 27, 36, 40, 83, and 283, by a rail system consisting of Union Pacific, Burlington Northern, and Kyle, and by limited air service from passenger line Air Midwest and freight carrier Pony Express.

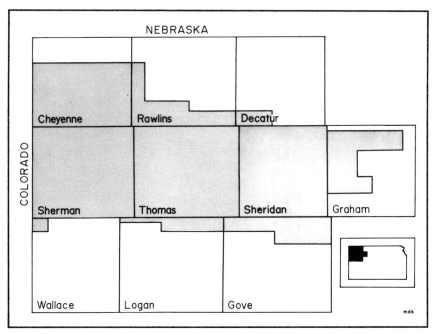

Figure 9.1. Northwest Kansas Groundwater Management District Number Four

Average annual precipitation ranges from 17 inches in the western tier of counties (Cheyenne, Sherman, and Wallace) to 21 inches in Graham County on the eastern edge of the district. Rain showers account for the majority of the annual precipitation during the growing season from April to September. Daily and annual temperatures vary significantly, with summer days being warm and summer nights generally cool; this is true when the relative humidity is low, even during the hottest periods of the summer. Weather records show that a low relative humidity and frequent cloudless or near-cloudless days are typical for the area, as are moderate-to-strong surface winds most of the year. The major climatic drawback is the occasional devastating episodes of hail and damaging winds associated with severe thunderstorms and tornadic activity, which generally occur in the spring or summer months when the storms tend to be most intense. These typical conditions result in the need for special soil and water management practices in order to protect and retain these resources. Moreover, the low annual precipitation led to significant irrigation development in the early 1960s, thus creating the overdraft condition experienced at the time of district formation.

The climate is generally well suited for grassland and certain agricultural crops, particularly if irrigation is developed to supply needed moisture during dry periods. Agricultural cropping within the district remains primarily wheat, corn, grain sorghum, soybeans, and sunflowers. As one would expect, the combined irrigated acreage of these crops, approximately 270,000 acres, places a heavy demand on the aquifer (Table 9.1). This demand peaked in the late 1970s and translated into significant groundwater declines. These eight counties do not represent the precise boundaries of the district but are considered to be a good approximation since portions of the district's area that are absent from these figures are roughly equal to the adjacent nondistrict areas that are included. Livestock (cattle, pigs, and sheep) are also significant to the economy of the area.

Most soils in the district developed on windblown loess deposited during the Pleistocene age. River valleys contain a more granular soil type resulting from stream-laid deposits. The primary soils are in the Ulysses-Colby and Holdrege-Ulysses associations. The Ulysses-Colby association has deep, grayish-brown to dark grayish-brown silt loams, nearly level to slightly sloping, and is found in the western three-fourths of the district. The Holdrege-Ulysses association consists of deep to moderately deep, dark grayish-brown silt loams and moderately deep gray clays that are gently sloping and is typically found in the eastern one-fourth of the district. With today's irrigation equipment and techniques, nearly all of these soils are potentially irrigable, as is evidenced by the classifying of most of the soils in the district as Class 1, 2, and 3 with

Table 9.1. Crop Acreage and Livestock, by County

County	Wheat Acreage			Corn Acreage			Sorghum Acreage			Soybean Acreage			Livestock		
	Irrigated	Dryland	Total	Irrigated	Dryland	Total	Irrigated	Dryland	Total	Irrigated	Dryland	Total	Irrigated	Dryland	Total
Cheyenne	8,900	139,100	148,000	14,800	100	14,900	3,200	6,900	10,100	4,800	0	4,800	57,700	4,700	400
Rawlins	2,000	126,400	128,400	4,600	900	5,500	6,400	30,900	37,300	700	0	700	49,800	8,400	3,000
Decatur	1,500	116,000	117,500	5,000	11,600	16,600	1,900	41,700	43,600	0	1,600	1,600	69,000	9,100	1,100
Norton	700	98,300	99,000	6,400	1,500	7,900	1,500	24,000	25,500	0	1,200	1,200	40,500	16,600	2,600
Sherman	21,000	164,500	185,500	33,800	800	34,600	5,400	4,400	9,800	4,300	1,100	5,400	39,600	3,100	1,800
Thomas	20,000	192,000	212,000	47,400	3,600	51,000	10,000	26,600	36,600	5,800	2,700	8,500	33,300	3,200	2,200
Sheridan	7,000	117,000	124,000	25,200	3,100	28,300	12,000	29,100	41,100	5,000	0	5,000	48,600	7,900	1,600
Graham	2,900	118,700	121,600	3,800	400	4,200	3,600	23,500	27,100	0	400	400	44,500	2,000	300
Totals	64,000	1,072,000	1,136,000	141,000	22,000	163,000	44,000	187,100	231,100	20,600	7,000	27,600	383,000	55,000	13,000

Source: Kansas Farm Facts, 1987.

respect to land-use capability. It is generally recognized that in many cases these soils do require special management in order to be irrigated effectively.

In the geologic past four drainage basins developed within the district's boundaries. The largest is the Upper Republican, which consists of the South Fork Republican, Beaver Creek, Sappa Creek, and Prairie Dog Creek. This basin's drainage trends northeast across the district and ultimately meets the Republican River in southwestern and south-central Nebraska. The Solomon Basin includes Bow Creek and both the North and South Forks of the Solomon River, which trends primarily east across the district. The Saline Basin contains the Saline River and its less substantial South Fork. Like the Solomon Basin, it trends east and leaves the district essentially in the extreme northeast corner of Gove County. The Smoky Hill Basin consists of the North Fork Smoky Hill and Smoky Hill River, Hackberry Creek, and Big Creek. This basin trends east-southeast and leaves the district along the eastern border of Gove County.

Surface water within the district is limited to runoff during and shortly after periods of moderate to heavy rainfall and base flows in the South Fork Republican and South Fork Solomon Rivers. Throughout most of the district the surface runoff is low and difficult to capture economically because of the nature of the rainfall, the soil characteristics, and the general topography. Locations where suitable dams could be constructed to capture and control surface runoff in significant amounts are somewhat limited. Currently, the cost-effectiveness of such large structures for both groundwater recharge and irrigation use is questionable. Studies have shown that the high evaporation rate in the area (as much as 72 inches of pan evaporation per year) would deplete much of the captured water before it could be recharged into the aquifer or used for irrigation purposes. Detailed future studies are expected to determine more accurately the amount of water that could be economically stored and used, however.

The streams, rivers, and creeks that originate in or flow through the district are largely intermittent and supply only a small percentage of the district's total water requirements. Many of the early surface water rights along these creeks and rivers are used only occasionally because of intermittent or absent base flows. The majority of surface water rights being applied for recently are being requested from retention structures collecting rainfall runoff and irrigation tailwater.

Groundwater resources supply a large percentage of municipal, industrial, domestic, and agricultural needs. The district overlies the High Plains or the Ogallala Aquifer, which is a Tertiary, fluvially deposited silt, sand, and gravel formation ranging in thickness from 300 feet in the west to 50 feet or less in the eastern portions of the district. Because the Ogallala was deposited on a preerosional surface, the thickness of the deposit can vary significantly within a relatively short distance. The saturated thickness of the Ogallala ranges from 225 feet in the west to 30 feet or less in the east. East of the district boundary there are areas where the Ogallala formation is unsaturated. This variability in formation and saturated thickness causes special complications in developing equitable management strategies.

The U.S. Geological Survey estimates that the district has approximately 40 million acre-feet of Ogallala water in storage, with a median saturated thickness of approximately 85 feet. Alluvial deposits, generally 30 to 80 feet thick along the major streams and creeks, supply water of varying amounts to wells. These deposits do not generally exceed 50 feet in saturated thickness, but their medium-to-coarse textures often yield enough water for limited irrigation. About 3,550 wells are registered with the Division of Water Resources and approximately 902,000 acre-feet of water are currently appropriated within the district boundaries. This development has resulted in declining water-table elevations within certain areas of the district (Revised Management Program, 1991).

The other potential source of usable groundwater is the Dakota formation. Lying beneath the western half of Kansas, this Cretaceous, predominantly sandstone aquifer supplies water ranging from fresh in the southwest portions of the state and in central Kansas near its outcrop area to highly mineralized in extreme northwest Kansas. Beneath GMD No. 4, the Dakota formation is classified as "usable water" over the southern one-third of the district but is not a major source because of its depth and relatively poor quality. It ranges from 900 feet below land surface in Graham County to nearly 3,000 feet below in Cheyenne County. The Dakota is consistently 200 to 300 feet thick under GMD No. 4 and contains highly mineralized water (greater than 10,000 ppm TDS [parts per million total dissolved solids]) under the northern two-thirds of the district.

DISTRICT OPERATION AND MANAGEMENT

Once organized and funded, GMD No. 4 began to develop its first management program. It soon became evident that the district's programs, policies, and other activities were centered around four fundamental issues: water quantity, water quality, public education, and conservation, including water use efficiency. In order to implement the ideas and preferences of the board, they established a management program that was carefully organized into four sections. These covered a description of the

As pump engines are outdoors, they are exposed to the severe climate conditions of the High Plains. A farmer in Thomas County, Kansas, has provided some shelter.

district, an assessment of its problems, the programs needed to address those issues, and the rules, regulations, and policies required for implementation and enforcement of those programs.

Depletion

Increased irrigation development that ignores available groundwater reserves is a major problem in certain areas within the district. Groundwater development was sluggish from its introduction into the area until approximately 1950. Since that time the rate of development increased steadily until the early part of 1980, when it began to slow significantly. By this time, however, most of the district had been developed in excess of any safe-yield criteria, and consequently the rate of the groundwater table's decline ranged from a few inches to 2.75 feet annually. Although these overdeveloped areas are not extensive in size, several are becoming intensive in nature. Importantly, groundwater depletion eventually affects surface water base flows, which in turn adversely affect surface water rights.

The process of solving or controlling groundwater depletion is complex and necessitates a holistic approach involving the control of future development, the regulation (when necessary) of existing use, and the design and implementation of programs for augmenting water supplies.

In addressing these problems, the district encounters legal, social, and economic obstacles. The control of new development means devising a fair and equitable method of processing new requests for groundwater appropriations. First, the district must define locally acceptable limits of development and then create a policy that will not allow new appropriations to exceed those limits. In this process, direct and regional impairment of existing rights must be a consideration. Additionally, the district must devise a method to determine the amount of unappropriated water supplies and decide on the best way to manage these reserves.

Regulation of existing development may necessitate policies that encourage or mandate more efficiency in current use or that require measures designed to reduce existing appropriations within overappropriated areas to locally defined limits. Regulating existing uses could prove to be the most effective way to ease the declines, and the possibility of implementing extensive programs such as metering, resource development planning, or intensive groundwater use control areas appears realistic. The variability of saturated thickness, well densities, and withdrawal amounts poses special problems in equitably designing programs to regulate existing water rights. For example, a single standard for regulating pumpage in areas of 50 feet of saturated thickness and in 225 feet of saturated thickness will not be considered fair treatment.

The design and implementation of programs augmenting water supplies could require policies and projects entailing artificial recharge and weather modification. A third possibility, water importation, is the most technically oriented and may also prove to be the most futuristic and expensive of the three.

Since 1977 the district has developed a series of programs, policies, and regulations designed to address all aspects of the depletion problem, including the control of future development, regulation of existing water use, and the augmentation of the current resource.

Controlling Future Development

Allowable Withdrawal. Water-table declines during the late 1960s and throughout the 1970s averaged .75 to 1.5 feet per year; clearly, some course of action was needed. The board considered a number of options and finally agreed on allowable withdrawal. This policy had the advantages of restricting future development and of addressing the regional impairment issue by setting limits for declines and allowable appropriations within a designated area. The allowable withdrawal policy enables the district to recommend denial of a new water-right application if the newly granted right would cause the water table to decline faster than a designated percentage of the current saturated thickness within a 2-mile radial area surrounding the proposed well. The policy first was implemented in 1980 when the designated rate was 2 percent per year—or 40 percent depletion of the saturated thickness in twenty-years' time. It was modified to 1 percent per year in 1987, which then made it twice as difficult to obtain new rights. A 1 percent rate allows only 1,943 acre-feet of water to be appropriated from within a 2-mile radial area (8,042 acres) where the average saturated thickness is 100 feet. In approximate terms, if more than eight wells exist within 2 miles of a proposed location, no additional water rights are likely to be approved. On August 19, 1991, the directors amended the allowable withdrawal policy again, reducing the designated rate to 0 percent, or safe yield (Revised Management Program, 1991).

The allowable withdrawal policy currently in effect has prevented the appropriation of additional water rights. Quantifying the amount would be impossible since nearly all prospective appropriators requested informal determination of the availability of water before they committed themselves to the application filing fee required by law. Approximately 80 percent of these workups revealed that no additional water was available, which would have translated into a district recommendation for denial if an application had been filed. The allowable withdrawal policy for new development encountered little if any resistance; everyone seemed inherently to know that the end of unplanned new development was necessary. Minor opposition came from a few young farmers just starting out, but they never went beyond voicing their concerns.

Alluvial Development. Additional groundwater development in proximity to any streams would undoubtedly affect alluvial groundwater and base flows. The board therefore developed a policy to prohibit further nondomestic, permanent well development near existing streams. The policy prohibits the approval of additional rights within specified corridors along the streams and alluvial aquifers within the district that have any hydrologic connection to the Ogallala. The corridors range in width from 1,500 feet (3,000 feet total width) to 5,000 feet (10,000 feet total width) on either side and are set so that no stream-associated alluvial formation would be omitted. They are sufficiently wide enough that in all cases they extend beyond the true contact between the alluvial aquifers and the Ogallala.

Currently the policy covers all or parts of thirteen creeks and rivers within the district. If vertical separation between an alluvial aquifer and a deeper aquifer can be proved, the policy does not prohibit the development of the deeper aquifer, provided the well construction prevents any alluvial water from being tapped. A well log from the proposed well site showing separate static water levels is required for proof. This policy also received virtually no opposition. An ad hoc committee formed by the board to study a future zero-depletion program for all water rights has recommended enhanced management of the alluvial aquifers within the district.

Well Spacing. Since the allowable withdrawal policy should control the new development and regulate the rate of regional decline, an effective spacing policy for wells need only prevent a proposed well from directly interfering with those water rights already in existence. Since the Kansas Water Appropriation Act already prohibits unreasonable impairment by new appropriators, any policy developed would also define the limits of reasonable impairment on a local basis.

The board developed a well-spacing policy that is based on hydrologic parameters common to northwest Kansas and the Ogallala Aquifer and that uses a variable-spacing system predicated on the amount of water requested (Revised Management Program, 1991). The larger the water-rights request, the greater the spacing between wells. The requirements for the various quantities of water are

0–175 acre-feet requested = 1,400 feet spacing
176–350 acre-feet requested = 2,000 feet spacing
351–575 acre-feet requested = 2,400 feet spacing
>575 acre-feet requested = 2,800 feet spacing

Additionally, all proposed wells must be spaced 800 feet from any domestic well not owned by the applicant unless written permission granting closer placement is obtained from that domestic well's owner. When additional rights are being applied for on an existing well, the combined quantity of water under both rights (or all rights if more than two) is considered in determining the spacing.

A series of wells and Dakota aquifer wells are handled differently. Dakota wells must be spaced 5,000 feet from all other Dakota wells. A series of wells must be spaced according to the required distances, which are measured from the outside of the 300-foot radial circle centered on the wells within. When this policy was being formulated, some landowners feared that they would become "well-locked" and not be able to drill a new well, while those against irrigation believed that the distances were too lenient.

Allowable Appropriations and Reasonable Use. This policy affects future development because it allows the exercise of local discretion in establishing acceptable amounts of water that can be appropriated for various uses. The Water Appropriation Act simply requires that all requests for water be reasonable for the intended use and allows the local board to set the limits at any level either equal to or more stringent than those set by the chief engineer.

The district limits irrigation to that amount of water in acre-feet that equals 50 percent of the approved diversion rate in gallons per minute or that does not exceed two acre-feet per acre on the land proposed for irrigation—whichever is less. The maximum amount of water that municipal/industrial water users can request is based on their projected population numbers for the ensuing twenty years and on a 10 percent increase in documented per-capita-use figures. Finally, reasonable needs for the watering of stock are considered to be 15 gallons per day per head of cattle based on the maximum five-year stock population. This policy also allows the board to review and determine reasonable-use amounts for any other uses on a case-by-case basis and to use specific information that may demonstrate that the established limits are unreasonable.

Metering. Because quantified water use is important to the well owner, to the district, and to the state, the board decided to begin the process of phasing in meters on May 1, 1980. The policy requires all new wells to be metered with a state-approved flow measurement device permanently installed and properly operating any time the well is diverting water. Since new wells can be more easily metered, little opposition to this mandate arose; however, well owners have opposed metering existing wells retroactively.

Resource Development Plans. Another concept the board examined in order to control future development was water use efficiency. Before the district developed its policy, the state of Kansas deemed that beneficial use was not "wasting of water"; because irrigation was a beneficial use, it was therefore not waste as long as it was done within the water-rights limitations. Rarely, if ever, had there been a consideration of efficiency attached to the definition of waste of water or to the approval or denial of a new water-rights application.

By specifically defining waste of water within the district, the board cleared the way for applying the concept of efficiency to water use in the processing of new water rights. The Resource Development Plan (RDP) calls for the prospective applicant to submit a plan of irrigation; its efficiency is then determined. If the goals cannot be attained by implementation of the proposed plan, the water right is denied until the plan is modified to achieve those efficiencies.

In order to implement the policy, the district designed a memorandum of understanding with each soil conservation district within the GMD. The agreement calls for the conservation district to provide the technical review of a submitted plan and for the District to provide the authority for and the enforcement of the plan's implementation. To date, all RDPs have resulted in new water-rights applications achieving at least an 85 percent water-application efficiency. The district policy was the first of its kind in the state and has been incorporated into the State Water Plan and expanded to other areas of the state. This policy received little opposition during its formulation and subsequent enforcement (Memo of Understanding, 1985).

Regulating Existing Development

Tailwater Control. Historically, irrigation tailwater (pumped water that flows through the lower end of the field in order to water it adequately) was rarely collected and reused because the energy costs of delivering new water were exceptionally low. But as the groundwater declines became ever more apparent, the public began raising the issue of tailwater control; the runoff was a visible form of wasting water. In 1978 the issue was included in the management program because of public demand—the district members made it clear they wanted all irrigation water controlled, collected, and reused on the fields where it was originally applied.

This policy states that noncontrol of irrigation tailwater is not permitted; any tailwater collected that can be reused economically must be. Violations of this policy can result in the board's requiring meters and resource development plans or issuing cease-and-desist orders or in other measures deemed appropriate to ensure the control of excess irrigation water. A local enforcement mechanism for this policy has been developed and provides the process by which the board continues to regulate irrigation-tailwater control over existing systems. The aggressive enforcement has caused some consternation among irrigators caught wasting water, but most district members continue to support the policy and its enforcement.

Changes in Points of Diversion. The issues of impairment are important not only in considering new development but also in creating any policy dealing with replacement wells. Thus the board developed a policy controlling the replacement of wells for any reason. Any well may be replaced within a 300-foot radius of the original well with the filing and approval of the appropriate application for change. When the change is approved, the new location assumes the conditions and limitations of the original water right. A replacement well may also be located more than 300 feet away from the original if it is spaced appropriately from all other wells at the new location. Since each water right is authorized and perfected within a "local source of supply," no replacement well can be located more than 2,640 feet from the original well; otherwise, it would be using a different "local source of supply" and might therefore impair existing water rights.

Resource Development Plans and Metering. This policy applies to existing irrigation systems having unresolved or chronic problems with irrigation tailwater. For the first time in Kansas GMD No. 4 has the power to mandate target irrigation efficiencies for those existing systems with chronic tailwater-control problems. Metering is required not only for new water-rights applications; it also regulates existing development. For example, existing wells are subject to metering when applications for a change in point of diversion are filed.

PUBLIC EDUCATION AND INVOLVEMENT

The whole concept of local control hinges on the public's awareness of and involvement with the district. This is particularly true in the formulation of management policies and other planning. The need to marshal and maintain public interest and involvement has been recognized since the district began and will require continuing attention from the board. A well-informed and active constituency is an important goal in groundwater management. The board believes that the public needs more knowledge about local groundwater conditions and problems, water-rights administration, general water doctrine in Kansas, the role of the local districts in managing water, and the different responsibilities of the various water-related agencies in Kansas.

The mainstay of the district's educational program is a bimonthly newsletter called the *Water Table*, which has covered virtually every issue and program undertaken by the board. It also occasionally publishes research results relating to irrigation and water use and has included editorial comments from water leaders across the state and from local water users within the district. Its circulation of approximately 4,400 includes all district members and local, state, and federal water-related agencies in an attempt to broaden both its appeal and its effectiveness. The board requires that the publication serve informational needs in both directions—to and from the office. It is free to any interested person who contacts the district office.

Other efforts toward public education include radio and television messages, special appearances, speeches before service organizations, clubs, schools, and local governments, and responding to day-to-day requests for information. In the past the district manager has developed and taught a college-level, six-weeks course (for credit) covering all aspects of water rights and local groundwater management in northwest Kansas. This course, offered by the district staff through the Colby Community College Outreach program, was reviewed and approved by the State Department of Education for regional outreach education and was taught for one semester in Goodland, Colby, and Hoxie.

WATER QUALITY

The district now recognizes the availability of water of a suitable quality as a problem. Human activities are the major threat to groundwater since no natural contamination within the district has yet been identified. Specifically included in GMD No. 4's list of concerns over groundwater degradation are problems with wells and with surface activities.

Unplugged, poorly constructed, or improperly maintained wells, including water wells, oil and gas wells, all test holes, seismic holes, core holes, injection wells, disposal wells, and all other drillings and borings, have the potential to induce water unnaturally into the subsurface. Wells that do not meet state and local GMD No. 4 standards are considered to be potential threats to groundwater contamination or leakage, possibly by allowing fluid migration inside or outside the casing(s), or up or down the well or the well bore. Surface activities requiring the collection or use of any substance that could possibly influence the quality of the groundwater would include feedlots; landfills and other waste dumps; underground fuel storage facilities; oil-field tank batteries and distribution systems; and all the agricultural-related storage, handling, and use of chemicals, including elevators, chemical plants, and chemigation systems. As materials, substances, or animals collect, the potential exists for infiltration and percolation of leachates, chemicals, water soluble by-products, and other organic and inorganic substances into the subsurface and the water table (Revised Management Program, 1991).

Water Quality Monitoring Network

When the board decided to tackle the issue of water quality, it realized the need for either a monitoring network to keep track of the baseline water quality or a sampling program to locate contamination cases. It opted for a sampling network designed to look for contamination at likely points and then established a monitoring network after all the potential contamination sites and activities were located and evaluated. For example, feedlots, landfills, chemical facilities, industries, gas stations, heavy irrigation areas (chemigation), oil and gas activities, and so forth were considered. Then a monitoring grid was placed around the most likely candidate for each potential source of contamination. An appropriate number of monitoring wells were then identified, and arrangements were made with the owners for an annual sampling for specific, expected constituents based on the particular activity. If nothing is found, then the grid can be considered an early warning system for that activity since it was located where contamination was first expected. Of course, if a problem is found, then it can be dealt with and the other locations representing the same activity can then be monitored as soon as possible.

Disposition of Abandoned, Unused Wells

Abandoned and unused wells are significant contributors to groundwater contamination. It is against district policy to have an abandoned, unused water well within its boundaries. Wells must be properly constructed and active, properly constructed and capped as inactive, or abandoned and plugged.

Once an abandoned well is located, the owner is notified and asked to contact the district within two weeks to discuss its disposition. If no contact is made, a formal district order is served by registered mail, which directs the owner to handle the well properly and to report within forty-five days. If the order is ignored, the staff alerts the owner that a petition for injunction will be served after ten days; if there is still no response, an injunction is filed. All locations are tracked via a computer data base, so most deadline dates are observed. A full-time field person has been delegated to find wells, and typically five hundred or more wells in the various stages of remediation are being processed.

Well Construction—Including Inspection of New Wells

Once any water-rights application is approved, the board wants to ensure that well construction is completed properly so that groundwater mixing and contamination do not occur. Currently all new nondomestic wells completed in the district must be installed with a check valve that meets or exceeds minimum state specifications. All wells must meet minimum state construction criteria, which include 20 feet of grout behind the casing, proper venting, an adequate surface seal, strong casing, and so on. All wells completed in the Dakota Aquifer are required to be constructed so that no mixing occurs between the Dakota and any other water-bearing zone.

In 1988 the board passed a resolution that all wells completed within the district must be constructed to state specifications. Since this is now a formal policy of the district, the staff may now enforce the state drilling regulations locally. Currently, the district can issue an order requiring any well contractor to return and to complete properly any well that the staff finds inadequately constructed.

Chemigation Memorandum of Understanding

Kansas recently passed the Chemigation Safety Law, which regulates the application of agricultural chemicals through irrigation systems. The board felt that the Chemigation Act was a good start but that its adminis-tration was hampered by the lack of adequate staffing and funding—only one full-time field person was to cover the entire state, from inspections to enforcement.

The GMD No. 4 board also recognized that improper chemigation was a threat to the groundwater and that the process had to follow the specific requirements of the Safety Law. To ensure that adequate field presence and enforcement were provided in northwest Kansas, the dis-trict created a system to enhance the state's effort. The board made it a policy that all chemigation within the district must be done according to the Kansas Chemigation Safety Law and must be subject to any sub-sequent regulations adopted and passed by the regulating state agency, the Division of Plant Health, State Board of Agriculture. This action al-lowed the GMD total discretion to issue district orders locally for any chemigation unit not in compliance with state law. However, preferring to work with the agency rather than simply to enforce its law in the district, the board proposed a Memorandum of Understanding (MOU) that offered its local field assistance to locate and turn in questionable operations. The MOU also made the GMD's efficient enforcement pro-cess available to the division, at the discretion of its director. This MOU provides the director, Division of Plant Health, with two avenues of monitoring and enforcement in northwest Kansas (Revised Management Program, 1991).

Protection Planning for Public Water-Supply Wellheads

In response to the 1986 amendments to the Clean Water Act, which prop-osed that state and local governments begin protection plans for public water supplies, the board saw a great opportunity for the district to provide the local cities with an important service. They authorized the staff to draft a planning strategy in order to gain knowledge and experi-ence. With the approval of the city of Oakley, the first Kansas wellhead protection strategy was completed under the direction of the GMD. This document used the well field of Oakley as a model, determining the overall area being influenced by its pumping wells. It further inventoried all potential contamination sources and called for the city council to ad-dress each potential source with a policy, an ordinance, or some other appropriate response. Other municipalities within the district have ex-pressed an interest in adopting such a strategy.

ENFORCEMENT

The enforcement of locally developed policies could pose problems in managing remaining groundwater reserves. The district believes that local enforcement is more effective, more efficient, and less expensive than state enforcement, but it anticipates a certain percentage of cases wherein local enforcement is not going to be effective and recognizes this as a possible problem. The district also sees the potential for trouble resulting from inconsistencies in enforcement when proper coordination is lacking between state and local levels. For the district, local enforcement is a primary endeavor; at the same time, it cooperates in an enforcement program with the appropriate state agencies in those cases where such an approach is warranted.

Noncompliance, Complaints, and Inspections

The board uses its policy for noncompliance, complaints, and inspections to enforce policies locally. Any alleged violation of district policy is to be field inspected by a member of the district staff. If a violation is found, the staff person will prepare a report and a district order outlining all obligations and corrective actions necessary for the violator to undertake in order to comply with district policy within a specified time. Failure to fulfill all the requirements of the district order automatically results in the district's filing a petition in district court for an injunction.

This process has been used successfully in violations involving irrigation-tailwater, metering, and abandoned-wells and is to be used for violations involving chemigation, abandoned underground storage tanks, water use reports, and new well constructions when programs for these activities begin. Potentially, any action or situation that the board deems to be against district policy would be a candidate for this simple but effective process.

Water Diversions

All groundwater diversions within the GMD must be conducted within the scope and limits of the Kansas Water Appropriation Act and the GMD Management Program. Although it sounds innocuous, this policy provides the board with significant potential to enforce state and local policies within the district.

POLICY EVALUATION

How well are these policies working? On the issue of quantity, allowable withdrawal and the other policies have slowed the rate of well development for at least the first four years after their adoption. How many wells it has prevented cannot be quantified. Yet a definite trend indicates the

Table 9.2. Number of Water Rights Approved, 1975–1991

Year	Number	Year	Number
1975	262	1984	19
1976	341	1985	15
1977	339	1986	2
1978	158	1987	16
1979	79	1988	12
1980	58	1989	25
1981	50	1990	8
1982	32	1991	0
1983	17		

Source: GMD No. 4 Water Rights Date File.

impact these policies have had, along with other external influences such as economics and federal farm programs (Table 9.2).

This trend is also evident in the number of water-rights appropriations available for pumping. For every year since exact records have been kept, the total number of approved water rights in the district has declined (Table 9.3). Thus there are 153,475 fewer acre-feet of water appropriated today than in 1980. Actual water-table declines from approximately 350 wells have been measured annually from all over the district (Table 9.4). The water table decline rate has slowed significantly since the early years of the district.

Water-quality indicators are much more difficult to display, and normally it takes many years to demonstrate any trends. The water-quality monitoring network has completed two years of sampling, and no

Table 9.3. Appropriations and Reductions of Water Rights, 1980–1991

Year*	Total Water Rights Appropriated	Reduction from Previous Year
1980	1,053,297	
1981	1,041,656	(−11,641)
1982	1,030,761	(−10,895)
1983	1,025,406	(−5,355)
1984	1,002,193	(−23,213)
1985	986,357	(−15,836)
1986	963,246	(−23,111)
1987	911,099	(−52,147)
1988	901,939	(−9,160)
1989	Unavailable	(N/A)
1990	Unavailable	(N/A)
1991	899,822	(−2,117)
Total		(−153,475)

*As of December 31
Source: GMD No. 4 Assessment File.

Table 9.4. Decline in Water Table, 1975–1990

Year*	Average Water-Table Decline	Year	Average Water-Table Decline
1975	−2.0 feet	1983	−0.6 feet
1976	−2.0 feet	1984	−0.1 feet
1977	−2.0 feet	1985	−0.1 feet
1978	−1.6 feet	1986	+0.1 feet
1979	0.0 feet	1987	−0.1 feet
1980	−1.0 feet	1988	+0.1 feet
1981	−0.3 feet	1989	−0.8 feet
1982	+0.9 feet	1990	−0.2 feet

*As of January
Source: Kansas Geological Survey.

definite trends are recognizable other than the indication that the water quality is generally very good throughout the district.

The abandoned-well program, as of December 1990, located and processed a total of 2,249 wells. Of this total, 1,816 have been completely taken care of and archived; the rest are still in the process. Of the archived wells, 1,454 have been plugged, 156 have been capped, 62 have been reconstructed and put back into use, and 144 have been vacated as GMD errors in an aggressive and sometimes hard-to-call field program.

THE FUTURE

In the board's opinion all but one of the immediate problems originally perceived by the district have been addressed, at least to some extent. New issues may arise. Future activity will most certainly be contingent on funding and other support demonstrated not only by the district members but also by the state and federal agencies responsible for groundwater concerns. Pending such support, the board has discussed and in some cases has already begun preliminary work on these potential programs:

- a program designed to stabilize groundwater declines, called Zero Depletion, which will include policies regarding mandatory water use efficiency, metering of existing wells, and the identification of economic support programs;
- local control and regulation of underground storage tanks;
- promotion and development of public water-supply protection plans for all public water supplies within the district;

- expansion of the GWMD 1 weather modification program into northwest Kansas;
- coordination and support of a regional environmental planning consortium for NW Kansas.

These are lofty goals, yet the objective of the district is higher still. Ultimately, the board would like to develop the programs and policies of this district into a national model for a comprehensive groundwater management program at a regional level. The board believes this kind of regional approach has the best chance of adequately protecting and managing the groundwaters of the nation—one area at a time, one aquifer at a time, one state at a time. Federal or state planning and programming from the top down cannot be successful in dealing with groundwater protection and the management concerns of the nation.

REFERENCES

Groundwater Management District Act. 1978. K.S.A. 82a-1020 et seq. Topeka.
Kansas Agricultural Statistics. August 1988. *Kansas Farm Facts.* Soil surveys listing. Topeka: 1987.
Kansas Water Appropriation Act. 1985. K.S.A. 82a-701 et seq. Topeka.
Northwest Kansas Groundwater Management District. 1985. Memorandum of Agreement. GMD4/SCS. Specific to each county. Colby.
———. 1985. Rules and Regulations. Colby.
———. 1987. Revised Management Program. Colby.
———. 1988. Proper Well Construction. Resolution 88–1. Colby.
———. 1991. Revised Management Program. Colby.
United States Geological Survey. 1975–1989. "Water Levels in Western and South-Central Kansas." Lawrence.

CHAPTER TEN

Texas High Plains

Lloyd V. Urban

GROUNDWATER IN THE TEXAS HIGH PLAINS

The High Plains of Texas extends approximately 300 miles south from the Texas-Oklahoma line and covers about 35,000 square miles. The subregion of the High Plains forms part of a relatively flat plateau extending west into New Mexico; its average width in the state is approximately 120 miles. Elevation ranges from about 2,700 feet above sea level in the southeast to over 4,500 feet in the extreme northwest. The region, comprising about 11 percent of the state's land, has been characterized as consisting of "about 22 million treeless acres" with a large part (approximately 5 million acres) being used for irrigation farming that produces primarily cotton, grain sorghum, and wheat (Knowles et al. 1984). About half of the area is cultivated, with the remainder in grass and pasture.

Major population centers in the region are found along Interstate Highway 27, including Amarillo, Plainview, and Lubbock. Primary economic activities are agriculture and petroleum-based industry, and major health-care and educational facilities are located in Lubbock.

Some 17,000 playa lakes are scattered throughout the region; these are natural, shallow, undrained depressions with relatively impermeable clay-silt bottoms that occur at a frequency of approximately one to two per square mile in the southernmost reaches of the Texas High Plains and at a lesser frequency as one moves north. Although often dry, the lakes fill during wet periods. If runoff is sufficient, the lakes will spill over to the next lake downstream; as a result, the playas form a relatively complex drainage system, with flow generally toward the southeast.

The Texas High Plains is semiarid, having a dry steppe climate with mild winters. Mean annual precipitation over the area ranges from about 14 inches in the extreme northwest and southwest to about 22 inches in the east. The majority (approximately two-thirds) of the rainfall occurs just before or during the growing season. Much of the precipitation occurs as thunderstorms resulting from warm, moist tropical air carried into the area from the Gulf of Mexico or the Pacific Ocean. Thunderstorms occasionally produce tornadoes, high winds, hail, and lightning. Intensity of rainfall frequently produces localized flooding and significant runoff into the area's playa lakes.

The major water-bearing unit of the Texas High Plains is the Ogallala formation, the principal geologic unit of the High Plains aquifer (Weeks and Gutentag 1984). The formation occurs at or near the surface throughout most of the area and consists of alternating beds of silt, clay, sand, gravel, and caliche, with a maximum known thickness of over 900 feet in Ochiltree County, on the Texas-Oklahoma border. Geologists estimate that before significant development of irrigation, the Ogallala held over 500 million acre-feet of drainable water. The saturated thickness of the Texas portion of the Ogallala ranges from only a few feet to over 500 feet, with the average recently reported to be approximately 112 feet. In general, greater saturated thicknesses are found in the northern sections. The water table slopes to the southeast with a gradient of approximately 15 feet per mile (Knowles 1985). Depth to the water table varies throughout the region, with about 30 percent of the aquifer at 100 feet or less and 81 percent of the water found within 400 feet of the surface (Sweeten and Jordan 1987). Greater depths to the water table are generally found in the northern sections of the Texas High Plains. Wells in the Ogallala yield water at maximum rates, ranging from less than 100 gallons per minute (gpm) to more than 2,000 gpm (Texas Department of Water Resources 1984), but most operating irrigation and municipal water-supply wells produce in the 100-to-500-gpm range. Water quality is suitable for most uses, with dissolved solids generally ranging between 300 and 1,000 milligrams per liter (mg/l) and hardness in the "hard" category.

Two minor aquifers are found in the southern portion of the Texas High Plains, the Edwards-Trinity (High Plains) and the Santa Rosa. The state considers an aquifer as minor if it can yield large quantities of water in small areas or relatively small quantities of water in large areas. The yields from wells in these aquifers are generally low but with some notable exceptions. The quality of water from both is poor, with dissolved solids in the 1,000–10,000 mg/l range (Texas Department of Water Resources 1984).

GROUNDWATER DEVELOPMENT
IN THE TEXAS HIGH PLAINS

Until the late 1800s the human inhabitants of the Texas High Plains were primarily Indians who were adept at hunting the great herds of buffalo that roamed the plains. Spanish explorers had passed through the region in the sixteenth century, but the vast majority of would-be settlers who followed shunned the area, finding that the lack of an adequate water supply made the region uninhabitable. The playa lakes were simply too unreliable, and no other alternative was known. By the 1870s, however, the people migrating west looking for land brought with them the technical ability to discover an alternate source of water, a source found only a few feet beneath the ground. Settlers began to homestead the area and were able to satisfy the water needs of both household and livestock with hand dug wells. The emergence of the windmill on the plains was another significant step in groundwater development. Coming into general use after the Civil War, these machines could be built by farmers and ranchers or purchased ready-made from a large and ever-growing list of manufacturers. The windmill provided a means by which food could be grown in sufficient quantities, allowing the settlers to "stick it out" during prolonged drought periods (Baker 1976). The windmill also supplied the lifeblood for the expanding railroad industry in the region during the late nineteenth century, since the steam locomotives were required to replenish their water supplies periodically. With communications, trade, and transportation centered at the water stops, the Texas High Plains became dotted with settlements as the railroads crisscrossed the area.

In many years dryland farming was successful, with cotton, wheat, corn, and forage crops; yet crop failures were frequent, and the desire for a reliable supplemental water supply grew. By 1908 the first steam-driven irrigation system was constructed, and by 1914 approximately 140 such wells were providing irrigation water (Judd n.d.). Growth in the irrigation industry continued throughout the first half of the decade, with large-scale development during the 1930s, and by 1940 2,180 irrigation wells existed in the Texas High Plains (White et al. 1946). During the 1950s and early 1960s wells powered primarily by gasoline engines pumped irrigation water to crops through conventional row and furrow application. The farmers generally perceived the groundwater supply as virtually limitless, assuming the aquifer to be a vast underground river, continuously recharged with snowmelt from the Rocky Mountains. They exchanged stories about purported incidents of blind trout, artificial flies, and other such evidence from irrigation ditches—obviously brought up from irrigation wells. Moreover, they knew little about the actual water needs for crops. Thus, when it came to irrigation, "if a little was good, more was bound to be better." Such beliefs and practices coupled with relatively low energy costs for pumping resulted in application rates that were usually excessive by today's standards. For example, farmers once commonly applied over 24 inches of supplemental irrigation annually to cotton; it is now generally accepted that cotton usually needs only 12 to 18 inches.

By the 1970s an estimated 71,000 wells in the region were supplying water to approximately 6.4 million acres of irrigated land. Farmers cultivated an additional 4.1 million acres using dryland crop practices. The High Plains had become Texas' most significant agricultural region, with 34 percent of the state's total cropland in production and 69 percent of its total irrigated cropland. The cattle-feeding industry had burgeoned, and corn and vegetable production became common in the central and northern portions of the region although cotton, wheat, and grain sorghum were the most significant crops. The region supplied about 66 percent of the cotton, 53 percent of the grain sorghum, 72 percent of the wheat, and 82 percent of the feedlot cattle production in the state. This output also compared significantly with respect to the national economy; the state closed the decade of the seventies ranking first in feedlot cattle production, third in dollar value of agricultural production, and fourth in value of agricultural exports (HPUWCD No. 1 1979).

Groundwater has played an important role in the development of municipalities and industry in the region. Industrial demands include steam/electric-power generation, manufacturing, and oil and gas recovery. Until 1968, when the Canadian River Municipal Water Authority began to supply Lubbock, Amarillo, Plainview, and ultimately nine other municipalities with water from Lake Merideth, groundwater was virtually their only source of water; similarly, the White River Municipal Water Authority has been serving Crosbyton and Ralls since 1965. These municipalities continue to use groundwater for a portion of their demands, and others rely solely on groundwater.

It is generally agreed that total groundwater use peaked in the 1970s. A study by the High Plains Study Council (1982) estimated that in 1977 a total of 8.24 million acre-feet of water was withdrawn from the Ogallala. Projections of annual water use from the Ogallala were made during that study based on the assumptions that no changes in water laws would occur and that more efficient technology would be adopted as it becomes available (Table 10.1).

In a related study the U.S. Geological Survey estimated that during

Table 10.1. Projections of Annual Water Use

Year	Million Acre-Feet	Percentage of 1977
1977	8.24	100
1985	5.605	68.0
1990	3.820	46.3
2000	3.575	41.4
2020	3.235	39.2

Source: High Plains Study Council (1982).

Cotton is a major crop in the southern plains of west Texas. Cochran County.

the 1980 growing season groundwater pumped from the Texas portion of the aquifer and used for irrigation totalled 5.17 million acre-feet, second only to Nebraska (6.395 million acre-feet) and ahead of Kansas (4.130 million acre-feet). Total volume pumped from the High Plains was estimated at 17.98 million acre-feet, applied to 13.70 million acres (Heimes 1984).

GROUNDWATER PROBLEMS IN THE TEXAS HIGH PLAINS

Historically, the groundwater of the region was replenished primarily by natural infiltration from infrequent and sometimes severe precipitation and from seepage associated with the playa lakes of the region. The water table was maintained at a relatively stable level through discharge in a series of springs near the base of the escarpment, which forms the eastern edge of the southern High Plains. Under the regime of irrigation for half a century, however, the natural recharge became only a fraction of

Cotton supports a variety of economic activities: gins in Lamb County (top), an oil mill in Lubbock (middle), and a denim plant in Littlefield (bottom).

the draft, and a commensurate drop in the water table and a reduction or an elimination of the spring flow resulted.

Among the first to recognize and document the extent of the problem was the Texas Board of Water Engineers; in 1954 it published maps depicting the decline of the water table in the Lubbock-Amarillo region. Over the period extending from March 1938 to January 1953 declines of 5 to 25 feet were common, with one area in Floyd County experiencing a drop of over 50 feet (Leggat 1954a). The board reported that in the following twelve months, most of this same area typically experienced declines of 2 to 6 feet, with water-table levels in several localities falling 10 feet or more (Leggat 1954b). Continued increases in irrigation and domestic demands over the ensuing decades caused further decline in the water table, bringing about concern among the agricultural, municipal, and industrial sectors. Irrigators saw the problem as affecting their own and their children's future; feedlot operators perceived a similar problem, and the siting of new operations and the phasing out of others resulted. Many municipalities using groundwater as their sole source of supply sought alternatives, leading to the development of surface supplies. Others sought supplemental groundwater rights, sometimes at considerable distance and expense. Lubbock, for example, supplements its summer supply from a well field near Muleshoe, some 90 miles to the northwest. Industrial users have been less affected although many, such as those in petroleum and power, have been forced to seek alternative solutions.

As the quantity of any resource becomes limited, its quality takes on an added degree of importance; water in the Texas High Plains is no exception. Improper protection and maintenance of the water quality in the Ogallala clearly can reduce the supply further and can increase the cost of consumption. Again, the agricultural, municipal, and industrial sectors share the general concerns. Ogallala groundwater is acceptable for the principle crops grown in the area—cotton, grain sorghum, corn, wheat, and vegetables—and for the watering of livestock. Ongoing issues in the agricultural sector include the potential impact on groundwater quality from agricultural chemicals (pesticides, herbicides, fertilizers, and so on) and from the runoff from livestock-feeding operations. To date, however, fears of widespread contamination from these sources appear to be unfounded.

Issues concerning the municipal sector are essentially the same as those affecting municipalities anywhere—safe drinking water, wastewater treatment and disposal, landfills, storm water, leaking petroleum storage tanks, and so forth. With respect to human consumption, Ogallala water in the Texas High Plains appears to have both good and bad characteristics. With its hard water, the region has one of the lowest cerebrovascular death rates in the United States—a characteristic often associated with areas having relatively hard water. On the other hand, Ogallala water in the region often contains very high concentrations of fluoride. Within a range of 0.6 to 1.0 ppm, fluoride protects against cavities, but amounts in excess of 1.0 ppm frequently cause discoloration of permanent teeth (Sweazy et al. 1978). Other concerns include questions about nitrates, radon, lead, and uranium.

Since Ogallala groundwater is generally hard, scaling is often a problem with boilers, water heaters, and laundry machines. In fact, it is not recommended for boilers, electroplating, tanning, dyeing, or textile manufacturing without treatment because of its high calcium or magnesium content or both (Sweazy et al. 1978). The potential effects of industry on water quality include petrochemical wastes, brine contamination from oil and gas production, and leaking storage tanks.

SOLUTIONS TO GROUNDWATER PROBLEMS IN THE TEXAS HIGH PLAINS

As the scientific community began to understand the nature and extent of the dwindling water supplies, the challenge grew to inform and educate the public, to initiate programs for conserving remaining supplies, and to seek long-range solutions to the problem. Water importation was one of the first alternatives considered for solving the region's shortage. In the late 1960s and into the 1970s residents responded with great enthusiasm to proposals ranging from the importation of water from the Mississippi River to west Texas and eastern New Mexico to the transfer of water from Canada to most of the western United States and Mexico. Water, Incorporated, was organized in west Texas and headquartered in Lubbock for the express purpose of encouraging political action and scholarly study of the feasibility of water importation (Urban and Whetstone 1987). The 1968 Texas Water Plan, developed and adopted by the Texas Water Development Board, called for the construction of sixty-seven major reservoirs and three major diversion arteries to form the "Texas Water System." A major component of the plan included the delivery of approximately 9 million acre-feet of water annually to west Texas and New Mexico from east Texas (Texas Water Development Board 1968). When the $9 billion plan came before the electorate in 1969, the voters were asked to consider the authorization of $3.5 billion in water-development bonds to finance the project, with the federal government bearing the remainder of the cost. Only 18 percent of the state's 3.5 million voters participated, and they defeated the issue by 6,277 votes (Rayner 1969). The U.S. Army Corps of Engineers reintroduced the issue in a report to the Six-State High Plains Ogallala Aquifer Regional Resources Study. Four routes were considered, with results indicating that 1.26 to 8.68 million acre-feet per year of imported water could be delivered to the Texas High Plains for costs (using 1981 energy prices in 1977 dollars) ranging from $430 to $569 per acre-foot (High Plains Associates 1982).

Because of the high costs and the political realities of water importation, even its most avid proponents have lost their enthusiasm. In the 1970s alternative solutions to the problems of a decreasing water supply began to take on an increasingly important role; water conservation was in the forefront. Farmers in the area learned to combine the natural precipitation with reduced draft on their underground water to save fuel and to conserve their groundwater supply. They were aided by extensive research on the local, state, federal, and international levels that was interpreted and taught in the schools and in field demonstrations by local underground water conservation districts and extension services. Conservation practices included

- close regulation of flow in furrows by dikes, which eliminate soil erosion and provide more uniform water distribution;
- recovery by low lift pumping of tailwater that escapes the ends of furrows and collects in playa lakes or constructed tailwater pits;
- irrigation by employment of alternative furrows;
- soil moisture testing to avoid excessive application of irrigation water;
- the employment of sprinkler systems with well-designed nozzles and drop lines that minimize evaporation of the water droplets between nozzle and furrow;
- conservation tillage in which herbicides are employed to minimize the loss of moisture that results from cultivation;
- basin tillage to facilitate the retention of rainfall;
- terracing and leveling to restrict runoff;
- use of underground pipelines to avoid the evaporation and deep percolation of open ditches.

In the municipalities of the region, long-range planning strategies have focused primarily upon acquisition of both surface and groundwater rights, often at a considerable distance. In some cases, the cost of conveyance of water from distant sources has led to the use of larger than immediately necessary pipelines in order to avoid subsequent expansion. Water use (with subsequent billing) rather than conservation is encouraged in order to help pay for the system and its operating costs. Fortunately, however, municipal residents in the region have generally developed a sound conservation ethic and are not prone to use water excessively or to waste it. In addition, recent activity by the Texas Water De-

Littlefield is a prosperous farm service center based on irrigated crops in west Texas.

velopment Board indicates that municipal water conservation will be emphasized statewide in the near future.

Most municipalities in the region practice some form of reuse of wastewater, with most of the effluent applied in irrigation. With the exception of some locally important water-reuse programs (e.g., wastewater reuse for cooling in steam-driven power plants), regional industry has not had a major impact on water conservation. Since problems of water quality are relatively new to the Texas High Plains, solutions to date have focused on addressing specific problems (point sources, leaking storage tanks, accidental spills, disposal sites, and so on) and the collection of data.

TEXAS GROUNDWATER LAW

Groundwaters of the state are divided into two legal classes: water flowing in definite underground streams and percolating groundwater (Hutchins 1961). Since it is quite difficult to prove the existence of water in underground streams, Texas courts presume that all groundwater is percolating (Templer 1983a).

Texas groundwater law is based on the English common-law rule of absolute ownership, giving the overlying landowners the right to capture and use percolating groundwater beneath their land. In 1904 the Texas Supreme Court firmly established the common-law doctrine in *Houston and T. C. Ry. Co. v. East*. Considering groundwater's existence, origin, and movement to be "secret, occult and concealed," the court ruled that it would be "practically impossible" to regulate it by any other means. Originally adopted in many western states (but not in Texas), this doctrine was subsequently replaced either by the prior appropriation doctrine or by modifications of the common-law doctrine that limited the extent of individual landowner rights (Templer 1983a). Subsequent court decisions have resulted in only minor modifications but have established that landowners can sell their groundwater rights, that groundwater can be used on the land from which it was pumped or at some other location, and that all groundwater is presumed to be percolating unless proved to be flowing in an underground stream, of which no claim has been sustained in the courts (Templer 1987).

Because Texas groundwater law remained one of strict common-law rule, separate and distinct from Texas surface water law, it has been termed "judge-made law" and "law of the biggest pump." Lacking any legal mechanism to control groundwater pumping effectively, Texas groundwater law permits one landowner to "dry up" an adjoining landowner's well, leaving the latter without legal recourse (Kaiser 1986). Exceptions to the absolute-owner rule have evolved. Kaiser (1986) described five situations in which an affected landowner may legally claim interference with his/her ground water rights:

1. If an adjoining neighbor trespasses on the land to remove water either by drilling a well directly on the landowner's property or by drilling a "slant" well on adjoining property so that it crosses the subterranean property line, the injured landowner can sue for trespass;
2. if there is malicious or wanton conduct in pumping water for the sole purpose of injuring an adjoining landowner;
3. if landowners waste artesian well water by allowing it to run off their land or to percolate back into the water table;
4. if there is contamination of water in a landowner's well. No one is allowed to unlawfully pollute groundwater;
5. if land subsidence and surface injury result from negligent overpumping from adjoining lands.

With Texas groundwater law "encouraging a race for the available water supply" among competing landowners, excessive pumping and wasteful practices are encouraged (Templer 1983b). The potential problem was well recognized by the 1930s, when irrigation with groundwater first became widely practiced. Legislation to alleviate the situation was unsuccessfully introduced in 1937, 1939, 1941, and 1947. In 1949 a statute established considerable local control through groundwater districts, but the validity of private ownership was upheld (Templer 1983a). Many proposals for revising and reforming Texas groundwater law have been initiated since 1949, with the most significant revisions becoming law in 1985 and 1989. As in 1949, these revisions dealt with the creation and powers of local management districts.

GROUNDWATER MANAGEMENT

The Texas Legislature authorized the creation of underground water conservation districts in 1949. Referred to as "chapter 52 of the Texas Water Code," the statute provided a mechanism for exercising control over landowner's rights. Underground water districts could be created to provide for the conservation, preservation, protection, recharging, and prevention of waste of underground water in reservoirs or in their subdivisions. In addition to these "general law districts," other "special law districts," such as those needed to control subsidence caused by withdrawal of groundwater, were created. Prior to 1985, only twelve districts existed in the entire state; none exercised its potential for complete regulatory authority or attempted to control groundwater production directly (Templer 1987). According to the Texas Water Commission (1989), six districts had been created in the Texas High Plains by 1985 (see Figure 5.1).

The 1985 legislation provided considerable impetus for the creation of general-law districts by eliminating the requirement that district boundaries coincide with an aquifer or an aquifer's subdivision, by allowing other factors such as political boundaries to be considered, and by expanding the powers of general-law districts to sell and distribute surface or groundwater and to exercise some power of eminent domain. Perhaps the greatest driving force was the authorization of the Texas Water Commission and the Texas Water Development Board to identify and delineate "critical" groundwater areas in the state and to promote the creation of underground water conservation districts in these areas. In order to give this provision teeth, the legislation prohibits any political subdivision in designated critical areas where voters have rejected state financial assistance for district water projects. The provision apparently had a significant effect; by the end of 1987 twenty-two underground water conservation districts were in operation, and an additional thirteen were authorized during the Seventy-first Legislature in 1989.

The recent trend is toward single-county districts. Districts are governed by an elected five-member board of directors, and when multiple counties (or portions of counties) are included, representation at the county level may be added. Each district has a manager, hired by the board of directors to carry out the day-to-day operations, and additional staff, depending on the level of activity in the district.

Districts are charged with mandatory duties dictating that they must

- develop comprehensive plans for water use and the control and prevention of waste and subsidence;
- require records to be kept of the drilling, equipping, and completion of water wells and the production and use of groundwater;
- require that driller's logs of water wells be kept and filed with the district;
- require permits for well drilling, equipping and completion of wells producing more than 25,000 gallons per day or for alterations to well size or pumps;
- publish rules;
- provide an annual report to the Texas Water Commission;
- operate on the basis of a fiscal year;
- have an audit of financial accounts prepared annually;
- prepare, hold a public hearing on, and approve an annual budget (Jonish et al. 1989).

Many duties and activities are simply encouraged:

- to make and enforce rules for conserving, preserving, protecting, recharging, and preventing waste of groundwater;
- to conduct surveys and collect data on aquifers, groundwater production facilities, and groundwater use;
- to conduct research;
- to engage in recharge operations;
- to regulate well spacing and production;
- to enforce rules by injunction or other appropriate means;
- to levy taxes on an annual basis to pay bonds and/or operating and maintenance expenses (Jonish et al. 1989).

In actual practice the programs and activities vary with the individual district's size, resources, management and staff, and major issues of concern. Jonish et al (1989) described some typical programs.

Well Permitting. Permitting of wells is accomplished through an application process; a typical form provides information on the proposed well's location, the landowner's name and address, the well's size and expected production rate, a legal description of the property, and the distance to legal boundaries and adjacent wells. Other forms are used to register wells and to acquire well logs and information about the well's construction and equipment. Such information becomes particularly useful to districts in developing and maintaining a data base to facilitate programs and objectives.

Water-Well Inventories. New or newly annexed districts present a particular problem since a complete, accurate inventory of all wells is essential for accomplishing objectives. Common methods for developing a water-well inventory include ownership reports based on questionnaires mailed to all landowners in the district, physical inspection through visits to each landowner and parcel of land in the district, aerial photographs and existing maps, and the well-permitting process. Most districts use some combination of these techniques and a computer-based system for storing and cross-indexing inventory files.

Well Spacing and Production. Since districts are permitted to regulate the spacing and the production of wells, those in the Texas High Plains exercise that option primarily to minimize the drawdown of the water table and to prevent waste. Regulation depends upon district rules and is a responsibility not taken lightly. Considerable studies on the effect of well spacing or the limitation of production typically precede formal rule-making. Rules generally cover the minimum distance from other wells or authorized well sites, the minimum distance from property lines, and the maximum number of wells in a specified area of land. Other options or refinements may be included, such as incorporating pump sizes into a formula for determining minimum distances or setting allowable cumulative production rates, although this is not currently practiced in districts on the Texas High Plains.

Abandoned Wells. As with other districts throughout the High Plains, districts in the Texas High Plains consider abandoned water wells to be a safety hazard and one of the greatest sources of groundwater contamination. Abandoned wells are regulated by the Texas Water Commission through its Underground Injection Control (UIC) program and by the Texas Water Well Drillers Board. Districts have become actively involved in open-hole location and in closing programs and are encouraged to establish rules requiring proper closing or capping, involve district staff in identifying and locating abandoned wells, involve the public in district-wide programs, establish active search programs, conduct site investigations, and ensure that abandoned wells are properly closed or capped.

Public Information/Education. Most districts appreciate the benefits of an active information/education program, and the High Plains Underground Water Conservation District No. 1, headquartered in Lubbock, provides a prime example, with its informational and educational programs and materials. The key to its informational program is a monthly newsletter, the *Cross Section*. With a circulation exceeding six thousand, the publication informs district residents, legislators, agency personnel, and other leaders and subscribers of the district's programs and activities. The district also relies on special mailings, news releases, and radio public-service announcements and actively participates in education programs for public schools from kindergarten through high school, using original educational materials such as activities booklets, comic books, supplementary textbooks, and water resources/conservation packets. District informational projects include presentations to service clubs and professional groups, informative displays at fairs and livestock shows, technical reports and brochures, and a series of "Water Management Notes" addressing specific techniques of water conservation.

Technical Assistance. Districts are in a unique position to develop expertise, data, and technical assistance for a wide range of potential users. Irrigators depend on the districts for planning new wells, planning for production from new or existing wells, and in making decisions about irrigation and its related equipment and management. The general public relies heavily on districts for answers to questions on drinking water, industrial supplies, and water quality. Lending institutions often turn to districts for information used in determining approval for loans. Other requests for data or for technical assistance can originate from conservation groups, educational institutions, or federal, state, and local agencies.

Conservation. District activities often center on conservation programs, and those in the Texas High Plains tend to focus on agriculture, since farmers are the biggest users and therefore have the greatest potential impact on water savings. Programs to inform irrigators about conservation techniques through demonstrations and services such as soil-moisture monitoring and pump-plant or irrigation-application efficiency testing or both are effective. Districts are also encouraged to target residential, industrial, and municipal sectors through public education, technical assistance, and voluntary or mandatory conservation programs.

Monitoring Water Quantity and Quality. An important function for most Texas High Plains districts entails developing and maintaining a data base of information on water quantity. Instead of attempting to monitor individual wells, district managers think that better information is obtained by measuring the annual changes in the saturated thickness of the aquifer. The district then uses the changes to determine the state of the aquifer, to project future supplies, and to develop goals, plans, and programs. Some districts are also actively involved in monitoring water quality by working with state agencies (e.g., the Railroad Commission, the Water Commission, the Water Development Board, the Department of Agriculture, and the Department of Health) and by developing in-house techniques for sampling and analysis. Because of the expense and training requirements, in-house programs are usually limited.

Research and Enhancement Projects. Chapter 52 of the Texas Water Code authorizes districts to carry out research projects, particularly in the area of artificial recharge. Districts may support such programs through direct or partial financing, cooperative efforts, or with technical assistance and other forms of support.

Although significant progress has been made in groundwater management in the Texas High Plains over the past few decades, new programs and trends are evolving, including augmentation (increasing the supply of available water), conservation (reducing demands and increasing the efficiency of use of water), and protection (preventing pollution and enhancing the quality of existing supplies).

Among those organizations actively involved in this research and development are the High Plains Underground Water Conservation District No. 1, the Water Resources Center at Texas Tech University, the Texas Water Development Board, the Texas Water Commission, and the Texas Agricultural Experiment Station.

Weather Modification. Although not a new concept, precipitation enhancement, or weather modification, continues to be viewed as a potentially significant tool for augmenting surface and groundwater in the Texas High Plains. Numerous studies have been conducted at various locations throughout the region since 1970, and data indicate that cloud seeding with silver iodide can be effective in reducing irrigation demands, increasing stream-flow and supplies in surface water reservoirs, and increasing crop yields. In one study that included all or parts of seven counties overlying the extreme southern Ogallala, an increase ranging from two to six inches in annual precipitation was noted from 1980 to 1987 compared to the thirty-year norm. (Kastner et al. 1989). A coincident rise in the water table in the area was measured and attributed to the increase in precipitation and attendant reduction in groundwater pumping.

Artificial Recharge. A significant amount of water in playa lakes throughout the region is soon lost through evaporation. With an estimated seventeen thousand playas typically capturing from 1.8 to 5.7 million acre-feet/year of runoff, an estimated 30 to 60 percent evaporation loss becomes momentous (Urban et al. 1990). Residents and researchers in the area have long recognized the potential for using storm water collected in playas for artificial recharge, but numerous attempts to capitalize on this potential through the use of wells, pits, and other techniques have run into problems. For example, the water normally contains particles of silt and clay held in suspension through wind and wave action, and such particles readily clog the receiving formation or recharge basin.

Since its inception in 1965 the Texas Tech University Water Resources Center has devoted considerable research to seeking practical solutions to this problem. Currently it is attempting to create technologies to use recently developed, commercially available geotextile materials in a system to recharge playa-lake waters quickly, efficiently, and economically before significant evaporation loss occurs. By incorporating these filtering materials in shallow trenches backfilled with sand and a thin 6-inch layer of original playa-bed material, researchers were able to achieve flow rates into a recharge well of 35 to 200 gallons per minute from three different configurations of test systems (Urban et al. 1989). Subsequent studies have indicated that a typical playa could be used to recharge from 20 to 50 acre-feet of generally good quality water, which would be available for future use at the same location (Urban et al. 1990).

Secondary Recovery of Groundwater. Spaces between the clay, silt sand, and gravel in a groundwater-producing formation may be completely saturated. As water is removed from an unconfined aquifer, gravity causes some of the water to drain down to replace that which was extracted, resulting in a lowering of the water table. It is generally known that considerable water remains in the "dewatered" zone but is held in a thin layer surrounding individual particles by forces such as surface tension. In the Ogallala formation, researchers found that approximately as much water remained in the dewatered zone as that amount drained by gravity. From 1980 to 1985 the Texas Water Development Board sponsored a project by the High Plains Underground Water Conservation District No. 1 in cooperation with the Water Resources Center at Texas Tech, Texas A & M University, and the Texas A & M Agricultural Experiment Station to investigate the use of artificial means to gain access to the water in the dewatered zone. Several approaches were evaluated; the technique determined to be the most promising incorporated the use of air pressure applied beneath semiimpermeable formations above the water table. Termed "secondary recovery of groundwater," since the approach is similar to that successfully employed in petroleum production, the method was found to be successful in laboratory and field tests at three locations. In addition to being technically workable, the system appears to be economically feasible for purposes of municipal and industrial water supply (Texas Water Development Board 1985).

Financing Conservation Improvements. Although much good work has been done in the development of equipment and techniques for promoting agricultural water conservation and in programs to demonstrate their availability, use, and effectiveness to potential users, the expense of the required capital equipment often inhibits widespread application. To further such efforts, groundwater districts may provide assistance through loan or grant programs.

Loan programs are designed to provide funds at relatively low-interest rates to qualified applicants. In an outstanding example of a loan program, the High Plains Underground Water Conservation District No. 1, using monies from the Texas Water Development Board's Agricultural Water Conservation Loan Program, loaned approximately $5.5 million between 1986 and 1990. The loans were used to help farmers purchase approximately $7.7 million in equipment, including center pivot sprinkler systems, surge-irrigation systems, furrow dikers, soil moisture monitoring equipment, computer software for use in irrigation scheduling, and laser land-leveling equipment. Grants, on the other hand, do not require repayment and are funds consigned from one agency or party to another. Districts may use funds originating from the district budget or may seek grants from other agencies or sources such as the Texas Water Commission and the Texas Water Development Board.

OUTLOOK FOR THE FUTURE

Groundwater and its use in the Texas High Plains continue to be essential to the long-term economic viability of the region. Although a considerable portion of the "original" amount in storage has been depleted through pumpage in excess of natural recharge, significant quantities remain. Through the programs of underground water conservation districts, agricultural experiment stations, universities, and state and local agencies, problems associated with water quantity and quality have been identified and documented, programs for addressing major concerns have been established, and research and development of new concepts and programs are being advanced. Residents of the area are keenly aware of the importance of groundwater and are highly supportive of programs and efforts designed to augment, conserve, and protect existing supplies. When it comes to groundwater and the outlook for the future, residents of the Texas High Plains are convinced that although many mistakes have been made in the past it is by no means too late. They are resolute in their conviction that this part of the country will not dry up and blow away; the hard part is convincing outsiders that "this just ain't so!"

REFERENCES

Baker, T. Lindsay. 1976. "History of Water Supply Projects in the Southwest." In Robert M. Sweazy, ed., *Water Utilization Studies in the Dry Lands*. International Center for Arid and Semi-Arid Land Studies. Lubbock: Texas Tech University.

Heimes, Frederick J. 1984. "The High Plains Regional Aquifer—Estimating 1980 Ground-Water Pumpage for Irrigation." In George A. Whetstone, ed., *Proceedings of the Ogallala Aquifer Symposium II*. Water Resources Center. Lubbock: Texas Tech University.

High Plains Associates. 1982. "Six-State High Plains Ogallala Aquifer Regional Resources Study." Austin, Tex.

High Plains Underground Water Conservation District (HPUWCD) No. 1 and Texas Department of Water Resources. 1979. "A Summary of Techniques and Management Practices for Profitable Water Conservation on the Texas High Plains." Report 79-01. Lubbock, Texas.

Houston and T. C. Ry. Co. v. East. 1904. 98 Tex. 146, 81 SW 279. Tex. Sup. Ct.

Hutchins, Wells A. 1961. "The Texas Law of Water Rights." Board of Water Engineers. Austin, Tex.

Jonish, James E., Bill Klemt, Lloyd V. Urban, and A. Wayne Wyatt, eds. 1989. *Groundwater Conservation District Operations Manual*. Vols. 1 and 2. Water Resources Center. Lubbock: Texas Tech University.

Judd, Patricia F. (No date.) "An Introduction to Water and Water Conservation with Emphasis on the High Plains of Texas." High Plains Underground Water Conservation District No. 1. Lubbock, Tex.

Kaiser, J. D. 1986. "Handbook of Texas Water Law: Problems and Needs." Water Resources Institute. College Station, Tex.

Kastner, William M., D. E. Schild, and D. S. Spahr. 1989. "Water-level Changes in the High Plains Aquifer Underlying Parts of South Dakota, Wyoming, Nebraska, Colorado, Kansas, New Mexico, Oklahoma, and Texas: Predevelopment Through Nonirrigation Season 1987–88." Water Resources Investigation Report 89-4073. Denver, Colo.: U.S. Geological Survey.

Knowles, Tommy. 1985. "The Ogallala Aquifer—Facts and Fallacies." In *Issues in Groundwater Management*, ed., E. T. Smerdon and W. R. Jordan. Austin: Center for Research in Water Resources, University of Texas.

Knowles, Tommy, Phillip Nordstrom, and William B. Klemt. 1984. "Evaluating the Ground-Water Resources of the High Plains of Texas, Vol. 1." Department of Water Resources. Austin, Tex.

Leggat, E. R. 1954a. "Summary of Ground-Water Development in the Southern High Plains, Texas." Board of Water Engineers Bulletin No. 5402 (Feb. 1954). Austin, Tex.

———. 1954b. "Ground-Water Development in the Southern High Plains, Texas, 1953." Board of Water Engineers Bulletin No. 5410 (July 1954). Austin, Tex.

Rayner, F. A. 1969. "Apathy Defeats Amendment 2." *Cross Section* 15, 15. High Plains Underground Water Conservation District No. 1. Lubbock, Tex.

Sweazy, Robert M., Lloyd V. Urban, C. C. Reeves, Jr., and George A. Whetstone. 1978. "Groundwater Resources of the Texas High Plains: State-of-the-Art and Future Research Needs." Water Resources Center. Lubbock: Texas Tech University.

Sweeten, John M., and Wayne R. Jordan. 1987. "Irrigation Water Management for the Texas High Plains: A Research Summary." Water Resources Institute. College Station, Tex.

Templer, Otis W. 1983a. "Groundwater Management Institutions in Texas." In R. J. Charbeneau, ed., *Proceedings of the Regional and State Water Resources Planning and Management Symposium*. Washington, D.C.: American Water Resources Association.

———. 1983b. "Legal Constraints on Water Resource Management in Texas." *Environmental Professional*. Vol. 5. New York: Pergamon Press.

————. 1987. "The 1985 Water Legislation and Groundwater Management in Texas." In James E. Jonish, ed., *Proceedings of the Association for Arid Lands Studies Annual Meeting*. El Paso, Tex. April 22–25.

Texas Department of Water Resources. 1984. "Water for Texas—A Comprehensive Plan for the Future, Vols. 1 and 2." Austin.

Texas Water Commission. 1989. "Underground Water Conservation Districts." Report to the Seventy-first Legislature. Austin.

Texas Water Development Board. 1968. "The Texas Water Plan." Austin.

————. 1985. "Investigation of the Feasibility of Secondary Recovery of Ground Water from the Ogallala Aquifer." Report to the Sixty-ninth Legislature. Austin.

Urban, Lloyd V., B. J. Claborn, and R. H. Ramsey. 1989. "Aquifer Recharge Utilizing Playa Lake Water and Filter Underdrains." Water Resources Center. Lubbock: Texas Tech University.

Urban, Lloyd V., R. H. Ramsey, and B. J. Claborn. 1990. "Artificial Recharge in the Southern Ogallala—Experiences with Playa Lake Water and Filter Under-drains." *Proceedings of the 1990 National Conference*. Sponsored by the Irrigation and Drainage Division of the American Society of Civil Engineers. Durango, Colo. July 11–13.

Urban, Lloyd V., and George A. Whetstone. 1987. In Jonish, ed., "Stretching the Ogallala: Technical Alternatives versus Economic Realities." *Proceedings of the Association for Arid Lands Studies Annual Meeting*. El Paso, Tex. April 22–25.

Weeks, John B., and Edwin Gutentag. 1984. "The High Plains Regional Aquifer—Geohydrology." In Whetstone, ed., *Proceedings of the Ogallala Aquifer Symposium II*. Water Resources Center. Lubbock: Texas Tech University.

White, W. N., W. L. Broadhurst, and J. W. Lang. 1946. "Groundwater in the High Plains of Texas." U.S. Geological Survey Water Supply Paper 889-F.

CHAPTER ELEVEN

Future Prospects

David E. Kromm and Stephen E. White

The High Plains is a region of constant change. This may be true of all places to some extent, but the High Plains is characterized by our changing perceptions of the region as well as by the realities of change. It has been an irrigated garden and a dust bowl. Humid times alternate with desert-like periods. The changes reflect instability in both the environmental and the human spheres, and land use reveals much of the change. Irrigated acres continue to decline in all states but not in all counties. Measures of economic and social vitality in the High Plains denote both growth and decline. Most counties that are stable or expanding share the commonality of sufficient water to sustain irrigation.

Two very different regions coexist in the High Plains, and their disparities may continue to widen in the future. One enjoys prosperous farms and service centers, relatively strong economic activity, and a sense of well-being. The other shrinks economically and demographically; each year fewer farmers come to town and more windows are boarded up on Main Street. Where irrigation is based on physically and economically dependable water supplies, much goes on. Implement and truck dealers flourish; town centers look alive; seed factories, beef processing plants, and other agriculturally related manufacturing enterprises thrive. Schools with modern playground equipment and well-supplied classrooms bustle with children. Where irrigation has sharply declined far less is happening. The shops and stores that remain open always seem to need a coat of paint; potholes deepen and weeds grow. Yet there is a middle ground, often outside the irrigation economy. Communities in the High Plains where irrigation never formed the economic base fare much like farm towns elsewhere, with a gradual decline for many and stability for few.

In considering the future in the High Plains, we believe that the availability of water is the key to economic survival in much of the region. Sustainability is the basic issue. Can the availability, the economical use, and the quality of water be sustained? For each negative answer in a given county or cluster of counties, a future of decline becomes more likely. The inevitable process previously experienced in other areas where irrigation could not be sustained will occur. The problem therefore centers on determining which counties cannot continue to irrigate at substantial levels.

The water limits are most serious in the southern reaches of the High Plains and least so in the north. Texas, New Mexico, and Oklahoma are most likely to experience the greatest groundwater depletion and the most significant reduction in irrigation, resulting in large areas of economic and population loss. Areas of Nebraska, with its substantial groundwater reserves and a modest depth to the water table, will fare much better. As an increasing proportion of feed-grains are grown in Nebraska, expansion in feedlots will probably take place there. Investment in large feedlots is high and they are not very mobile; thus many will remain where they are.

Beef-processing plants would be even less likely to move. The large feedyards and packing plants of western Kansas are close enough to the relatively expanding feedgrains of Nebraska to remain where they are. Cotton will continue to support gins and a denim mill further south, but an increasing proportion will be grown dryland. We expect that the highest percentage of small towns to remain vital will be in the Platte River valley of Nebraska and in southwestern Kansas and north Texas, between Lubbock and Amarillo. Small towns closely tied to nonagricultural activities such as the petroleum industry or the provision of services associated with interstates and other highways are also likely to prosper. In general, areas will grow if they have added people over the past twenty years as a result of irrigation expansion and if they have gained advantages in economy of scale and agglomeration at the expense of their less fortunate neighboring counties.

THE IRRIGATOR'S PERSPECTIVE

A multitude of concerns hover about the future of agriculture, regional economic viability, demographic stability, and the sustainability of many communities throughout the Ogallala region; much of it centers on irrigation. High Plains irrigators are generally more optimistic than pessimistic about the economic future of their home counties. In a ten-county survey conducted by the editors, 672 irrigators responded to the following statement: "As compared with the past five years, I believe that the economic future of my county over the next five years will be much better, slightly better, about the same, slightly worse, or much worse." Over 46 percent indicated that the future would be either much better or slightly better. About 40 percent said the future would be about the same as the past five years, and less than 14 percent felt that economic conditions would get worse.

Optimism varies substantially according to place. It was greatest in Dawson County, Nebraska, where more than 67 percent of the irrigators thought that the future would improve and was lowest in Wichita County, Kansas, where only 31 percent shared that view. Interestingly, Dawson County, located in the Platte River valley, has the greatest water availability; Wichita County has encountered the most severe depletion problems among the ten counties surveyed. Although ten counties constitute a small sample, the results suggest that a positive correlation exists between level of optimism and water availability.

The irrigator is the key agent in any program to extend the life of the aquifer, and most irrigation farmers take the responsibility seriously. Nine out of ten of those we surveyed believed that they should voluntarily conserve groundwater. Nonetheless, the respondents ranked low crop prices and high energy costs as concerns more important than groundwater depletion. Almost half the irrigators indicated that groundwater quality is more important than depletion, and less than half (37.1 percent) thought that local, state, or federal governments should do more to encourage groundwater conservation (Kromm and White 1990a). In short, irrigators feel a need to conserve, but groundwater depletion is not their most important worry. Unless energy costs decrease and crop prices increase sharply, the irrigator's concern about groundwater depletion will probably not change much in the future.

Irrigators are adopting a wide assortment of water-saving practices. The typical irrigator uses an average of nine methods from among a list of thirty-nine possibilities listed in a survey. Many of the technologies to conserve water in the High Plains were discussed by Musick and Stewart (see chap. 6) and are generally available to irrigators throughout the region. The information base is not uniform, however, and practices used widely in one area are almost ignored in other places. We have found that location explains this variability better than socioeconomic characteristics, farm variables, or hydrologic characteristics (Kromm and White 1990b). Irrigators do different things at different locations, and more work is needed to understand the diffusion of water-saving practices so that the information can be distributed uniformly, the optimal mix of practices adopted, and conservation efforts encouraged (Kromm and White 1991).

What prompts efforts to conserve groundwater? Depth to water is strongly associated with whether or not irrigators adopt water-saving practices, whereas the amount of water as measured by saturated thickness of the aquifer is not (Kromm and White 1990b). Conservation efforts result more from the high costs of energy than a from fear of a declining aquifer. Irrigators who pump water from over 200 feet and pay higher energy bills are more likely to adopt water-saving practices than those who have less water that is nearer the surface. In our past research we found that a majority of irrigators adopted water-saving practices to conserve energy, to reduce labor, and to increase yields or when they had to replace existing equipment—not just specifically to save water, although saving water was viewed as a positive advantage. Perhaps an effective way to promote future water conservation in the High Plains would be to encourage high energy costs, even though it is an unrealistic and unpopular suggestion. Efforts to conserve water in the future may be affected by at least four forces: (1) external agribusiness variables such as energy costs, interest rates, and crop prices; (2) irrigators' attitudes and predisposition to conserve; (3) the legal basis for administering and restricting water use; and (4) the effectiveness of local groundwater management institutions and policies. In designing and enforcing restrictions, institutions and water law vary significantly in the High Plains as Templer and Roberts point out (see chaps. 4 and 5).

In some areas, past legislation may discourage water conservation. Duncan (1987) has argued that irrigators operate within a legal framework that sometimes encourages depletion rather than conservation. For example, in recognizing that as the water table subsides the value of farm land declines, the IRS ruled in 1982 that Ogallala irrigators were entitled to a cost-depletion deduction for the exhaustion of their capital investment in groundwater. Thus "government policy not only encourages irrigation of the Ogallala, it also subsidizes it" (Duncan 1987, 27). Duncan also argued that the Kansas Water Appropriation Act of 1945 can be characterized as anticonservation because it provides that "allotments not used beneficially for three successive years are deemed abandoned" and thus "irrigators are encouraged to use it or lose it."

Irrigators' decisions about water use in the Ogallala region will be influenced by many factors: hard economic realities, complex geohydrologic conditions, sophisticated information systems, and regionally variable regulations and management. These operate within a heterogeneous physical and cultural landscape and are constantly subjected to the winds of uncertainty. The High Plains will continue as a region of change.

LOCAL MANAGEMENT'S PERSPECTIVE

What will be the role of local groundwater institutions and managers in the future? For several reasons we believe that their powers to influence the management decisions of irrigators and to regulate water use will increase substantially. First, public opinion throughout the High Plains supports decision making at the local level more than at the state or federal level (Kromm and White 1986). Second, although institutional arrangements take on varying forms in different parts of the High Plains (see Roberts, chap. 5), the majority of citizens in the Ogallala region are pleased with the current institutional structure for managing groundwater in their respective states. Nowhere does there appear to be a desire to limit or to reduce the regulatory powers of existing local institutions. Third, although Gaul, Bossert, and Urban (chaps. 8, 9, and 10) demonstrated that much still remains to be done to improve the effectiveness of water use locally, institutions from Texas to Nebraska have intensified their efforts to manage groundwater better and are achieving measurable success. The satisfaction of irrigators and of the public with current local-management efforts, a preference for local rather than for state or federal control, and the demonstrated success at reducing water consumption have combined to strengthen the local water-management agencies as they orchestrate future plans to lengthen the life of the aquifer significantly.

Local groundwater management will benefit doubly from technological advancement. First, the range of technologies for water conservation available to irrigators has rapidly expanded over the past twenty years, and many experimental efforts appear promising (see chap. 6). One of the major tasks of groundwater managers in the future will be to encourage the adoption of appropriate technologies from an increasingly long list of options. The optimal choice of the mix of technologies will be difficult for individual irrigators to determine because the feasibility of any one water-saving practice will be influenced by field characteristics, hydrologic conditions such as the availability of and the depth to water, farm scale characteristics, external factors such as crop prices, energy costs, the availability of capital, and importantly, the nature of the water-saving technology already adopted.

In addition, water managers will increasingly be able to measure irrigated acreage, assess crop-water needs, estimate water use and demand, and identify potential problems of groundwater quality with remote-sensing and geographic-information systems (see chap. 7). Researchers are currently working on ways to apply these technologies in meaningful, cost-efficient ways locally.

Local water management within the High Plains region seems secure in the future from a spatial perspective as well. Because local conditions associated with field, aquifer, farm, topography, and energy vary tremendously within the High Plains (see chaps. 1 and 3), detailed water-management plans will be necessary subregionally to adjust adequately for local conditions that might influence the efficacy of water restrictions or the adoption of specific water-saving practices. Roberts argued that environmental differences may be more important in explaining water use than management differences (see chap. 5). Based on our field observations, different management approaches in different areas have worked to improve groundwater conservation. A comprehensive, homogeneous approach to local water management in the High Plains would prove ineffective because environmental differences do affect water use and must be accounted for in successful water management plans.

We anticipate that much will be done to reduce the rate of groundwater depletion in many areas, but the grim reality of economic depletion will undoubtedly continue to spread across the landscape. Greater competition for water, frequently for habitat protection and enhancement, and an increase in water marketing will also emerge. As the demand for water grows, we assume that pressures to encourage research for water-enhancement strategies such as interbasin transfer, playa-lake modification, recharge structures, weather modification, and air-injection technologies will continue to increase. People in regions nearing the depletion stage will continue to hope and to fight for technological breakthroughs that will enable them to sustain their way of life rather than willingly accept the return of the "buffalo commons."

REFERENCES

Duncan, Myrl L. 1987. "High Noon on the Ogallala Aquifer: Agriculture Does Not Live by Farmland Preservation Alone." *Washburn Law Journal* 27, 1 (Fall): 16–103.

Kromm, David E., and Stephen E. White. 1986. "Variability in Adjustment Preferences to Groundwater Depletion in the American High Plains." *Water Resources Bulletin* 22, 5 (Oct.): 791–801.

———. 1990b. *Water Conservation in the High Plains.* Manhattan: Kansas State University.

———. 1990a. "Adoption of Water Saving Practices by Irrigators in the High Plains." *Water Resources Bulletin* 16, 4: 999–1012.

———. 1991. "Reliance on Sources of Information for Water Saving Practices by Irrigators in the High Plains of the U.S.A." *Journal of Rural Studies* 7, 4: 411–21.

CONTRIBUTORS

WAYNE A. BOSSERT has managed Northwest Kansas Groundwater Management District Number 4 since 1977. He is a graduate in geology of the University of Oklahoma and past president of the Groundwater Management Districts Association.

ROBERT "STEVE" GAUL serves as state water planning and review process coordinator for the Nebraska Natural Resources Commission, where he has been employed since 1979. He has degrees in geography from Kansas State University (B.S.) and the University of Nebraska (M.A.).

DONALD E. GREEN is a historian and dean of the College of Humanities and Social Sciences at Chadron State College. He has published widely on the historical development of irrigated agriculture in the High Plains and is author of *Land of the Underground Rain.*

DAVID E. KROMM is professor of geography at Kansas State University, where he has taught since 1967. He has authored or coauthored publications dealing with water management and policy in the U.S. High Plains, the Canadian Prairie West, and Great Britain.

JACK T. MUSICK has been an agriculture engineer at the USDA Agricultural Research Service Conservation and Production Research Laboratory in Texas since 1963, serving as research leader of the Water Management Unit since 1977. Musick is an authority on limited-irrigation management practices for drought-tolerant crops in the Great Plains.

M. DUANE NELLIS is head of the Department of Geography and director of the Institute for Social and Behavioral Research at Kansas State University. His research interests include the application of remote sensing technologies to natural resource management.

REBECCA S. ROBERTS teaches in the Department of Geography at the University of Iowa. Professor Roberts's major research contributions have focused on water resources, natural resources, and agricultural policy.

B. A. STEWART is laboratory director and research soil scientist at the USDA Conservation and Production Research Laboratory at Bushland, Texas, a position he has held since 1968. His area of expertise is the influence of weather and climate on moisture supply for crop growth and improved soil and water management.

OTIS W. TEMPLER is an attorney and professor and chair of the Department of Geography at Texas Tech University. He has published widely on the legal ramifications of groundwater development in the southern High Plains.

LLOYD V. URBAN is director of the Water Resources Center at Texas Tech University and teaches in the Department of Civil Engineering. His professional expertise lies in the areas of water resources, environmental engineering, and environmental impact assessment.

GILBERT F. WHITE is Gustavson Professor Emeritus at the University of Colorado Institute of Behavioral Science. The dean of water resource scientists in geography, he has authored numerous books and directed many domestic and international research projects in flood control and water management.

STEPHEN E. WHITE is professor of geography at Kansas State University. His published research includes works on population geography, environmental perception, groundwater depletion in the High Plains, and regional development in central Appalachia.

INDEX